CONTEMPORA
UTOPI/

Contemporary Feminist Utopianism is a study of, and an exercise in, utopian thought. Its specific focus is current feminist utopian thinking. Feminism is identified as being in crisis. This book sets out to explore utopianism as both a cause of and a potential solution to this crisis.

Lucy Sargisson rejects approaches to utopianism which insist upon utopia as a perfect blueprint for the future. Instead, she identifies a new transgressive utopianism which destroys old certainties in favour of a new and more unsettling vision of a feminist future. This transgressive utopianism stresses process over product and is informed by contemporary poststructuralist theories of language.

The book is split into three parts: the first is concerned with approaches to utopianism, the second with an exploration of current debates in contemporary feminism and a study of the relation between utopian and poststructuralist thought, and the third with a thematic discussion of feminist utopian literature.

Contemporary Feminist Utopianism is a stimulating, original and accessible survey of some of the more complex strands of contemporary thought. Its interdisciplinary nature will make it a book of great interest to students and scholars of political theory, feminist theory, utopian studies and literature.

Lucy Sargisson is Lecturer in Politics at Nottingham University.

WOMEN AND POLITICS
Edited by Haleh Afshar and Mary Maynard
University of York, UK

Series advisers:
Kum-Kum Bhavnani, University of California, Santa Barbara
Haideh Moghissi, Queen's University, Kingston, Canada
Afsaneh Najmabadi, Harvard University
Pippa Norris, Harvard University

This new series will present exciting and accessible books covering both the formal public domain and the informal and practical strategies and organizations that women throughout the world use to obtain rights, to meet their needs and to improve their situation in life. The series will combine theoretical and empirical work, revealing how and why the political experience of women has been neglected, and contributing to the ongoing reconceptualization of the political.

Also in this series:

NO MORE HEROINES?
Russia, Women and the Market
Sue Bridger, Rebecca Kay and Kathryn Pinnick

WOMEN AND POLITICS IN THE THIRD WORLD
Edited by Haleh Afshar

Forthcoming titles include:

WOMEN'S PLACES
Gender, National Identity and Political Ideology
Edited by Nickie Charles and Helen Hintjens

RATIONAL WOMAN
Raia Prokhavnik

CONTEMPORARY FEMINIST UTOPIANISM

Lucy Sargisson

London and New York

First published 1996
by Routledge
11 New Fetter Lane, London EC4P 4EE

Transferred to Digital Printing 2004

Simultaneously published in the USA and Canada
by Routledge
29 West 35th Street, New York, NY 10001

Typeset in Garamond by Routledge

British Library Cataloguing in Publication Data
A catalogue record for this book is available from the
British Library

Library of Congress Cataloguing in Publication Data
Sargisson, Lucy, 1964–
Contemporary feminist utopianism/Lucy Sargisson.
p. cm. – (Women and politics)
Includes bibliographical references and index.
1. Uto ias. 2. Feminist theory. 3.Feminist criticism.
I. Title. II. Series.
HX806.S25395   1996
305.42–dc20   96–7014
                                                        CIP

ISBN 0–415–14175–3 (hbk)
ISBN 0–415–14176–1 (pbk)

For Mike Craig and Hilary Sargisson

CONTENTS

CONTENTS

SERIES EDITORS' PREFACE

We are delighted to be able to include *Contemporary Feminist Utopianism* in our new series on women and politics, particularly since it is the first theoretical text to be published in it. The notion of 'theory' is a much contested and somewhat polarized area of discussion in feminism, women's studies and political science more generally. Whereas some argue that it is important to engage with and challenge existing forms of theoretical knowledge, others regard theory as an arid, abstract and masculine form of activity, one bearing little relationship to everyday lives and experiences. Lucy Sargisson's book, however, demonstrates that it is possible to adopt the former position without ignoring the concerns of the latter. While reviewing and critiquing a variety of sophisticated and complex theoretical ideas in an extremely accessible way, she also remains sensitive to the relevance of these to questions about the body, sexuality, identity and power in relation to feminist politics more generally.

Sargisson's concern with utopianism is, indeed, timely. As she demonstrates, feminist writing on the subject is extensive and there is a snese in which most forms of feminist theorizing have utopian aspects. However, many of these do not fulfil the definitions and criteria by which utopias are usually defined. This led Sargisson to ask the question as to whether these texts were not utopias, or whether, instead, the idea of utopia needed to be reconceived. She eventually opted for the latter point of view. *Contemporary Feminist Utopianism* proceeds, via a critical angagement with both feminist and non-feminist utopian writing, to argue for a new feminist understanding of what utopias involve. It is critical, in particular, of approaches which emphasize perfection and the ideas that utopias constitute blueprints for the perfect polity. Instead, it argues that while some feminists have satirized the concept of perfection, most simply avoid clusure of their utopian vision. They avoid unnecessarily restrictive definitions, leaving the possibilities open-ended.

As Sargisson shows in this book, feminists' writing on utopianism draws on a wide spectrum of material – fiction, science fiction, history, political analysis and social commentary. Sargisson herself weaves and synthesizes these ideas into a fascinating and compelling account of the ways in which transformations in gender relations might be envisaged. What she calls the 'new' approach to utopianism focuses on dynamism and unending process. In this she calls for a new kind of feminist political theory, one which in transgressing and rendering meaningless the division between mind and body also elevates and values the physical, the emotional or the 'feminine'.

Haleh Afshar and Mary Maynard
Series editors

ACKNOWLEDGEMENTS

Love and thanks to Pauline Weston, Jill Allaway and Andy Dobson without whom this book would never have been finished.

INTRODUCTION

Utopia: the good place which is no place. This book is a study of and exercise in contemporary feminist utopian thought. Discussion is presented and undertaken in three distinct but related parts. The first is concerned broadly with defining utopianism. The second explores new ways of contextualizing and understanding utopianism. The third is thematically based, and tests and expands the thesis advanced in the second from within the context of feminist utopian fiction and theory.

I should, perhaps, begin with a clarification of terms: I shall be using the word 'utopianism' in a similar sense to Lyman Tower Sargent's (1994). Utopianism, throughout this book, is an umbrella term referring to a way of seeing and approaching the world and to subsequent ways of representing what is perceived of the world. For Sargent, utopianism is social dreaming (Sargent, 1975, 1994). Ruth Levitas uses the word 'utopia' in the same umbrella sense; for her it refers to the expression of a *desire* for different (and better) ways of being (Levitas, 1990). Both of these positions owe something to the work of Ernst Bloch, whose encyclopaedic study *The Principle of Hope* richly details, in three volumes, the presence of what he perceives to be a utopian *impulse*.[1] For Bloch, this impulse or propensity is grounded in our capacity to fantasize beyond our experience, and in our ability to rearrange the world around us (he calls this 'forward dawning' – Bloch, 1986: p. 3). He reaches these conclusions through a beautifully written and complex engagement with the Freudian notions of the unconscious, the pre-conscious, the ego and the id (Bloch, 1986: esp. pp. 55, 114–17). These conclusions about a utopian impulse are not Bloch's only contribution to the debates around utopianism, and I shall be returning to his work again later when discussing both form and function.[2]

1

'Utopianism', then, the umbrella term, concerns the propensity or phenomenon, and under this umbrella I place utopian thought, utopian theory and utopias. Also under the umbrella are eutopias, dystopias and utopian satire. Utopian thought I take to be the experience and expression of utopian desires, or the engagement in utopian dreaming. The terms 'utopian theory' and 'utopias' are variously used, but unless otherwise stated they refer to the genres of political thought and literature which are specific *forms* of utopian thought.[3] (In Chapter 7 I shall be arguing that feminist interventions have significantly problematized these genres.) Finally, wherever possible, I use 'Utopia' to refer to the desire or vision in question, and *Utopia* to refer to the book by Thomas More (1975).

The first two chapters of this book represent a survey and assessment of existing approaches to utopianism, which is undertaken systematically by working through analyses which privilege form, content and function. Approaches to utopianism in terms of its form or content are found to be problematic methodologies and are largely rejected in the first chapter, although the formulaic approach to the content of utopias is found to be of some use in narrowing the field to create an identifiable concept. Chapter 2 examines and finds broadly useful those approaches which identify and privilege a utopian function.

These opening discussions are informed by my belief that the dominant commonplace understanding of a utopia as 'a place, state, or condition ideally perfect in respect of politics, laws, customs and conditions'[4] is mistaken, and, further, that this view, which I call 'the standard view', is the result of certain approaches to utopianism and to the practice of theoretical thinking which are discussed and rejected in Chapter 1.

One component of the commonly held view of what constitutes a utopia that is particularly puzzling is the assumption that utopias are blueprints for the perfect polity. Strangely, this description is not appropriate to contemporary feminist utopianism, or to many historic utopias. When surveying recent fictional and theoretical manifestations of feminist utopian thought, I could not help but notice the absence or redundancy of the concept of perfection.[5] Many commentators who privilege formulaic content assume a representation of a blueprint to be an ingredient of utopian thought. This blueprint is an image of a future that is idyllic and perfect in all senses. The absence, though, of a detailed plan for a perfect society is a characteristic of many of the texts that I have studied. Some writers treat such a plan as synonymous with death (Cixous and Clement, 1986; Slonzcewski, 1987). Others satirize the concept of perfection (Carter, 1969: p. 19). Most simply avoid closure of their utopian vision and leave it openended.

These observations led me to consider that either these feminist texts were not utopias, or utopia needed to be reconceived. Looking at historical utopias firmed up this conviction and also informed my belief that the approach taken to theoretical thinking helps shape the eventual conceptualization. I therefore stress the *process* of conceptualizing in these opening chapters and find the methodology of many approaches to be constraining and to result in unnecessarily restrictive definitions and unacknowledged closure.

To perfect is to make complete. On a superficial level, the equation of perfection with finality and death can be read as expressing fears that utopianism has traditionally evoked. Utopia as the death of politics is sometimes related to absolutism and totalitarianism. Dystopian representations of all-powerful and omnipresent governing bodies are generally grounded in these fears. George Orwell's *Nineteen Eighty-Four* and Zamyatin's *We* are examples of texts of this kind. Briefly, these critiques of utopianism evoke an apparently eutopian state which either becomes or is oppressive. If a utopia represents the end of change then these dystopias are the end of politics. Other related concerns are of a Burkean or conservative nature and have do to with the perceived danger of large-scale social engineering and the unpredictability of such projects.

This book advances a critique of utopianism as perfection-seeking that is different from those mentioned above. It hinges on a critique of the equation of perfection with closure and is related to (and should be contextualized within) debates on the construction of meaning. Whilst the arguments and discussions advanced in the following chapters are broad-ranging and diverse, this concern is the central theme of the entire book. The chapters in Part I, then, argue for a new approach to utopianism that should be contextualized within these debates on how meaning is constructed.

Moving on to the second part of the book, the third chapter focuses on current debates within contemporary feminism and argues that these provide a useful context from which a new understanding of utopianism can be advanced. Debates concerning equality and difference, the construction of meaning through language, and the construction of subjectivity, it is argued, provide a backdrop to this new approach to utopianism. It is suggested that current concerns about *essentialism* and *female* subjectivity create a tension which threatens the coherence and existence of feminism itself. This tension is explained by reference to related debates about the transgressive discourses of poststructuralism and postmodernism. The fourth chapter offers a number of readings of utopianism which permit multiplicity to exist in a definition of that genre and which resist closure. In this chapter I undertake an engagement in transgressive utopian thinking that illustrates the new approach that I am advocating.

Part II of the book has a number of complexly related functions and themes. It asks *why* much feminist utopianism is not marked by closure. In so doing it builds, advances and applies a new approach to utopianism. These moves of building, advancement and application are sometimes simultaneous. This is intentional and represents an attempt to enact or practise the utopian thinking which is theorized. This practice makes for dense reading and is rooted in an understanding of poststructuralism which insists on engagement.[6]

It is suggested that feminist utopianism is, in many cases, transgressive of the standard view of utopia as perfection because of a desire to escape closure, and that this desire is informed by (or can be read through) theories of the construction of meaning. Meaning is said to be constructed by a complex and hierarchical system of binary oppositions. The utopian thought with which this book engages attempts to transgress this system and to open new conceptual spaces for exploration and exploitation in projects of emancipation. I argue that emancipatory projects are doomed to failure and to conservatism unless they challenge and provide alternatives to this conceptual system, which rests on dualistic thought and hierarchical relations.

Part III of the book tests and explores this hypothesis by textual application. This part represents a shift in focus, as the majority of its primary sources are fictional or literary rather than theoretical. In this sense it practises the political theory which has been advanced in the chapters above. The use of literary sources is deliberate. First, utopian studies cannot help but be cross-disciplinary, as many (but not all) manifestations of utopianism are presented in a literary form: some consideration of these texts is therefore essential. Secondly, and within the context of feminist utopianism, it has traditionally been a tactic of (radical branches of) feminism to explore theory in and through fiction.[7] There are, however, problems associated with any project which attempts to prove a hypothesis by reference to literary texts. It is easy to 'lift' a section of literary text and use it to substantiate a theory, regardless of context. In this case, though, the practice is defensible. In the first instance, as noted above, the move is made deliberately: that is, intentionally and carefully. The texts are not taken out of context. Indeed, the context is explained and provided in the discussion of informing debates in Chapter 3. Further, the theory of utopia which is promoted has some of its roots in the very texts which I explore. It was when reading them initially that the germ which grew into a hypothesis was first generated. This part, then, represents a return to the texts with and from which the book began. Discussion here is thematically arranged and asks and answers questions of how and why feminist utopian texts transgress binary oppositional thought.

The new approach suggested by this book enables us to identify what I call a new utopianism emerging from contemporary feminist theory and fiction. At its most radical, I suggest that it undermines not only the concept of utopianism but the concept of conceptualization. At the very least, it forces the field of political theory on to new ground: utopian thought journeys into uncharted and unfamiliar territory, and creates spaces in which visions of the good can be imagined. It is the good place that is no place. This book stresses the 'ou' – the 'nowhere' element – of utopianism and addresses fundamental questions of conceivability; it urges the theorist to let go of the stability and certainty of the search for conclusions in favour of an approach that is resistant to closure.

Part I

APPROACHING UTOPIANISM

1

FORM-BASED AND CONTENT-BASED APPROACHES TO UTOPIANISM

INTRODUCTION

I shall be arguing, in this part of the book, in favour of a new approach
to utopianism; 'new', that is, in contrast to some of the dominant
(historical) approaches which have contributed to the erection of the
myth of utopianism. This myth, the 'false' or inappropriate view of the
phenomenon, is present in many definitions and outlines of the
colloquial usages of the terms 'utopia' and 'utopianism'. Perusal of
the reference section of any library tells us that 'utopia' means
something along the following lines:

> 1. An imaginary island, depicted by Sir Thomas More as
> enjoying a perfect social, legal and political system. . . . 2. Any
> imaginary, indefinitely remote region, country or locality. 3. A
> place, state, or condition ideally perfect in respect of politics,
> laws, customs and conditions. . . . 4. An impossibly ideal
> scheme, esp. for social improvement.

This comes from the *Oxford English Dictionary*. The *Encyclopedia
Britannica* provides a similar characterization, in which a utopia is
described as 'An ideal commonwealth whose inhabitants exist under
perfect conditions'. This is clearly the standard colloquial view of
utopia.

I shall make the mythical character of these understandings of
utopianism clear later in the chapter. First, though, I should like to
return to the first sentence of this chapter in order to make two
important preliminary points:

> 1 Not all historically previous utopias have contributed to this
> myth. Thomas More and William Morris are both cited later in

the chapter as providing utopian visions which transgress these definitions.

2 The importance of the term 'approach' should be noted at this early stage. Descriptive statements perform creative acts. Naming a thing – giving a concept, idea or entity a name, description or category – is an act of creation. Descriptive, defining statements bring into being that which they (claim to) describe.

These beliefs inform my text and are informed by Derridean post-structuralism. Hence 'approach' is an important concept within the confines of this book: the nature of the approach taken towards an idea or phenomenon affects the eventual product of conceptualization – the concept (as conceptualized). This, if you like, is a methodological claim; and I shall be adopting a transgressive approach (or methodology) towards what I shall identify as the transgressive phenomenon of utopianism.

Utopianism, then, needs to be reconceived. At the root of these arguments are three justificatory claims which will inform the discussions below. Utopianism should be reapproached because:

1 what I shall call the standard view of utopia is fundamentally flawed;
2 the standard view is inappropriate to much of contemporary feminist utopianism and is, therefore, unnecessarily exclusive;
3 the new approach offered in this book is more appropriate to contemporary feminist utopianism.[1]

The most comprehensive study of utopian thought to be published recently is Ruth Levitas's *The Concept of Utopia* (1990). Levitas states that utopianism has historically been approached in terms of one (or more) of three aspects: content, form and function (Levitas, 1990: pp. 4–5). Levitas's scheme is a useful one, and I shall adopt and adapt these headings in order to give shape to the discussions that follow.[2] This chapter will identify and assess those approaches to utopianism which privilege form and content and will identify the (problematic) implications of these approaches. Chapter 2 will look at approaches to utopianism which privilege function. Approaches of this type are cautiously supported.

Part I, then, is concerned to look behind the question 'what do (feminist) women want?' – what are the desires and hopes and aspirations of contemporary feminism(s)?[3] – to the more interesting question 'how are these desires and hopes and aspirations formulated?'

and, finally, to the root or heart of this book: 'how can we (as political theorists, theorists of utopian studies – we, the recipients/readers/audience) best approach these desires as scholars?'

FORM

Does form represent the best approach to utopianism? The answer must be 'no', because approaches that take form as the primary defining characteristic of utopianism tend to assume that the form in question is that of literary fiction.[4] The assumption that utopianism is a literary genre is common in utopian studies and is perhaps dominant in colloquial understanding.[5] This approach, I suggest, results in an unnecessarily restrictive definition of utopianism and of utopias (constructions of utopian thought). Lyman Tower Sargent, the main bibliographer of the field, veers, albeit self-consciously, in this direction (Sargent, 1975, 1994). An early and influential definition comes from Darko Suvin (Sargent himself found this definition to be 'by far the best' (1975: p. 140)) and situates the phenomenon firmly within the field of literature:

> The verbal construction of a particular quasi-human community where sociopolitical institutions, norms and individual relationships are organized according to a more perfect principle than in the author's community, this construction being based on estrangement arising out of an alternative historical hypothesis.
>
> (Suvin, 1973: p. 132)

This definition is reached after careful and elaborate consideration of previous definitions, and I shall return to it again later in this chapter. For the present, it is illustrative of a definitional assumption that utopia – the expression of utopian thought – is a verbal construction, a literary or textual artifact. This view is, as I have said, common. Even Frank Manuel, infamous for shunning definitions, describes utopias as 'speaking pictures' (Manuel, 1973: p. viii). The image of the word is clearly present in this phrase, which is evocative of an image captured in textual form. A.L. Morton adopts the following as a definition for his work: 'an imaginary country described in a work of fiction with the object of criticising existing society' (Morton, 1952: p. 10). Krishan Kumar is even more specific; for him, utopianism belongs to the field of science fiction:

Utopia distinguishes itself from other forms of the ideal society,
and from other forms of social and political theory, by being in
the first place a piece of fiction. It is, using the term in its
broadest sense, a species of science fiction.

(Kumar, 1991: p. 20)

Of course, these definitions do not take just the form as being the
defining characteristic – they do not, in other words, approach
utopianism purely through a methodological route that privileges
form. Morton's definition alludes to content, form and function.
Likewise, Darko Suvin, cited above, does not approach utopianism
solely in terms of form: content and function are also components of
his definition. These thinkers do, however, privilege form in their
various approaches. Peter Alexander and Roger Gill begin the
introduction of their edited collection *Utopias* with this:

Utopian constructions may take the form either of a picture of an
unrealisably ideal social order criticizing an existing order,
teaching us lessons about organization and promoting understanding of the concepts involved, or, alternatively, of a blueprint intended to guide the actual reorganization of a society.

(Alexander and Gill, 1984: p. xi)

Here, again, we find an approach to utopianism which relies on form,
function and content. Also present in this last definition is a negative
and prescriptive element. For Alexander and Gill, the picture or vision
which represents a 'utopian construction' *contains* an 'impossibly ideal
society'.

I shall return to discussion of content later. The point that I should
like to raise now is that made by Ruth Levitas: that defining
utopianism/utopia in terms of form in this way is too restrictive an
approach, and one that issues in an unnecessarily narrow definition
(Levitas, 1990: p. 4). This point can be illustrated by reference to the
work of Ernst Bloch, who has perhaps been most persuasive in
broadening the field of utopianism beyond the literary (Bloch,
1986). He finds utopianism (a utopian impulse) to be immanent in
popular culture, in the fashion industry, dance, film, adventure
stories, art, architecture, music and even medical science. Each of
these fields contains its various Utopias – visions of a better or more
desirable way of being, a desirable future or present.

Vincent Geoghegan uses Bloch's work alongside that of Karl
Mannheim (who also argues for a utopian disposition) to broaden

our understanding of what constitutes utopianism. For Geoghegan, 'the "classic" utopia [which he describes as the literary model established by More] is but one manifestation of utopianism' (Geoghegan, 1987: p. 2). The implication here is that approaches which privilege form are mistaken, because utopianism and Utopias are expressed in many forms. Geoghegan rejects form in favour of function, which is discussed further below.

I mentioned above the fact that Levitas rejects approaches which privilege form. She is also critical of those which take More's *Utopia* as their starting point. I will cite her in full on this point as her statement raises a number of other, related issues:

> Some commentators take the form of More's *Utopia* as a model and argue that the utopia is a literary genre, involving the fictional depiction of an alternative society in some detail. However, ... depictions of the good society do not necessarily take the form of literary fictions – and indeed this form is only available under certain very specific historical conditions; is it then to be assumed that when these conditions do not exist, there are no utopias?
>
> (Levitas, 1990: pp. 4–5)

I should like to note two of the points being raised here. The first is a concern brought up earlier by Levitas, which arises from the multi-disciplinary nature of utopian studies, when she states that 'there is a temptation to try to delimit the field [of utopia] to one's own area of interest and set up boundaries which exclude large areas of material as not properly utopian' (1990: p. 4). The disciplinary imperialism and exclusivity of such an approach must be resisted.[6]

The second point relates to another danger of a similar ilk, that of *cultural* imperialism and exclusivity. Because literary utopias are rare in cultures other than 'Western' ones, does this mean that utopianism and Utopias do not exist in other cultures? Lyman Tower Sargent makes passing reference to an ongoing project in which he is involved: studying and cataloguing the Utopias of indigenous societies (Sargent, 1994). One of the questions that he poses is 'Are utopias, as many (Krishan Kumar most recently) have argued, a phenomenon of the Christian West or are there indigenous pre-contact utopias outside the Christian West?' He responds:

> No, utopias are not solely the product of the Christian West, but utopias as a genre of literature that has certain formal

13

characteristics are most common in the West, almost certainly because the genre is identified with Thomas More, a person from the Christian West.

(Sargent, 1994: p. 2)

These last points can be related to something which emerges repeatedly throughout this book: that is, a concern about the function and nature of definitions and the act of defining – and, consequently, a concern about the function and nature of political theorizing. Definitions exclude that which is not the subject of the definition in question; this is their primary function. But it is possible, as I shall suggest below, that definitions may be constructed in such a way as to *exclude* that which should be *included*. A route around this problem, which is advocated in many sections of this book, is to strive for openended definitions, or, to borrow Sargent's phrase, to seek definitions with 'porous boundaries' (1990: p. 5). This is a project with its own problems,which will become increasingly clear as I proceed and with which I shall grapple in the concluding chapter. The implications for political theory are methodological ones – political theory has traditionally sought classificatory systems and schemas in order to make sense of the world. A political–theoretical approach to feminist thought, for instance, divides it into liberal, socialist, marxist, radical and, latterly, black and postmodern feminisms, which are then analysed for their own differentiating ideological content. (Books of this type fill the shelves of university bookshops. Examples are Jagger (1983) and Bryson (1992).) The fact that these categories are themselves artificial constructions into which few actual feminists 'fit' – or indeed that some people may wish to occupy more than one position, or none of the above, yet still regard themselves as 'feminist' – is worrying. At the root of these concerns is the inadequacy of the original system of definition or classification: the approach.

To conclude this preliminary discussion of approaches which privilege form, I should like to note that many of the texts referred to in the discussions in later chapters of this book are not of the literary-fictional form. Form as literary (or other) genre, then, represents too restrictive a starting point for comprehensive analysis of utopianism.[7] In making this argument it is not my intention to close debate of the fictional status of utopian thought and other manifestations of utopianism, and I shall be discussing the function of a fictional format below.[8]

So, whilst this book is concerned with 'verbal constructions' or with textual utopianism – speaking pictures – we cannot presume to define utopianism, Utopia or utopian thought in these terms. Utopia, the literary genre, will be discussed further below, but this particular manifestation of utopian thought cannot be taken as the definitional point of departure for its other forms.

CONTENT

Formulaic content

Approaching utopian expressions in terms of their content is perhaps the most common way of looking at and defining utopia(nism). The question asked by commentators who take this approach is 'what is *a* utopia?' – and the answer comes in a formula that specifies the common or necessary 'ingredients' or criteria that a text needs in order to be defined and categorized as a utopia. Given then that utopianism is not (just) a literary genre, but given too that the subjects of this book *are* textual (written) utopias and utopian theory, investigation of approaches to utopianism which stress the importance of formal criteria is necessary. This ground has been well covered, though, and I shall keep discussion brief on this point.

Approaches to utopianism which take this form tend to distinguish 'the utopia' from other forms of ideal society. Indeed, this differentiation of utopia is the basis of most projects of definition. J.C. Davis and Krishan Kumar both adopt this approach and both identify five types of ideal society, of which utopia is only one. The first is characterized as 'Cockaygne', from the medieval poem 'The Land of Cokaygne'.[9] In Cockaygne desires are instantly gratified; it is a world containing self-roasting birds, rivers of wine, fountains of youth, wishing trees and ever-available and desirable sexual partners. It is a hedonistic paradise. Cockaygne privileges material and sensual satisfaction and assumes natural abundance. Its inhabitants symbolize satiated desire.

The second ideal society is said to be the arcadia: a pastoral setting of natural abundance to which are added morally or aesthetically motivated humans. Appetites in arcadia are temperately satisfied. The third ideal is what Davis calls 'the perfect commonwealth', a society with a prescriptive moral order, perfectly realized by all of its members. This complements but is different from the millennium, the fourth type of ideal society, in which men and women are transformed, usually for the better, by an external force. This force

15

is a god-like figure whose strength is greater than that which it is believed is the force causing evil thoughts and behaviour.

Only the fifth type of ideal society is identified as the utopia, that in which there is 'no invocation of a *deus ex machina*, nor any wishing away of the deficiencies of man or nature' (Davis, 1984: p. 9). Rather, says Davis, the utopia creates systems which will cope with these deficiencies, systems that are recognizable as pertaining to the modern state: 'Such systems are inevitably bureaucratic, institutional, legal and educational, artificial and organisational' (Davis, 1984: p. 9). Utopia, says Davis, idealizes organization.

I should like to begin discussion of this 'formulaic' approach by questioning the validity of this type of methodology. 'The Land of Cokaygne', for instance, clearly does contain a utopian vision and expresses utopian desires – its exclusion from the field of utopia appears groundless. A.L. Morton's discussion of Cokaygne persuasively presents it as containing what he calls 'a Utopia of the folk' (Morton, 1952: p. 10).[10] I shall return to this point later; its significance at this juncture is that it introduces an important methodological point at an early stage. Further exploration of this concern is not possible until the key elements of this kind of approach are extrapolated. I shall focus on Davis, as his work clearly exemplifies this approach, which has come to be associated with the standard or colloquial understanding of the word 'utopia'. This, in other words, is typical of the approach which conceptualizes the myth of utopia.

Utopias for Davis are, as stated above, inherently political, whereas other forms of ideal society are not. The first two criteria identified by Davis, then, are (1) utopias' organizational preoccupations, and (2) the political nature of the genre. Some consideration of his concept of politics is necessary before proceeding further:

> If politics is about the distribution of opportunities, rewards and satisfactions, the setting of human behaviour and policing the abnormal, then ideal societies are, in a sense, all about the end of politics. . . . Utopia, by contrast, accepts the distributional problems posed by the deficiency of resources and the moral disabilities of men. Unlike the others, therefore, it accepts the bases of the problem from which politics arise. Out of the minds and wills of human beings must come organisational forms and practices which will guarantee the just distribution of finite

resources and contain the anti-social proclivities of men and women.

(Davis, 1984: pp. 9–10)

This definition of politics is from both feminist and political–theoretical perspectives inadequate and superficial. Politics is, in feminist analyses, read in terms of the distribution of power, be it power structures in a society that may affect the distribution of wealth and resources, or power relations between and within different groups and classes or between states. Whilst agreeing with Davis that utopias can be characterized partly by their political nature, I would deepen his concept of the political. Some feminist utopian work contains elements to do with the superficial power structures about which Davis is concerned. Shulamith Firestone's *The Dialectic of Sex* (1971), for instance, proposes institutional arrangements to protect the freedom and autonomy of children and women, and Marge Piercy's *Woman on the Edge of Time* (1979) has a kind of communal council through which disputes are settled. In both of these cases, however, these structures play a secondary and perhaps supportive role to the redressing of the balance of sexual power.

All feminist utopias are political in the sense that I outline above. All are concerned to some extent with power relations, all with sexual power, some also with the exploitative relations between patriarchy and nature. Their concerns are with diverse manifestations of sexual power relations. Psychoanalytic utopias, for instance, are concerned in part with the gendered power relations embodied in language, whereas others focus on social and reproductive relations.

It is, perhaps, unfair to criticize Davis's view of the political from the perspective of late twentieth-century feminism. I should, therefore, also like to suggest that his view of politics is inappropriate *per se*. 'The Land of Cokaygne', for example, can legitimately be read as a political text, although not in Davis's terms. Although it has been frequently dismissed (as Kumar and Davis dismiss it) as fanciful wish-fulfilment, Cokaygne does engage critically with some of the dominant political issues of its day. Its anti-clericalism, for instance, in a fourteenth century context, constitutes a political commentary: Morton notes the context of 'monastic gluttony and evil-living' (Morton, 1952: p. 11). A second theme of the poem, also noted by Morton, is the debate in which it engages between Celtic mythology and Christian theology:

17

> Fur in see bi west of Spaygne
> Is a land ihote [called] Cokaygne

This westward placing clearly connects Cokaygne with the earthly paradise of Celtic mythology. Throughout the Middle Ages the existence of such a paradise was firmly believed in, but the church always placed its paradise in the East and strongly opposed the belief in a western paradise as a heathen superstition.

(Morton, 1952: p. 13)

Also in the Middle Ages, of course, there was a close relation between church and state, thus making engagement in this particular debate a political act. (Further, the claim of an earthly western paradise would have been a radical one.)

Even this brief consideration of the context of Cokaygne and of its engagement in two contemporary debates shows it to be a subversive, critical and, in a straightforward sense, political text. The underbelly of this hedonistic paradise with its fanciful poetics is, I suggest, a serious critique of the corruption of the church and an engagement in the doctrinal dispute between church and people. Davis's understanding of politics is inadequate to this context.[11] This (playful?) engagement in contemporary political debates is, I suggest, one lasting feature of utopianism that can actually be considered a 'utopian convention' or ingredient of utopian expression.

Curiously, Davis's definition of politics is also inadequate to the task of describing texts that Davis *does* consider to be utopias. Two examples of such texts are Edward Bellamy's *Looking Backward* (1957), and William Morris's *News from Nowhere* (1891). The organizational–institutional interpretation of politics fits *Looking Backward* perfectly – the 'socialist' Boston of the year 2000 as imagined by Bellamy is mechanistically organized and concerned with the just distribution of goods; the system imagined is highly complex and state-run. It is perhaps ironic, but certainly relevant, that it is this very state centralism to which Morris objects in both his 1889 review of *Looking Backward* and in his own utopian vision, *News from Nowhere*: 'This scheme may be described as State Communism, worked by the very extreme of national centralization. The underlying vice in it is that the author cannot conceive . . . of anything else than the *machinery* of society' (Morris, 1889: p. 250). The world presented in *Looking Backward* is sterile and hollow, and Morris attributes this to the type of politics by which it operates. And indeed, *News from Nowhere*, with its broader conception of politics, does present a more fluid and full vision of a utopian society.

On this count, then – the assumption that utopias are of a political nature and that 'politics' means institutional and bureaucratic arrangements – this approach to utopianism results in a definition that is too narrow and unnecessarily exclusive. A restricted and narrow approach to utopianism produces a restricted (restrictive) and narrow definition, understanding or concept. The act(ivity) of conceptualization thereby becomes an exclusionary one.

A further conventional ingredient in the content of the narrative form of utopianism is, according to Davis, the commonly held belief that utopia is finite. The depiction of a Utopia, he says, is:

> a once-for-all political act; a set of decisions against which there is no appeal.... Once the utopian has solved the political problem by organisational means, there is no longer need for politics in utopia.... When politics stops, so does change. Perfection is not relative. *The dynamic utopia is a myth.*
>
> (Davis, 1984: p. 10 my emphasis)

This view of utopianism as finite and static occurs in much of the literature on utopias that takes this content-focused approach, and informs the standard view of what constitutes a utopia. Barbara Goodwin, for instance, includes it as a characterizing feature in her work on utopia. She also connects utopian perfectibility with its finality:

> Furthermore, 'perfect' connotes a superlative state which must be considered beyond the reach or necessity of change, since there is no progressing beyond the perfect. This syntactical dictate, literally obeyed, gives many utopian states a static, unreal quality, which detracts from their credibility.
>
> (Goodwin, 1978: p. 5)

In terms of common usage, as well as in the works of theorists of utopian studies, perfection is frequently associated with utopia. This connection, however, is, I suggest, mistakenly made. This approach constructs as its performative act a myth of utopianism which is characterizable by reference to perfection. We saw, in the introduction to this chapter, that colloquial understandings of utopia perceive it as desiring to represent a perfect society, or to blueprint the perfect polity. Actual utopias of this kind are, I have suggested, rare, and do not represent utopianism *per se.*

19

Utopias that do appear to be formed by reference to perfection have a static feel to them (Bellamy's *Looking Backward* is one example). Most (contemporary) feminist utopian works lack this sense of stagnancy, being instead fluid and dynamic constructions. The depiction of multiple worlds is in actuality a recurrent characteristic of many modern feminist utopias.[12] I return to this theme of the static and universal utopia later in some detail. For the sake of the present discussion, however, it is enough to note that many feminist utopias do not 'fit' into a definition which relies on finality of end. The utopianism that Goodwin and others outline needs to be reconceived. Progress, movement and the perpetuation of struggle take the place of finality in many (contemporary and historical) utopian texts. An approach is needed that is open to these facts. A flexible and open-ended approach may go some way towards enabling conceptualization of a multiple and openended utopianism.

Utopias that do represent perfect worlds appear to function as a didactic device. Francis Bacon's *New Atlantis* (1629) will serve as an example. Bacon clearly intended his Utopia to be taken seriously as a model from which lessons about future society could be learned. It may even be the case that he intended the society that he depicted to serve as a blueprint for change. He was clearly preoccupied with perfection. This, I should like to suggest, is due to the nature of the debates and historical context in which he was engaged: Bacon wrote in a revolutionary age and shared a widespread belief that social and political transformation was achievable in the here and now. This is historically associated with the idea of a God on Earth. I stated above that engagement in current debates was a hallmark of utopian thought, and, as I read Bacon, he was clearly preoccupied by those mentioned.

In contrast, it is more common to find in contemporary feminist utopian literature and theory several worlds, often contrasting, none perfect. These worlds play speculative, meditative or critical roles rather than instructing as to the creation of a perfect world. Angela Carter's utopian/dystopian satire *The Passion of New Eve* (1982) is representative of this move, which is discernible in many feminist utopias: they are openended texts that let go of the notion of perfection. By so doing, they escape the finality of utopias of perfection. Their content tends to be marked by various manifesta-tions of discontent or wariness towards the concept of perfection. Rather than waxing lyrical about the nature of the perfect society that is imagined, these texts tend to focus instead on satire, on speculation, on ridiculing past universals. The function of these texts, I suggest, remains that of political opposition to the status quo, and of transgression of that which maintains the dominant relations of the political present. Put simply, these texts break and transform societal and cultural rules. In so doing they exploit the 'ou' of utopia and create new conceptual spaces in which radically different ways of being can be imagined. This, I suggest, is their definitive function.[13]

Like most of Carter's fictions, *The Passion of New Eve* is immensely complex. The following reading suggests that it can perform as an openended and satirical speculation. Its subject is Evelyn the man, who becomes Eve the woman. It can be read on one level as an exploration of the construction of female identity, on another as a satire of that which is America. I propose to concentrate on the former reading. The plot follows the adventures and misadventures of the central character Eve/lyn. As a man, in the early stages of the book, this character is callous, self-obsessed and self-loathing. The passion of Evelyn is twofold, involving on the one hand a tragic star of old films called Tristessa ('tristful', sad) and on the other himself. These passions intertwine to the extent that Tristessa, the ideal woman about whom he fantasizes, is an unreal figure, a simulacrum of his self-reflexive desire. The Tristessa by whom Evelyn is impassioned is a shadow. Her beauty is that of cracked and ancient celluloid: 'She had been the dream itself made flesh though the flesh I knew her in was not flesh itself but only a moving picture of flesh, real but not substantial' (Carter, 1982: pp. 7–8). Her appeal is her tragedy – she is 'necrophilia incarnate' (1982: p. 7), a symbol (an anti-symbol as it turns out) of the romantic heroine. He dreams of her as a victim and despises her pretences towards reality in the form of a publicity photograph in which she assumes the pose of a 'normal' woman, playing golf:

> I only loved her because she was not of this world and now I was disillusioned with her when I discovered she could stoop to a pretence of humanity. I therefore abandoned her. I took up rugby football and fornication.
>
> (1982: p. 8)

Images of Tristessa haunt the book, and reappear at incongruous moments throughout the experiences of Evelyn and Eve. In the later stages of the narrative, we discover that she (Tristessa) is a man. By this time, Evelyn has become Eve and is well on the way to being a woman.

The plot is bizarre and the ending is open – opening, if you like, with Eve's metaphorical birth as a woman. Evelyn (an Englishman) flees the apocalyptic city of New York after leaving his temporary lover, Leilah, with a crass bunch of red roses in an abortion clinic. He heads out into the desert (not quite for forty days and forty nights, but the metaphor is resonant), where he is captured by a matriarchal sect who rape and castrate him (turn him into Eve) and plan to impregnate him with his own semen. Eve escapes, and the remainder of the plot concerns her (mis)adventures in a female form, and her progress towards 'becoming' a woman. She is 'psychologically reprogrammed' by the women of the sect, but only after a number of concrete experiences – such as enslavement and repeated rape by Zero the misogynist poet, a love affair with the man who was Tristessa, and a journey into the womb of the earth – does she start to 'be' feminine. This is a utopian text that ends with a metaphorical rebirth in a truly open and unprescriptive finish.

Much of the content of *The Passion of New Eve* is satirical. The utopian convention of a perfect society, for instance, is ridiculed in the form of the matriarchal world of Beulah and the city of reason which was New York. In both of these locations form echoes function: the city is built to a grid on a rational basis:

> the streets had been given numbers and not names out of a respect for pure function, had been designed in clean, abstract lines, discrete blocks, geometric intersections, to avoid just those vile repositories of the past, sewers of history, that poison the lives of European cities. A city of pure reason – that had been the intention.
>
> (1982: p. 16)

In a classically ironic move, this city suffers dissolution. The evangelical fusion of form and function means that when reason breaks down and order dissolves into chaos, the city's sewers do overflow, and the structures and infrastructures of the city are inadequate to the disintegration and decomposition of social order that are occurring. Beulah also reflects its function in its form, and here Carter appears to satirize the inversion of logic practised by early radical feminists. Beulah represents the female body, and particularly the womb (from whence the biologically feminine Eve emerges). Rooms are round, passages curve and swoop inwards and downwards towards the belly of the earth. Beulah fetishizes the feminine form; New York was phallocentric in form, Beulah is shaped after the circle. This world of women is not presented as perfect, ideal or a blueprint. Rather, it is a place of madness, the madness born of fundamentalism and blind faith. The women of Beulah volunteer to donate one of their breasts to their spiritual leader, the goddess incarnate who is Mother:

> It is the home of the woman who calls herself the Great Patricide, also glories in the title of Grand Emasculator; ecstasy their only anaesthetic, the priests of Cybele sheared off their parts to exalt her, ran bleeding, psalmodising, crazed through the streets.

(1982: p. 49)

Mother is grotesque:

> Mother has made herself into an incarnated deity; she has quite transformed her flesh, she has undergone a painful metamorphosis of the entire body and become the abstraction of a natural principle.

(1982: p. 49)

Echoes of the radical vanguard feminism of the 1970s permeate the text. Parallels could be found, were we seeking them, between the female-centred spirituality advocated by writers such as Mary Daly and this horrific creation of Carter's. That is not the function of this discussion, but it is worth mentioning this satirization of a feminist text that is utopian in the standard, colloquial sense: Mary Daly's *Gyn/Ecology* (Daly, 1987). The books are roughly contemporaneous and whilst no direct reference is made to *Gyn/Ecology* by Carter, she does use many of its ideas in her depiction of the town of Beulah. Much of Daly's text is devoted to the 'exorcism' of masculinity from women's heads, and whilst undergoing her psycho-surgery, Eve is instructed into the misogyny of world religions in a typically Dalian fashion. The repetitive structure and horrific tone of *Gyn/Ecology* are mimicked when Eve is told about Chinese footbinding and Indian suttee: 'hour after hour was devoted to the relation of horrors my old sex had perpetuated on my new one' (1982: p. 73).

The Passion of New Eve rejects all attempts to force one's vision of perfection on to the world. It refutes the ideal society and shows one result of competing utopias: chaos, civil war and mass destruction. It is not, however, a conservative text – much of its content is concerned also to expose and ridicule the ways in which femininity is characterized and constructed in the present.

Another utopian text that evokes multiplicity rather than an all-encompassing perfection is Doris Lessing's *Marriages Between Zones Three, Four and Five* (1980), in which the central characters, Al*ith and

Ben Ata, move between them in and out of the book's four zones. The utopianism of this text is regarding social relations rather than institutions. Likewise, Angela Carter's *Heroes and Villains* (1969) presents two modes of existence in the one world, those of the Professors and the Barbarians, self-contained and with no contact between the two apart from the occasional Barbarian raiding party on a Professor village. Neither of these societies is ideal, and the stress in this novel is on process and change, which occur when the inhabitants of the two worlds begin to interact. Ursula Le Guin's *The Dispossessed* (1975) is a further example of a utopian text in which the concept of perfection is challenged. *The Dispossessed* privileges harmony and unity and represents an ambiguous utopia that has perhaps more links with ecology movements than with feminism. None the less, Le Guin is clearly wary of the stagnation of process, and this concern is reflected in the attitude of the central character Shevek, the utopian dissident. Further examples of openended utopianism will be cited in later chapters; I offer these merely as an introduction to the phenomenon that I shall later be calling 'transgressive utopianism'. At this early stage, we can see that one way in which this 'new' utopianism differs from the standard (mythical) model is in its transgression of accepted definitions of what it is to be a utopia.[14]

Not only are assumptions of a finite, static blueprint and perfect utopianism exclusive of most contemporary feminist utopias, but they are also mistakenly applied to some utopias of past decades and centuries. They cannot, for instance, be accurately applied to even the apparently uncontroversial example of Thomas More's *Utopia*.[15] We cannot justify the statement that this text represents a static or finite vision of the perfect polity. Its subtitle describes it as 'Concerning the *best* state of a commonwealth and the new island of Utopia', and 'best' need not be perfect or even ideal. *Utopia* is full not of perfection but rather of irreconcilable tensions, and is, I should like to suggest, self-consciously not perfect.

The 'flaws' of More's best commonwealth are well documented. Liberal commentators often remark upon the restrictions on individual freedoms to speak and travel, and upon the uniformity of the towns and households. More convincingly, perhaps, More's scholastic use of the pun – Hytholoday, pedlar of nonsense; Utopia, the good place that is no place; the river Anyder, without water – points to a construction more subtle than a simple blueprint for perfection. At the end of the book comes More's own disclaimer which, again, is often cited: 'Meantime while I can hardly agree with everything he

[Hytholoday] said ... yet I freely confess that in Utopian common-wealth there are many features that in our own societies I would like rather than expect to see' (More, 1975: pp. 110–11). Whilst often read as expressing the 'ou' of *Utopia*, this passage can also, of course, be taken as an expression of desire, cautiously phrased perhaps because of More's own political–historical context. Either way it reads as a curious ending to a blueprint for social change.

I stated above that *Utopia* is an apparently uncontroversial example of a utopian text, but if we stay with the standard view of what constitutes a utopia (what, in other words, a utopia contains) then we arrive at a complex position which is neatly summed up by Robert Adams:

> The meaning that 'utopia' has come to have as a common noun – a perfect society, or a literary account of one – seems authorised by the full title of the book which is (translating from the Latin) 'Concerning the Best State of a Commonwealth and the New Island of Utopia' ... When we begin to read the book itself, though, the plausible supposition that *Utopia* is a utopia is rapidly undermined.
>
> (More, 1975: p. xi)

I shall return to these tensions later, in the section on function. I mention them now to illustrate the imperfection and openended unresolvability of *Utopia*, *contra* Davis and the approach which identifies perfection as an ingredient of utopian thought.[16]

I have made much of this issue of perfection because I believe the imperfection and consequent openended and dynamic nature of many utopian texts are of key importance, and that these features need to be recognized. Hence, in the new, or different, approach to utopianism that I shall be proposing, these factors are understood as contributing to what I identify as utopian characteristics of engaged political speculation and debate. Earlier I stated that 'The Land of Cokaygne' could be read as engaging in serious political debates of its time. More's *Utopia* clearly does the same, and attention to this fact tells us about both the historical and the intellectual context of the book. This ground is well covered by other commentators and I have little to add to existing debates, except to stress the importance of these acts of engagement. Briefly, then, More's *Utopia* engages in contemporaneous debates about the relation between the crown and church, the role and nature of the state, the relation between the crown and people, and social implications of the changing economic infrastructure. It engages as well in intellectual debates with which contemporary humanist thought was preoccupied, namely the relation between morality and expediency, and the function of counsel.

Book I, Hytholoday's commentary on the problem of theft in England, sets the scene for entry into these debates. The context is one in which the enclosure of common land is having a profoundly alienating effect upon the income and stability of many livelihoods. Idle mercenaries added to this problem, as did rising food prices. Theft had become a social problem of some magnitude, and the penalty for theft was death. Hytholoday has to say of this that:

> this penalty is too harsh in itself, yet it isn't an effective deterrent...Severe and terrible punishments are enacted for theft, when it would be much better to enable every man to earn his own living instead of being driven to the awful necessity of stealing and then dying for it.
>
> (More, 1975: pp. 15–16)

He says of the social causes of widespread theft:

> If you don't try to cure these evils, it is futile to boast of your severity in punishing theft. Your policy may look superficially like justice, but in reality it is neither just nor practical.
>
> (1975: p. 21)

Hytholoday's style is rhetorical, and the enactment of rhetoric was common in sixteenth-century humanist debate. We shall see poststructuralist attempts to employ style as enactment of argument in later chapters. I mention this practice now just to show some of the subtlety and complexity of More's approach in *Utopia*. Hytholoday's rhetoric and the social construction of Book II both enact the moral/expedient debate with which humanism was engaged:

> If the moral and the expedient are ultimately identical [as Stoics believed], then it is theoretically possible to design a commonweal that would always act morally. But if the moral and the expedient cannot be fully reconciled [as Italian humanists such as Machiavelli would have it], then this ideal could never be achieved, even in theory.
>
> (Morton, 1952: p. 63)

Hytholoday's comments above show an inclination towards the belief that justice is a meeting of the moral and the expedient. In terms of its content, then, More's *Utopia* can, even from this short discussion, be seen to engage in political debate, and further to engage in a debate which took an ambiguous view of the attainability of perfection. Surely, though, the form or shape of *Utopia* also represents an enactment of this debate: is it possible to theorize perfection in this sense? Can it be conceptualized? *Utopia*, I suggest, is fruitfully read as exploring this debate at many levels. It is not a closed text but rather one that struggles to maintain an open end (or mind) by inhabiting the spaces and tensions between two ideals that are created by such debates as the moral/expedient rhetoric.

Other historical utopias can also be seen to engage critically with contemporaneous political debates: Morris's *News from Nowhere* (1891) examines debates within Marxism (as he understood it) on such topics as historical materialism, change as a positive and creative force, and revolution as an agent of widespread social change; and he does this by attacking the state communism of Edward Bellamy's *Looking Backward* (1951). Francis Bacon (1629) and Campanella (*c.* 1600) engage in debates concerning the human potential for progress; hence their shared stress on research, exploration and science. Even Bishop Hall's hilarious satire 'Mundus Alter et Idem' has a clearly serious edge to it: this piece was first published in 1607, and the preposterous tales of Crapula, Virginia, Moronia and Lavernia reflect early seventeenth-century concerns about discipline within the church. The world of Crapula is 'the Land of Inebriate Excess'; its two provinces, Pamphagonia and Yvronia, translate as 'Omnivorous Gluttony' and 'Drunkenness'. The discipline of the clergy may appear an unpolitical matter, but the excesses of monastic life had provided fuel for Henry VIII's dissolution of the monasteries (1536–1540). That, of course, helped to shape the role of the state and crown in the sixteenth and seventeenth centuries.

I digress, for whilst the historical utopias provide a source of endless speculation, they are not the subject of this book. I make these references, though, in order to reinforce my arguments *contra* Davis and the colloquially dominant view of utopianism as a blueprint for a perfect world. Utopianism has always been much more than this.

Engagement in debate and critique of the status quo remain characteristic features of utopian thought. Debate is engaged because the author is politically or ideologically committed in some way to the project in question. A primary function of feminist utopian thought is, unsurprisingly, to criticize patriarchal society. Critique is a characteristic of all utopian writing that is, I suggest, related to its political nature. For Goodwin, this function contributes to the value of utopianism to political theory:

> If a culture is to be criticised radically, by reference to alternative values outside its own ideology, a utopian model is a valuable device. When the theorist wishes to refashion society wholesale, utopia offers to him a useful space, devoid of preconceived features, within which to work.
>
> (Goodwin, 1978: p. 3)

Two points are being made here: the first relates to the critical function of utopia, while the second asserts that utopia presents a perfect space for radical criticism. I shall return to these points later in my discussion of approaches that privilege function. For now, though, I should like to include a critical function as an ingredient of utopian thought.

So far this discussion of approaches that focus on content has been restricted to formulaic content. A number of conventions have been discussed and explored, and this kind of content-based approach is certainly of some value to establishing definitions of the literary genre of utopia. The central problem with this approach, which has contributed so much to the dominant view of a utopia, is that often criteria have been established that are not appropriate to their subject. Utopian texts are, I have suggested, of a political nature in that they are engaged in political debate and with political issues. They have a critical edge in that they challenge the political present. Perfection is not a utopian convention, and I have argued that the dynamic utopia is not a myth. Many of these points will be developed further in the subsequent discussions of approaches which privilege function. I should like, for now, to set aside this approach and to shift focus slightly to approaches that use content in a broader sense.

Narrative content

Much feminist commentary on utopianism is cast in terms of the narrative content of utopias, and it is on this approach that I propose to focus now. By discussing feminist approaches of this sort, the flaws of this (content-based) methodology can be identified clearly. There is a popular argument amongst commentators who favour this approach that the common ground that can be found in many feminist utopias is what distinguishes these works from the male/mainstream text. Before discussing this in any detail, however, it is important to note that feminist utopianism is no more a homogeneous body of thought than is feminism itself, and, more importantly, that feminist utopianism, whilst firmly rooted in the present in its various critiques, is not representative of feminism in general.[17] There exist, for instance, differences amongst women's utopias that reflect the writers' differing circumstances and environment (in the larger sense). Marijke Rudnik-Smalbraack, for example, finds distinctive differences between French and American feminist utopianism. American utopianism, she states, is more practically orientated, more accessible, whereas the French tradition she finds more abstract, more extreme. She concludes that utopia is: 'a rich and fruitful land for many feminist writers and critics, hospitable not only to the wild dreams and theoretical projections of the French, but also to the literary ambitions and intellectual explorations of [US] writers' (Rudnik-Smalbraack, 1987: p. 178). There is in her discussion a clear preference for the American approach on the grounds that it is more practical and, therefore, more practicable. She is, I suggest, mistaken in this conclusion, whilst correct in her generalizations of the differences between the two traditions.[18]

Nan Bowman Albinski raises similar points regarding the differences amongst women's utopias. Albinski has undertaken a comprehensive historical analysis of American and British feminist utopian literature. She finds some striking differences between these works that comprise different literary traditions. To summarize broadly, she finds the American tradition to be concerned with a 'belief in social rather than political change, in internal rather than external influences, and in religious and moral rather than secular evolution' (Albinski, 1988: p. 5).

Differences in narrative content can be found, therefore, within women's utopian theory and fiction. These traditions tell different stories. Apart from such broad national/cultural variations, it should also be noted that differences exist within and between the various ideological manifestations of feminism. The move observed by Albinski and others towards a certain fragmentation and dislocation is illustrative of this.[19] Whereas Shulamith Firestone's work is a(n overly) self-confident proclamation of the radical socialist feminism of the 1970s, later works reflect in their lack of cohesion the (troubled) state of contemporary feminist theory.[20] It should be noted furthermore that the vast majority of the works under discussion are the product of white Western feminism. This 'movement's' recent self-consciousness regarding its historical racism and cultural imperialism can be seen to be reflected in its ambivalent attitude towards race.

Black and white feminisms are not yet comfortable with other; and the consequent tension between the pull of integration on the one hand, and separation on the other, is an important theme of this work. Any approach which insists upon criteria of narrative content runs the risk of burying this diversity.

Levitas has objected to definitions reliant upon content on the grounds that 'definitions in terms of content tend to be evaluative and normative, specifying what the good society would be, rather than reflecting on how it may be differently perceived' (Levitas, 1990: p. 4). Instead of relying upon function, form or content, Levitas proposes that utopia be considered in broad terms as the expression of the desire for a better way of life. I suggest that the nature of the desire expressed is of some defining value in distinguishing the feminist from the mainstream utopia. Whereas utopianism *per se* cannot be defined with regards to function, form or content alone, these aspects do, I suggest, play a role in identifying specifically feminist utopias. (In the following section I suggest that the relevant factor is not so much what the book in question is about as how and why the material is used; hence form and function cannot be divorced from content.)

A content-based approach, then, may be of some value in identifying feminist utopianism but is problematic to a project of redefinition of the field of utopia. In the following discussion I propose first to argue that focusing on content in this way falsely homogenizes feminist thought.[21] Further, I suggest that the writers under discussion promote an understanding of feminism which is dualistic and which is perceived to operate in simple binary opposition to the patriarchal present. In Chapter 3 I propose a new (and utopian) conception of the function of feminism.

> A feminist utopian novel is one which *a.* contrasts the present with an envisioned idealized society (Separated from the present by time or space), *b.* offers a comprehensive critique of present values/conditions, *c.* sees men or male institutions as a major cause of present social ills, and *d.* presents women not only as at least the equals of men but also as the sole arbiters of their reproductive functions.
>
> (Gearhart, 1984: p. 296)

Often the content of a feminist utopian text is what delineates it as specifically feminist, but, as suggested above, content alone is inadequate with regard to definition. Sally Miller Gearhart's definition is offered here as an example of this inadequacy. Whilst it may serve to cover work that she herself has produced, it is insufficient as a general definition on several counts.

The first concerns utopian content and is fairly straightforward: implicit in Gearhart's point (a) is the assumption that the feminist utopian novel is representative of eutopia, other elements of the field, such as dystopia, being disregarded. I follow Sargent in insisting that the field of utopianism contains the eutopia, the dystopia and utopian satire. Moreover, there is no room in this definition for the openended utopia. In this reading, therefore, Gearhart's understanding of utopia is over-restrictive.

Point (b) of the above quotation is satisfactory as a broad defining characteristic of utopianism in general but adds nothing to those definitions discussed already. A combination of points (b) and (c) results, according to Gearhart's reasoning, in a text of a feminist nature, although I would argue that point (c) itself is unnecessarily exclusive, because it relies on a universalism of the narrative content of utopias. Her understanding of what constitutes feminism is clearly free from the subtleties of the French analyses. Use of the words 'male' and 'men' points to a biologically determined enemy camp, whereas the concepts of cultural and libidinal masculinity, whilst more complex, allow a less clumsy analysis.[22]

Point (d) again restricts utopia to eutopia but in a dangerously exclusive and prescriptive manner, not least because not all feminist utopian novels concern themselves with reproduction, let alone centre upon this issue. Levitas's worry about normative definitions that are formed in terms of content is, I suggest, well illustrated by this point. Its implications are twofold: first, a novel, according to this definition, cannot be considered feminist unless women are depicted as at least equal to men and in control of reproduction; second, a feminist text, thus defined, cannot be said to be utopian unless it contains an idealized society in which such a scenario is considered.

Gearhart's definition or outline of the feminist utopian novel adds nothing to the approaches to utopianism that have been discussed above. Further, it invokes and invites unnecessary closure – a twofold closure that restricts utopianism to conventional understandings, and restricts feminism to Gearhart's limited (and limiting) conception. The problematics of such an approach are further explored in the next chapter. Briefly, though, Gearhart is (unwittingly?) erecting an exclusive model of what it is to be a feminist: to be a feminist is to think and desire what she (and people like her) think(s) and desire(s).[23]

In a short but influential essay, 'Coming Home: Four Feminist

Utopias and Patriarchal Experience', Carol Pearson proposes a content-based outline of feminist utopianism that also stresses function: 'Feminist utopian fiction implicitly or explicitly criticizes the patriarchy while it emphasizes society's habit of restricting and alienating women' (Pearson, 1981: p. 63). She argues that the works she studies: 'assume that patriarchy is unnatural and fails to create environments conducive to the maximization of female – or male – potential. Upon discovering a sexually egalitarian society, the narrators have a sense of coming home to a nurturing, liberating environment' (1981: p. 63). Pearson is careful to separate her first statement, that which is applicable to all feminist utopian fiction (in the narrow sense of that word), from the second, which she finds applicable to the four works which she considers.[24] In general terms, the critical function of utopia is stressed. In the second sentence, though, which may be read as relating to these specific texts or not, a constructive role is assigned to utopia. The nature of this construction is one of rediscovery.

'Coming Home' identifies 'surprisingly numerous areas of consensus among such seemingly divergent works' (Pearson, 1981: p. 63). These areas of consensus are ones of common narrative content. Amongst those identified are critiques of the low status of women's work in the present and the subsequent revaluing of traditionally 'feminine' occupations such as teaching; assumptions about an innate female nature are, she says, challenged, and stereotypes are countered by the emphasis on women's strengths. Violence is treated as male and is thus 'antithetical to a feminist vision' (1981: p. 64). The public/private divide is challenged by patterning society after the family; respect for the individual is given precedence over issues of race and class and social order is achieved by persuasion rather than force.

The central hypothesis of the piece concerns the metaphor of motherhood. Pearson states that 'In these novels, reclaiming the self is often associated with coming home to mother' (1981: p. 65). The mother in question is not the neurotic and smothering mother of patriarchy but, she suggests, 'a fully human, free person'. It is interesting to note the choice of the non-gendered noun 'person' to refer to the utopian mother, particularly when combined with the revaluation of culturally traditional feminine values and attributes outlined above. The utopian child is not the property of its mother, this newly empowered ultra-feminine being: rather child-care and birth are identified as a communal function; non-claustrophobic and non-repressive. The mother is also used by Pearson as metaphor for woman's experience, which, she seems to suggest, given the right situation, can result in empowered individuals and a better way of being for all. She refers to a new consciousness which 'fuses thought and feeling', in a reversal of patriarchal denigration of woman (1981: p. 69).

Pearson's approach is deeply essentialist and, like Gearhart, she presents a vision of feminism that is marked by unacknowledged and inappropriate closure. This, I suggest, is a worrying consequence of approaching utopianism through its narrative content. The problems regarding Pearson's essentialism are also noted by Sarah Lefanu, who states that it 'denies social and ideological construction of the self, and fall[s] back on the idea of a "natural" woman' (Lefanu, 1988: p. 54). However, Lefanu is not unduly worried about this apparent essentialism:

> The point is that 'woman' in conventional contemporary science fiction is an absence, at best a pale imitation of 'man', if not actually the feared castrating other. So to imagine a woman as having a self that can be liberated from the strictures of male dominance, of narrative form as well as the real world, as these feminist utopias do, is itself a liberating experience.
>
> (1988: p. 54)

I argue in Chapter 4 that, when located in a libidinal *and* cultural context, the valorization of femininity can be an emancipatory tactic, and even a utopian goal in itself. I also explore feminist utopian visions of a non-repressive relation between mother and child that might, perhaps, be located in what I call a feminine libidinal economy. These projects must not, however, be undertaken from a position of naivety, in a simple reversal of 'what is': that is, the acceptance of the given role, nature, function and form of an essential woman.

Whilst having some sympathy for Pearson's approach, then, I am worried about some of her methods. The advocacy of a simple reversal and universalism about 'human nature' is apparent in her discussion of, for example, the attitude towards women's work in the novels upon which she focuses. Women's work is given high utopian status and work is done 'naturally' for love rather than profit: 'Ironically, it may be women's experiences in a sexist society which have enabled them to see truths about human motivations' (Pearson, 1981: p. 64). There is an apparent confusion here between a self formed by experience and a self which is independent and naturally, or inherently, existing. There is a similar confusion of experience and innate essence or truth in her extension of the 'coming home' metaphor: 'The metaphors for the birth of feminist consciousness and society are patterned after women's actual procreative experiences' (1981: p. 70). If woman is formed by her experiences, there can be nothing natural to which to refer.

Related to this but of more concern are her assumptions regarding class and race. Within the narratives she studies she finds similarity of content regarding these areas. Of the utopian family she says 'Economic and racial prejudice are absent from these families. In fact, respect for the individual is an integral aspect of the feminist utopian vision' (1981: p. 67). To insist upon sexual difference whilst denying a role to other differences, is as implicitly imperialist as is the traditional treatment of woman as absence.

I have suggested that there are some serious flaws in the approaches of Gearhart and Pearson and that these flaws result from a normative focus on content. Analyses in these terms produce warped visions of feminism and do not contribute to the project with which this book is concerned. Utopianism itself needs to be reconceived.

Nan Bowman Albinski (1988) works from Sargent's definition of utopia, which is, as stated above, divided into the eutopia, the dystopia and the utopian satire. For her, the eutopia represents a 'good' place, and involves a common belief in the malleability of human nature. Eutopias she finds to be often set in the future but always directly connected to the imperfect present. The dystopia evinces a shared belief in the flexibility of human nature but shows it being manipulated for the worse, often in the name of eutopia. Dystopias may be, but are not necessarily, anti-utopian. Sargent characterizes the explicitly anti-utopian work by its focus on satire, but utopian satire is not always directed against utopia as such. The anti-utopia is, according to Albinski, unique in its approach towards human nature which is presented in works of this kind as fixed and immutable.

Albinski's analysis is in terms of content and form, and she manages to avoid problems of overgeneralization by keeping the focus of her work context-specific. With regard to form, she finds that the British and American eutopias of the 1960s and 1970s show declining realism and a shift towards allegory and ambiguity, whilst clear-cut images are the property of the modern dystopia. The bulk of her analysis is a thematic study in terms of narrative content. She finds that British eutopian visions of the 1960s–1980s never associate women with nature; science and technology are mocked rather than feared; and nuclear holocaust, whilst present in many eutopias, operates only as an instrument of social change. In the American eutopia she finds devastation via nuclear power to have a similarly minor role. Women in these eutopias are in control of their own and, occasionally, male destinies (examples can be found in some separatist societies). Androgynous societies minimalize gender differences, stressing the commonality of human experience. Violence is minimal, usually being associated with male rule; laws are generally presented as similarly oppressive. Both American and British utopias, she finds, celebrate reproduction, and sexual permissiveness is the norm.

Albinski's survey is more comprehensive than those of Pearson and Gearhart, but the observations made are generalizations which are not applicable to a project of definition. Whilst we can say that feminist utopias tend to treat these issues in similar ways, we cannot, as I argue above, use them as defining characteristics. Albinski does not attempt to do so; rather she works through Sargent's categories, noting that splits within and between feminist movements in the two countries correspond to the different ways in which these themes are treated. Her approach is useful, showing the connections between and differences amongst feminist theory and feminist utopian thought. Those distinctions are, I suggest, important, and they are explored in more detail in Chapter 3 where I suggest that differences should not be buried for the sake of providing a coherent thematic schema or framework of intellectual study.

Definitions which are established in terms of content attempt to identify politically grouped 'types' of utopia. The use of a politically defined adjective such as 'feminist' to describe a certain type of utopianism (eutopia, dystopia and utopian satire) does have some advantages. It makes for a definition that is descriptive whilst allowing flexibility to the genre of utopia(nism) itself. It also has limitations which I suggest outweigh its advantages, for if the characteristics of this form of utopianism are taken to be representative of the genre as a whole, familiar problems of exclusion will arise once more. Again, we can see how a closed methodology or approach produces an unnecessarily closed concept.

In conclusion, then, it is possible to make the generalization that definitions merely in terms of content cannot be universally applied and are therefore inadequate.[25] Normative definitions may enable us to distinguish the feminist utopia from other types, but not to define utopianism (or feminism). Approaching utopianism in terms of its content, therefore, may be of more value than privileging form, but is still a problematic route to understanding utopianism.

CONCLUSION

I stated in the introduction to this chapter that my argument for a new approach to the concept and phenomenon of utopianism was grounded in three justificatory statements. Utopianism, I said, should be reapproached because:

1 the standard view of utopia is fundamentally flawed;
2 the standard view is inappropriate to much of contemporary feminist utopianism and is, therefore, unnecessarily exclusive;
3 the new approach offered in this book is more appropriate to contemporary feminist utopianism.

The first two of these statements in particular have informed the discussions in which this chapter has been engaged, and I should like, by way of temporarily concluding this debate, to summarize with direct reference to them.

I began my discussion of the various approaches to utopian thought by looking at those which focus on form.[26] This approach, although common, was rejected because it was found to restrict discussions unnecessarily, and because these restrictive approaches can have the insidious functions of disciplinary or cultural imperialism. In other words, this approach is constructed in such a way as to exclude that which should and could be included. Utopianism and the expression of utopian thought have always been transgressive of disciplinary boundaries: attempts to capture it within the bounds of one discipline will inevitably result in both inadequate readings of utopian texts and inadequate conceptualizations of utopianism itself. The performative acts of this approach are essentially and eternally exclusive ones.

Focuses on formulaic content have also been found to contribute to a flawed conception of utopianism. In the first instance, some of the conventions or ingredients that are identified by theorists who take this approach are, I have suggested, mistakenly identified. The checklist of conventions that I identified included a statement that utopian thought is of a political nature: this I accepted, whilst considerably broadening the definition of what constitutes the political.[27] Many utopias were, however, found not to be finite or static, or to represent or desire perfection. These are the fundamental characteristics of any encyclopaedia or dictionary definition, and as such they form the keystones of the standard view of utopia. This, I suggest, is the standard approach to utopianism. By looking at historical utopias and by referring to contemporary feminist ones, I have shown that this approach is flawed in that it fails to capture the richness and diversity of utopian thought. This approach easily leads to misrepresentations of utopianism. It creates a view of utopia(nism) which sees it as closing debate, ending progress and process, and generally providing the ideal conditions for stagnation and decay. Perfection, I suggest, symbolizes death: the death of movement, the death of progress and process, development and change; the death, in other words, of politics. To strive for perfection is to strive for death. I have indicated an alternative, dynamic and vibrant model of utopianism that retains many of the traditional conventions. Primarily, I claimed that utopian thought represents a critical engagement with political issues and debates of its time.

This formulaic, content-based approach, then, has been found to be problematic, on the one hand, and useful on the other: it has invoked inappropriate closures but can enable us to begin building a picture of what utopian thought might look like. The discussions engaged in in this section also serve to illustrate my conviction that the approach taken to a subject (in)forms the subsequent theories about that subject.

I have also considered approaches to utopianism that privilege narrative content. These I found, following Levitas, to be unsatisfactory because they lead to misrepresentative (hence unnecessarily exclusive) ideas about the content of utopian thought. Not all Utopias are the same, and so this approach simply does not work in a definitional sense. It can, perhaps, be employed to enable separation of one 'type' of utopian thought (such as feminist) from others; but again, I have identified flaws in this approach, which lie in the tendency to misrepresent (and hence erect exclusive understandings of) feminism.

The new approach that I am advocating does not misrepresent utopian conventions, and I believe that those identified in the discussions above represent the first steps in narrowing down the field to an identifiable concept. My approach is not, in other words, averse to a focus on formulaic content. On the question of critical engagement in contemporary debates, for instance, which I have identified as a lasting utopian convention, consideration of this characteristic can throw light upon the nature of both utopianism and contemporary feminism. I shall be pursuing this sort of approach in Chapter 4; briefly, though, because critical engagement is a speculative activity, it does not (inevitably) create a desire to end debate. Contemporary feminist utopias often leave 'the end' unwritten or open. Contemporary feminism itself is a multifaceted phenomenon. Within the context of contemporary feminist thought, which is characterized by complexity, diversity and multidimensionality, utopian thought is, I believe, best approached in this way.

This approach that I am calling 'new' does not approach utopianism solely or exclusively in terms of formulaic content; it also privileges a certain focus on function, which I shall discuss in the next chapter. It is an approach that comes (simultaneously) to the subject from a number of perspectives, privileging whichever is appropriate at the given moment. Indeed, the approach for which this book argues (and which later chapters explore) represents a deliberate and principled avoidance of rigid definitions. Whilst acknowledging the considerable problems with this, I would like to suggest that it is less likely to lead the scholar into the methodological traps and exclusions that other approaches entail.

2

FUNCTION-BASED APPROACHES TO UTOPIANISM

INTRODUCTION

In Chapter 1, approaches to utopianism that privilege its form and content were found to contribute to what I have called the standard colloquial view of what constitutes a utopia. These approaches were, in the large part, rejected because I found them to produce inappropriate and unacknowledged closed representations of utopianism (and of feminism). They construct what I have called the myth of utopia. Utopian thought is far more interesting and complex than is allowed by the standard view of utopia as a genre that represents a perfect society and offers a blueprint for change.

I have identified a number of criteria that I find appropriate to historical and feminist utopias and that represent a new approach. This does not claim utopianism for any one discipline or field, and looks at it initially as a space for speculation and critique. In the discussions that follow I shall identify a number of 'ingredients' to utopian thought that give it a creative function to complement the critical one established above.

In this discussion of commentaries on utopianism which focus primarily on identifying or stressing certain functions to the phenomenon, I propose to discuss only those which *privilege* function. Definitions which are formed in terms of the function of utopianism tend to be more sophisticated than those which refer to form and content,[1] and the attention paid by commentators to the function of utopian thought both suggests and represents new approaches or attitudes towards utopianism. Approaches of this sort find oppositional and/or transformative functions for/in utopian thought and its expression, and I shall be focusing largely on the various ways in which these functions are thought to operate and be constructed.

CONTENT, FORM AND FUNCTION: SEEPAGE

I should like to begin this discussion of function-based approaches from the margins where seepage occurs between the three areas of content, form and function. It is at these moments of methodological overflow that some of the most interesting points of observation are made regarding the nature, function and implications of utopian thought. For the sake of manageable discussion, I shall focus primarily on approaches which ascribe a function to what are thought to be generic conventions of utopianism. Here, formulaic content and function overlap and intertwine. This discussion will not hope to be exhaustive; my aim is to evaluate the potential and implications of such approaches.

I stated in Chapter 1 that one commonly identified utopian convention is that of politically engaged discourse and critique. The metaphor of a mirror is often employed when illustrating these points. Utopian writing is said to place in front of the society that it criticizes a construct (theoretical or literary), which reflects back to that society the writer's perceptions. Like the queen's in the story of Snow White, this mirror is not compliant; rather it tells the viewer/reader that the fairest of them all is actually elsewhere, and it may or may not say where. I should like to suggest that this is the function of the common utopian 'ingredient' of the imaginary society. Rather than invariably reading these constructs 'straight', as depictions of the desired future or as blueprints for perfection, I suggest that we would do better to introduce greater subtlety to our reading and see them as critical artifacts.[2] Hence, I suggest, the reputation of utopia as a subversive genre.[3]

The utopian mirror can also have a function in the way that a text is constructed and, consequently, read. Luce Irigaray's theoretical texts, for instance, are profoundly utopian. She employs a tactic of textual mimesis that reflects a vision of the current situation that is just as exaggerated as is the presentation of an actual utopian ideal or dystopian mirror. Mimesis, for Irigaray, allows critique to occur concurrently with debate. She assumes exaggeratedly 'feminine' writing tactics, such as 'flirting' with the philosophers with whose texts she is involved. Thus she highlights the artificial position of femininity which they dictate, whilst engaging in scholarly debate with the texts. Like More's humanistic rhetoric, Irigaray's mimesis represents the use of style as enactment of a theoretical position. Mimesis produces a strangely estranged text, and this estrangement is another of the utopian conventions to which can be attributed an oppositional or transformative function.[4] Kumar links the estrangement of the utopian text to its subversive function: 'Utopia challenges by supplying alternatives, certainly. It shows what could be. But its most persistent function, the real source of its subversiveness, is as a critical commentary on the arrangements of society' (Kumar, 1991: pp. 87–8).

Feminism too has radically subversive potential, and for this reason it finds utopia a comfortable position from which to critique. Utopian estrangement moreover allows distance from the present world. As is often pointed out, the etymology of the word contains a double pun – outopia is a nowhere, eutopia a good place – which the spoken word condenses and compresses. Utopian thinking is thinking that creates and operates inside a new place or space that has previously appeared inconceivable. Writing from or towards a good place that is no place, glancing over her shoulder at the place whence she came, the utopian feminist escapes the restrictions of patriarchal scholarship. New and inventive languages can best be imagined and employed in a new space, as can different social, sexual and symbolic relations. The link with (perceived) reality, though, is of central import for the creation of utopian thought.

Northrop Frye identifies a further convention of utopianism, which is the explicit presence of imaginative and inventive thought:

> Utopian thought is imaginative, with its roots in literature, and the literary imagination is less concerned with achieving ends than with visualizing possibilities.... The word 'imaginative' refers to hypothetical constructions, like those of literature or mathematics. The word 'imaginary' refers to something that does not exist.
>
> (Frye, 1973: p. 32)

This convention too has an interesting and double-edged function. Because they are explicitly imaginative, utopian theory and literature have been devalued in the schools of political theory and philosophy as escapist, fanciful and, above all, unscientific in disciplines which favour rational debate, logical argument and serious scholarship. It is, perhaps, ironic that within this undervalued genre the contribution of women writers should in turn be denied voice, as, for the main part, women writers of earlier centuries are rendered invisible by concentration on their male counterparts. It is also, perhaps, ironic that the words used to depreciate utopianism are those which Western binary

thought designates 'feminine' as opposed to the rationality of masculine, 'scientific' debate. Its imaginative nature, its literary rather than
explicitly theoretical form, contribute to what I later call utopia's
cultural and social femininity.[5]

It is also apparent from the Frye quotation that the connections
between utopia and the imagination and literature have specific
consequences, in his analysis, for the function of utopian writing.
Reference to More's *Utopia* may be of some illustrative value regarding
this point. In the 1517 edition of *Utopia*, after Book II has ended, there
appears 'A Letter from Thomas More to his friend Peter Giles' which
concerns a(n imaginary?) critic who has asked whether the book is
fiction or fact. More's ironic response is as follows:

> But when he questions whether the book is fact or fiction, I find
> *his* judgement quite awry. There's no denying that if I had
> decided to write of a commonwealth, and a tale of this sort had
> come to my mind, I might not have shrunk from fiction through
> which truth, like medicine smeared with honey, might enter the
> mind a little more pleasantly. But I would certainly have
> softened the fiction a little, so that, while impressing on vulgar
> ignorance, I gave hints to the more learned which would enable
> them to see through the pretence.
>
> (More, 1975: p. 113)

Utopia (like utopian writing generally) is different from 'straight'
philosophy in that it enjoys a different status and has a different and
more explicitly subversive function. It sweetens the pill of a serious
'message' whilst playfully letting us in on the joke. Serious (philosophy) is dressed up as trivial (fiction), which is undressed as serious
(philosophy).[6] Utopian writing is ironic and satirical rather than
perfection-seeking. Visualizing possibilities is not the same as providing a blueprint for the future. Peter Alexander likens this to the
attempts by philosophers to test a concept by stretching it to its limits
(Alexander, 1984). Philosophy, he says, is the art of the possible in that
it is concerned with that which is conceivable. Utopian writing can
also be read thus, that is, as an intellectual expansion of possible
futures, not necessarily as a plan of campaign for action. The utopia,
then, can be read as metaphor or myth rather than literal blueprint, as
catalytic to revolutionary thought rather than as didactic. Linked to
the literary connection is the supposition discussed above that a
Utopia is a fictional construction or artifice. This view, as mentioned
in Chapter 1, is common in approaches which focus on form. I have

suggested that approaching utopianism in terms of its form is unhelpful, but would like now to reconsider this point. We can, quite usefully, consider what function this fictional status might have.

The *Concise Oxford Dictionary* defines the word 'fiction' as follows: 'Feigning, invention; thing feigned or imagined; invented statement or narrative; literature consisting of such narrative; conventionally accepted falsehood (esp. legal, polite, ~)'. For 'fictitious' the dictionary gives the following explanation: 'counterfeit, not genuine; (of name or character) assumed; imaginary, unreal; of, in, novels; regarded as what it is called by legal or conventional fiction'. These definitions are clearly appropriate to More's *Utopia* and also have resonance when applied to many feminist utopian texts. The imaginative nature and literary form of many feminist utopias earn them the title 'fictitious'. The inclusion in the definitions of the word 'feigned' is provocative. To feign is to invent, but the word 'feign' does not have particularly positive or favourable implications. To feign is to pretend or simulate, and from its etymological root, the French 'feindre', also comes the word 'feint'. Implied, then, in the statement that 'utopias are by definition fictions' is that utopias are shams, pretences, falsehoods.

This ambiguous and double-edged status is exploited by some writers to produce anarchic and rule-breaking texts with subversive potential. Angela Carter's work provides perhaps the clearest examples of the 'sham' utopia. Illusion and allusion, densely punning language and multiple metaphors, all seep through her texts so that nothing is as it first appears. With her tongue firmly in her cheek, she keeps the line between eutopia and dystopia fine. 'Outopia' as non-truth has power and strength. If fiction is understood in the terms expressed by Kumar ('All utopias are, by definition, fictions; unlike say historical writing, they deal with possible, not actual worlds' (Kumar, 1991: p. 25)), then opacity of form or content in utopian writing gives it enhanced fictional or subversive status. A text that is not unidirectional explores and extends what may be possible to a greater extent than one that is. Such a text is transgressive of what is described in later chapters as the logocentric pursuit of truth: further, such a text allows avoidance of the imperialistic imposition of a singular truth in the guise of a model society. Openended (multi-directional) fictive utopias do not desire or function to evoke the death of process.

Peter Alexander, in a discussion of the fictional settings of many utopias, introduces a contentious proposal. He suggests that both

utopian theory and philosophy are closely related at a functional level
to the fairy tale:

> Philosophers, too, may be thought of as writing fairy-tales when
> in pursuit of conceptual clarity they invent conceivable but
> highly improbable situations. They deal in problems which are
> *ex hypothesi* unlikely to arise. . . . I think it important to regard
> utopians as foster-siblings of the Brothers Grimm, working in
> their tradition although their messages are directed at adults.
> The Brothers Grimm played upon the fears and longings of
> children and no doubt intended to teach them certain things
> about morality as well as to entertain. Utopians play upon the
> fears and longings of adults and intend by rational argument to
> lead them to a better understanding of political and moral
> matters and, with the help of entertainment, to incline them
> towards valuing certain things.
>
> (Alexander, 1984: p. 41)

Angela Carter is perhaps the feminist writer most commonly
associated with the fairy tale. She has worked with them in *The Bloody
Chamber* (1981), for instance, reworking the old stories. Echoes of the
fairy tale flood through her utopian satires. The settings are fantastic,
the characters lack depth and magic pervades. The fairy tale can also be
found in Hélène Cixous's work. She presents close analyses of Little
Red Riding Hood and Sleeping Beauty, for instance, in her essay
'Castration or Decapitation?' (Cixous, 1981b). The following lines are
from 'Sorties', and are highly evocative of the fairy tale in both style
and the allusion in the last sentence to the warning of Little Red
Riding Hood's mother: 'Your continent is dark. Dark is dangerous.
You can't see anything in the dark, you're afraid. Don't move you
might fall. Above all don't go into the forest' (Cixous and Clement,
1986: p. 68).

The incorporation of the fairy tale or fable into such texts lightens
their tone and gives the reader a familiar handle to grasp. It also
deepens their speculative mood, providing meditative focal points,
combining the commonplace with the fantastic. Like the fairy tale,
blueprint utopias seek a happy ever after. They also share concerns
with universal themes and are emotional or romantic in appeal. The
following statement from J.C. Cooper can be read to draw together
functions that are shared by the fairy tale, the utopia of the standard
approach and traditional philosophy: 'The fascination of the fairy tale,
for all ages, lies in its revelation of one's own inner nature, with its

infinite moral, psychic and spiritual possibilities. It is the search for meaning in life' (Cooper, 1983: p. 21).

Philosophy seeks meaning and truth, and the standard colloquial understanding of utopia sees the genre as attempting to embody the truth of/as perfection. The metaphor should not, however, be over-extended, for whilst traces of the fairy tale can be found in the (sometimes fantastic) utopian works of contemporary feminists, it is in a form that does not seek unity or desire perfection. Rather, the fairy tale is inverted as a rhetorical device by writers such as Carter and Cixous, and the kind of sentiment expressed below by Cooper is satirized rather than echoed: 'The sufferings, trials and tribulations are necessary for total fulfilment, for the development of the individuals involved, until they achieve personal integration and then final realization in unity' (Cooper, 1983: p. 21).

The texts of Carter and Cixous are profoundly disintegrationist, and the subversion or inversion of the fairy tale as unifying force has the effect of shattering established myths and universals. This is, I suggest, related to the nature of contemporary feminism itself. The realization that has dawned upon many feminist theorists over the past ten or so years is that no single voice can speak for all women and that feminism must recognize this fact if it is to claim ethical and intellectual validity. Hence, I suggest, the increasing use and popu-larity of these and other tactics of separation.[7] The functional link between utopianism and the fairy tale, then, is in their shared use of the fantastic, and not in their shared pursuit of universal solutions to universal questions. This latter link is mistakenly made by taking the standard view of a utopia as given.

An approach that pulls together some of these observations about the function of the conventions of utopian writing is what I propose to call the generic one. Sarah Lefanu, Anne Cranny Francis and Rosemary Jackson all adopt this. Their concern is largely with literary genres (in the strict and proper sense of that phrase). Utopianism is often entwined in literary practice with science fiction, an area explored in greater detail in Chapter 7. Science fiction is considered by many feminist commentators to be that best suited to utopian exploration and critique. Sarah Lefanu, for instance, states that whilst science fiction has traditionally reflected the authority of men over women, as a literary genre it has emancipatory potential:

> It is able to break through the parameters of realism: in literary terms to enjoy the freedom of the fantastic mode, or to employ

modernist techniques to challenge the hegemony of the mainstream novel, or again, importantly, to centralise the short story
as a literary form that is both viable and popular. In social, or
political terms, it is able to extrapolate from, to comment on, to
satirise the real.

(Lefanu, 1988a: p. 87)

This potential Lefanu identifies in terms of (generic) form rather than
function or content, but the form of the text has a specific effect, and
hence her focus on function. The functions of form are also the subject
of Anne Cranny Francis's analysis. She finds that the generic conventions of science fiction allow exploration and critique that are
potentially free of patriarchal traditions. The treatment of science as
a strategy of estrangement, for instance, leads to displacement in time
and/or space, thus allowing different temporal and spatial perceptions
to come to the fore. The conventional presence of the alien, for
example, allows further displacement of that which is considered
normal and real: 'Because the alien is not formed within the ideology
of its found world, it (she/he) is able to re-vision that world for the
reader' (Cranny Francis, 1990a: p. 223). The distance of science fiction
from reality, such analyses suggest, foregrounds other perceptions of
the present.

Rosemary Jackson has made similar observations of fantasy and the
fantastic form in general. Fantasy, says Jackson, interrogates unitary
perception: nothing is taken at face value. She further argues that the
fantastic mode dissolves ordered structures, favouring openendedness
and thus dis-covering 'emptiness inside an apparently full reality'
(Jackson, 1981: p. 158).

Such analyses are, I suggest, of considerable value when discussing
utopian science fiction from a feminist theoretical perspective, and I
shall return to further discussion of generic disruptions in the last
chapter. This approach should not, however, be taken to comprise a
project of definition. In saying this I do not mean to reject the generic
approach as inappropriate. It goes beyond definition and is an
explanatory approach that I personally favour over the categoriza-
tional ones discussed above. Utopian transgressions of generic boundaries are discussed in a later chapter.

OPPOSITIONAL THEORIES OF FUNCTION

In the preceding section, utopianism was approached through the functions of its generic conventions. In this section, the focus is more explicitly on function *per se*, and I shall be discussing the work of theorists who attribute various functions to utopianism itself. Utopian thought is believed by these thinkers to be transformative, subversive or oppositional, or to have some other radical or political function. The first approach to be considered comes from the socialist tradition, which perceives utopian thought to oppose what is termed ideological thought. This is perhaps the most familiar of the function-based approaches, and I shall be suggesting that its weakness lies in its conceptualization of opposition. I shall then look at several interesting accounts which all focus in different ways on the oppositional and transformative function of utopianism. These positions are less familiar but, I suggest, more persuasive. Thinkers to be included here are feminist theorists Margaret Whitford and Angelika Bammer. This approach is, I suggest, leading in the same direction as that of Tom Moylan, whose concept of a critical utopia occupies a place of central importance in this book. In conclusion I shall propose that we consider utopianism to have a transgressive function, and will illustrate this point by looking at the effects of utopian thought upon political theory.[8]

Socialist oppositional approaches

Socialist commentaries on and critiques of utopianism are various and manifold, but I shall focus on two approaches. The first sees the function of utopia as making concrete a radically different vision of the good life. From this approach comes the idea of utopia not as 'no place' but rather as 'not yet'. Karl Mannheim has perhaps been most influential in this respect, and in the following discussion his work will be taken as representative. The second approach attributes a less revolutionary but equally radical function to utopianism and reads the genre as a space for speculative opposition. The connecting link between these somewhat diverse approaches is not so much their socialism as their bias towards function.

Mannheim, in *Ideology and Utopia* (1936), is primarily concerned with a socialist analysis of ideology. His conception of utopia, however, has, much to the discomfort of critics such as Krishan Kumar, been of widespread influence (Kumar, 1991). For Mannheim, utopianism anticipates reality – this is its function. This is a common assumption amongst commentators from the political left. This stress upon utopian realizability, which reads the utopia of the age to be that of socialism, has, according to Kumar, provided fuel to anti-utopians whose perception of socialism in practice as a nightmare of centrally planned authoritarianism contributed to their viewing utopia in the same light.

Mannheim's understanding of utopia is essentially oppositional in a simple, dualistic sense. He perceives a dialectical relation between ideology (which favours the status quo) and utopia (which favours radical change). He defines utopia as 'A state of mind [which] . . . is incongruous with the state of reality within which it occurs' (Mannheim, 1936: p. 173). This broad understanding is limited thus: 'Only those orientations transcending reality will be referred to by us as utopian which, when they pass over into conduct, tend to shatter, either partially or wholly, the order of things prevailing at the time' (Mannheim, 1936: p. 173).[9]

The form of utopian expression – that is, the concrete form – is not of concern to Mannheim; rather his focus is on the function of utopianism. The ideological is, for Mannheim, that which transcends existence or reality (that is, which is not achieved in reality) yet which functions to maintain the existing order of things. The function of utopia is destructive; it shatters that order:

> By this is meant that every age allows to arise (in differently located social groups) those ideas and values in which are contained in condensed form the unrealized and the unfulfilled tendencies which represent the needs of the age. These intellectual elements then become the explosive material for bursting the limits of the existing order. The existing order gives birth to utopias which in turn break the bonds of that existing order, leaving it free to develop in the direction of the next order of existence.
>
> (Mannheim, 1936: p. 179)

Describing the relationship between ideology and utopia in these terms is, I suggest, of limited value. Utopian thought is clearly desirous of change, but, for Mannheim, such thought must *achieve* change of revolutionary proportions in order to be considered utopian. Focusing on the effect of utopia in this way makes it difficult to distinguish from revolution, and the words become in effect synonymous. This is clearly problematic.

To describe the relationship as dialectical, in traditional marxian terms, implies that the ideological forces pull in one direction and the utopian in the other in binary opposition. This simplifies the function and substance of utopianism, which presents multifaceted opposition. Even within what can broadly be described as a feminist perspective, oppositional stances reflect the diversity of that movement. Socialist utopias reflect similar diversity.

The central problem with Mannheim's analysis is, I suggest, not so much that it fuels anti-utopian critiques as that it oversimplifies and inaccurately represents the function of utopianism. He is correct in arguing that utopian thought cannot exist independently from the real – it depends on and results from dissatisfaction with the present. It does not, however, comprise a coherent body in dialectical opposition with the dominant ideology.

This trend within socialist thought – of making utopianism in some way useful, practical or politically efficacious – seems to have its roots in orthodox marxist criticisms of utopian socialism. Socialist advocates of utopianism have, since the 1850s, been wary of this phenomenon, whilst desirous of the effects which they attribute to it. The work of E.P. Thompson exhibits this tension, and also illustrates the second socialist approach that I wish to introduce.

Thompson has written extensively on William Morris and in 1955 described *News from Nowhere* in the following terms:

> The key to the artistic power and unity of *News from Nowhere* lies in the fact that it is a Scientific Utopia. The contradiction implied by the coupling of these two words was intuitively perceived by Morris, and was quite deliberately turned into a fruitful source of tension, underlying the whole tale.
>
> (Thompson, 1977: p. 693)[10]

Utopianism is made 'respectable' here by being given the status of scientific socialism. Thompson is criticized by later socialist commentators who wish to retain the importance of utopianism without the 'scientific' rider.[11] He acknowledges his slip in the 1977 postscript to *William Morris: Romantic to Revolutionary*, and, writing of Miguel Abensour, he says:

> he chides me for evasion in accepting the formula, 'Scientific Utopia', for *News from Nowhere*. Behind this formula he detects a rejection of the validity of the utopian mode in any form: a

49

'Scientific Utopia' may be condoned only because it is not *really* utopian.

(Thompson, 1977: p. 787)

This ambivalence towards utopianism may help to explain the functional bias of some socialist approaches to the field, and contemporary critiques from this perspective tend to be more self-conscious. Abensour is cited by Thompson as one thinker who rejects the dichotomy science/utopia, and Thompson draws upon this approach to conclude that post-1850 utopianism represents a new genre, the function of which is not to offer societal models, but rather to educate desire:

> His intention was to embody in the forms of fantasy alternative values sketched in an alternative way of life. And what distinguishes this enterprise is, exactly, its *open* speculative quality, and its *detachment* of the imagination from the demands of conceptual precision.... Nor does it matter (as a first criterion) whether the reader approves of his approximations. Assent may be better than dissent, but more important than either is the challenge to the imagination to become immersed in the same open exploration. And in such an adventure two things happen: our habitual values (the 'commonsense' of bourgeois society) are thrown into disarray. And we enter into Utopia's proper and new-found space: *the education of desire*.

(Thompson, 1977: pp. 790–1)

This is a new and different function to that offered by Mannheim: here, the 'ou' of utopia is privileged and read as having a positive and enabling function. I mentioned a similar approach in the section above when discussing the role of fiction, or the fictional status in/of utopian thought. 'Ou' – 'non', 'no', 'not' place, the place that is not – is an ideal space in and from which to speculate upon radically different ways of being. This is a function of utopianism that I shall stress throughout this work. It is, I suggest, the most radical function, as new and different social arrangements can be best imagined in a space free from the constraints, norms and codes of present society.

Feminist oppositional approaches

Moving away from socialist 'oppositional' approaches to utopianism, but remaining with a bias towards function, I should like to turn now to the second approach mentioned above, the 'feminist oppositional' one. Utopianism, as presented by what I have called the standard approach, has a universalizing function. This is related to the assumed convention of a perfect society which is depicted in some detail. This representation of perfection negates process and offers a universal solution to the problems of political society. The avoidance of the blueprint that is so common in contemporary feminist utopias can, I suggest, be connected to current debates within feminist theory centred upon the issue of essentialism. Hence comes my insistence that an openended approach to utopianism is the most appropriate.[12]

More particularly, the emergence of the openended feminist utopia is, I suggest, related to an unease within feminist theory with any ascription of a fixed nature to man and woman. The assumption of a fixed human nature, such as that found in the 'state of nature' theory of, for instance, John Locke, has traditionally been the starting point for the imaginary and philosophical construction of ideal societies and polities.

If human nature is thus fixed then a universalizing utopian blueprint will unproblematically propose *the* good life for all. The universalizing tendencies of utopia are, however, seen to be based upon the attribution to a supposedly generic 'man' of a universal nature which is labelled 'human'. Within utopian literature and theory of the mainstream, this subject is possessed in abundance of qualities commonly associated with masculinity. The ideal utopian subject, for instance, conquers passion by the exercise of reason, and his mind conquers his body.[13]

Feminist commentaries have taken a variety of oppositional stances to this approach, ranging from the expression of unease with the perceived masculinity of the generic subject to a questioning of the existence of any cohesive subject, let alone of a generic and universal 'human' nature. Other fields of contemporary theory also express these concerns. Postmodern and poststructuralist theory in particular address questions of universalism and discussion, and the next chapter, is focused in this direction. Wariness of the blueprint in these terms can be found in the work of Margaret Whitford, whose work traverses all of these fields: 'Feminist philosophy is political and committed; it explicitly desires change, but to provide a blueprint in advance, explaining exactly what the nature of those changes will be, is to fall back into completely traditional methods of philosophy' (Whitford, 1991a: p. 13).

Against this desire to blueprint, Whitford sees emerging a utopia of process. This is a non-static utopianism that works to change the present rather than programme a future:

> Feminist utopian visions, then, are mostly of the dynamic rather than the programmatic kind; they do not seek to offer blueprints of an ideal future, still less of the steps to attaining it. They are intended more to bring about shifts in consciousness (paradigm shifts).
>
> (Whitford, 1991a: p. 20)

This approach to utopianism is radically and profoundly different from that taken by commentators who privilege form or content. Like the approaches above, it gives to utopianism a transformative function that goes beyond material change – it is a reading of utopian thought that perceives it as evoking and permitting conceptual change. It is this approach which I build on in the chapters that follow. The majority of the texts studied within this book are representative of this kind of utopia of process, which is dynamic and shifting. Movement and flexibility are their keynotes. The function of utopianism, thus approached, is not to blueprint and enclose the future but to explore alternative states of being to those presently existing – to stretch and expand our understanding of the possible, thus making a multiplicity of radically different futures not only desirable but also conceivable. The utopian conventions identified in the section above are therefore mobilized for a new purpose: tactics of estrangement, stretching concepts to the limit, and the use of imaginative and creative thought are all re-employed to subversive and transformative effect.

The function of utopian thought, thus approached, is to anticipate the possibility of radically different 'nows' (hence utopia as a paradigm shift in consciousness). This new utopian function operates in the political present, not in a desired future. This is an important shift that moves utopia from a speculative (or concrete) future to a no place/ good place that is an alternative reading of the present. In this way the dominant understandings of what is possible are undermined, new conceptual spaces are opened and different perspectives of the possible are forged.

CRITICAL UTOPIANISM

I have, more than once, mentioned approaches to utopianism which attribute to it a critical function, and have suggested that this is a useful way of understanding utopian thought and utopias. One commentator whose work is of considerable value when reapproaching utopia is Tom Moylan. Moylan's position is not without problems but occupies a central place in this book. His understanding of utopia is formed by reference to content, form and function, the last being the element to which he pays most attention. In the ensuing discussion I propose to highlight both the strengths and weaknesses of his thesis. For Moylan, utopian thought is rooted in discontent: 'It is, at heart, rooted in the unfulfilled needs and wants of specific classes, groups, and individuals in their unique historical contexts' (Moylan, 1986: p. 1). Its function is the opposition of what Moylan terms the affirmative culture: 'Utopia negates the contradictions of a social system by forging visions of what is not yet realized either in theory or practice. In generating such figures of hope, utopia contributes to the open space of opposition' (1986: pp. 1–2). The influences of Bloch and, to a lesser extent, Mannheim upon Moylan's thinking are apparent, yet the central hypothesis of his *Demand the Impossible* is distinct from that of any other thinker. Moylan, desiring to see the apparent uniformity and universality of twentieth-century capitalism shaken, delights in the new multiplicity of what he names the 'critical utopias' of the 1970s. The critical utopia is so in two senses:

> 'Critical' in the Enlightenment sense of *critique* – that is expressions of oppositional thought, unveiling, debunking, of both the genre itself and the historical situation. As well as 'critical' in the nuclear sense of the *critical mass* required to make the necessary explosive reaction.
>
> (Moylan, 1986: p. 10)

In order to critique contemporary society, the critical utopia must, according to Moylan, destroy, transform and revive the utopian tradition, which, in its present/past state, is/was inadequate to the task of provoking social transformation. A fixed, finite and universal utopia of perfection cannot, says Moylan, adequately critique a fixed, finite and universal capitalist system. Only an understanding of utopia that destroys old perceptions of the genre, transforms them into something new and thus revives utopianism can adequately reflect the concerns, needs and wants of contemporary malcontents. The critical utopia does not blueprint: social change in process is privileged even in the alternative societies it presents. Difference and imperfection are retained. This is more appropriate to contemporary feminist utopianism than were many of the previously discussed theories of utopia. It also moves towards the kind of view of

53

utopianism that I am proposing. It not only reconceptualizes utopia, but also (and importantly) approaches utopianism from a fresh angle.[14]

Moylan ties this new literary utopia to what he names a new historic bloc of opposition to contemporary Western(izing) culture and capitalism:

> the critical utopia is part of the political practice and vision shared by a variety of autonomous oppositional movements that reject the domination of the emerging system of transnational corporations and post-industrial production and ideological structures. . . . The new historic bloc of opposition is one that draws together an alliance of various groups and interests.
>
> (1986: p. 11)

This then is an historic bloc of autonomous groups, linked partially by that which they oppose but diverse in their manner or mode of opposition. Thus Moylan allows for a multiplicity of opposition, not one of binary simplicity such as that of Mannheim. He names certain values, manifested in democratic socialism, feminism and ecology, as deeply infusing this bloc:

> Whatever the particular set up of social images each text sets forth, the shared quality in all of them is a rejection of hierarchy and domination and the celebration of emancipatory ways of being as well as the very possibility of utopian longing itself.
>
> (1986: p. 12)[15]

Drawing on a Jamesonian idea of utopia as the expression of an emancipatory collective view,[16] Moylan sees the act of expression itself as the strength of utopia: 'The strength of critical utopian expression lies not in the particular social structures it portrays but in the very act of portraying a utopian vision itself' (1986: p. 26). The way in which this vision is presented is, as intimated above, of political importance for Moylan. The stress, in this approach is, I suggest, on process. Multiplicity of narrative structures, of worlds presented, and a general feel of dislocation all move these texts away from the binary oppositional expression that is, for Moylan, characteristic of the monolith of contemporary capitalism.

The function of such an act is considered in terms of what it does to the present rather than by direct reference to the future:

> The task of an oppositional utopian text is not to foreclose the

54

agenda for the future in terms of a homogeneous evolutionary plan but rather to hold open the act of negating the present and to imagine any of several possible modes of adaptation to society and nature based generally upon principles of autonomy, mutual aid, and equality.

(Moylan, 1986: p. 26)

Critical opposition is not in the classical binary tradition but opposes the existing space of opposition; its function is not to provide an alternative but to deny that existing options are the only ones. Opposition thus understood is a bigger concept than the either/or position; it is comprised of multiple critiques of a(n) (omni)present structure of exploitation, hierarchy and alienation. This leaves Moylan's concept in a position of considerable strength with regard to the transgressive feminist utopianism discussed in later chapters.

Of greatest concern in respect of Moylan's approach are his optimistic(?) assumptions not just regarding the potential unity between these autonomous groups (of which feminism is counted as one), but of the existing unity amongst them:

Similar to Bloch's concrete utopia, the plebeian public sphere is not an institution but rather a contradictory and non-linear space which unites the fragmented experiences of the opposition movements. It is a liberated cultural and ideological zone seized from the totalized society from which the anti-hegemonic forces can attack the present and move openly towards an emancipated and radically open future.

(Moylan, 1986: p. 28)

This cannot, I suggest, be offered as a descriptive analysis of the current state of affairs within the socialist, feminist or ecological movements, which Moylan argues constitute the new historic bloc of opposition. Whilst opposition within feminism can be aptly discussed in the terms outlined above, unity, thus considered, cannot be said to exist in any stable or meaningful form. Indeed, a desire to 'unify' (universalize?) feminism in such a way would be treated by many contemporary feminists with suspicion. A key theme of feminist thought today is the maintenance of diversity and differences.[17] Divisions within ecological movements, whether in theoretical terms of ecology or environmentalism or in practical terms of the gradualism of the British Green Party versus the radicalism of Earth First!, leave this movement similarly fragmented. Similarly, socialism, which has always been a broad church, in its late twentieth-century manifestations cannot be said to be pulling in one direction.

I suggest that the situation may be better represented by the metaphor of a spider: the body being those ideological and cultural structures that dominate the West and thus much of the world, the legs representative of the tensions of the multiple oppositions of feminisms, socialisms and other cultural movements, such as black political, gay and lesbian groups. Also existing of course are oppositional groups broadly grouped around the right wing of politics, as well as specifically religious fundamentalist and pressure groups. Some of these have shared interests, and membership is not limited exclusively to one group. The spider, though heuristically useful, is itself an oversimplification of the situation.

There is, then, a normative prescription in Moylan's approach to utopia which is not unproblematic. The tone of his work, though, is useful, as he is the only commentator to attempt to explain *why* the main body of contemporary utopian fiction looks so different from what is often assumed to be the standard utopian text: the utopia of perfection: 'There can be no *Utopia*, but there *can* be utopian expressions that constantly shatter the present achievements and compromises of society and point to that which is not yet experienced in the human project of fulfilment and creation' (Moylan, 1986: p. 28). Utopian thought not only points to the not-yet-become but opens receptivity to new and radically different/other ways of being and thinking: the ultimate function of utopianism is, for Moylan, the development of an open consciousness of the present: 'It can only offer itself as an activity which opens human imagination beyond present limits' (1986: p. 40).

In Chapters 3 and 4 I explore some other ways in which this new approach to utopianism can be employed. These readings are drawn from other discourses that are receptive to multiplicity and which are not grounded in a dualistic conception of the utopian function.

TRANSGRESSIVE UTOPIANISM

The final approach to utopianism that I propose to discuss is also one that privileges function. In the section above on 'Content, form and function: seepage', I concluded by looking at the work of people who see the genres in which utopian thought is sometimes expressed as having emancipatory and transformative potential. In a later chapter I shall explore these ideas further. For now, though, I should like to look briefly at the effect that utopianism has on one genre through which it is studied: in this case, political theory.

One person who moves towards this kind of approach is Carol Pearson. Pearson's work was mentioned earlier, and her bias towards content was criticized. She has, though, also examined the overlaps that occur between the fields of feminist theory and science fiction. From this area of overlap she identifies a new kind of emergent political theory. This theory is characterized by and grounded in three paradoxical principles. Examination of these principles leads Pearson to a theory which is transgressive of traditional ways in which the possible is conceived. The first concerns time, which, she says, can be perceived as being both linear and relative: 'To the degree that we live only in linear time, we are locked into a world governed by laws of causality, dualism, linearity, and struggle.' Relative time is emancipatory as linear time is restrictive: 'In this dimension, time and space are not separate, and time/space is curved. It then becomes possible to understand that we can change not only the future but the past' (Pearson, 1984: pp. 260–1). Feminist wilful transgression of time and space is a theme of a later chapter. For present purposes, Pearson's work serves to indicate how the function of achieving paradigm shifts in consciousness is to be achieved. It further places the moment of (utopian) change in the present, which is conditional (not enclosed by certainties).

Pearson's second principle concerns the point in time at which change can be achieved: the future and the past, she says, are enclosed within the present. 'Although past, present and future co-exist [as shown by the relativity of time] and are equally real in the present, the only point of action in which anything can be changed is in the present' (Pearson, 1984: p. 261). This observation can also be usefully linked to Whitford's concept of the utopia of process, the function of which is to cause (conceptual) change in the here and now. For Pearson, this can only be done by stepping into relative time: 'Paradoxically, widespread social change occurs only as a result of the solitary decisions of individuals to step outside linear time into the "eternal now"' (1984: p. 261).

Pearson's third principle relates to consciousness. Only once a paradigm shift has occurred can social transformation occur: 'The move into a new, utopian future occurs when we simultaneously take responsibility for our own lives and relinquish all illusions that we control anything – others, the flow of history, or the effects of our own actions' (1984: p. 261). This, perhaps, is the most paradoxical of her three principles. It is possible, she appears to say, to change our perceptions of the past, present and future by denying the linearity of time, yet real movement into a utopian future is not possible until collective acceptance of our ultimate impotence is made. Letting go of the notion of control appears paramount, for only then can utopian thought exist in the present.[18] The new kind of political theory that Pearson claims to identify is one that lets go of the quest for truths, certainties and fixed categories. It moves away from traditional philosophy and closer to what might be called fiction.

Another feminist theorist who argues that utopianism effects theory is H. Lee Gershuny. Gershuny has identified a common pattern in textual utopias, which consists of three phases, each with a particular function. Her analysis is focused on utopian work on language but can, for the moment, be usefully considered with reference to utopian texts in general. Phase one is concerned with analysis and criticism of the present; phase two with transformation, manifested, for example, in the creation of alternative worlds; and the third phase is focused on transcendence of what she calls androcentric forms of expression, an example being that of dualistic thought (Gershuny, 1984: pp. 189–203). Close analysis of feminist or feminine transcendence of dualism will be made in Parts II and III of this book. Analysis and criticism can be found in all feminist utopian texts and are, I have argued, a convention of utopian thought. Transcendence is a concept of which feminist theory is particularly cautious, as it is traditionally associated with the valuing of mind over body. I prefer the term 'transgression', partly for this reason. The transgression of boundaries such as that between mind and body by the feminist utopian text can, as I suggest in later chapters, change the way in which we theorize our relation to the world. Briefly, this transgression renders such boundaries redundant and opens the previously (masculine) world of the mind and theory to the body and emotion. The important point to note at this stage is that wilful transgression of generic or conceptual boundaries is both an effect and a function of utopian thinking.

CONCLUSION

The focus of this chapter has been on approaches to utopianism that privilege its (perceived) function, and I have found these approaches to be, on the whole, more useful than those discussed in the last chapter. I should like, by way of concluding this chapter, to turn to my third justificatory claim: utopianism should be reconceived because the new approach offered in this book is more appropriate to contemporary feminist utopianism.

The new approach that I suggest should be taken towards utopianism does privilege function, but not in any simple sense. A number of function-based approaches have been considered, and in general this approach has been found to be more complex, interesting and appropriate than those which privilege form or content. I have, for example, found useful those approaches which focus on what I have called seepage between areas of content, form and function. In this section I made a suggestion that will be further explored in Chapter 3: that utopia is a particularly good place from whence to think about and create sustainable feminist political theory. I have also suggested, and again will be expanding on this claim in Chapters 3 and 4, that the most appropriate approach to contemporary feminism(s) is through an understanding of utopian thought that is flexibly constructed and open to change.

From socialist and feminist approaches I have extracted a view of utopianism as having oppositional and transformative dynamic functions. I have challenged the simplistic dualistic conception of opposition and have replaced it (conceptually) with something multisourced and multidirectional. This creates new paradigms. Utopianism has a speculative function which is located in part in its conventions of critique, estrangement and imaginative writing, and I have suggested that utopias are often better read as metaphors than as blueprints. In poststructuralist terms, which I shall explore further in Chapter 4, this approach facilitates a reading of utopianism that operates with a certain lightness of touch that is entirely appropriate.

Utopian thinking, then, creates new conceptual spaces – outopias – in which can be imagined different ways of conceptualizing the past, present and future. This different and new imagining, in order to be really different and new, needs to transgress the structures and ordering of our present ways of thinking, conceptualizing and theorizing. It is for this reason that I have stressed the paradigmatic nature of the transformative effect of utopian thought: if utopian thought can change the shape and scope of our consciousness then the unthinkable can be thought and desired. In the absence of blueprints the future is openended:

> The transition to a new age comes at the same time as a change in
> the economy of desire. . . .

Our age, which is often thought to be the one in which the problematic of desire has been brought forward, frequently theorizes this desire on the basis of observations of a moment of tension, or a moment in history, whereas desire ought to be thought of as a changing dynamic whose outlines can be described in the past, sometimes in the present, but never definitely predicted.

(Irigaray, 1993b: pp. 7–8)

Part II

NEW APPROACHES AND A NEW UTOPIANISM

3

FEMINISM
Setting the tone for a new utopianism

INTRODUCTION

In the previous chapter I began to suggest and construct an approach
to utopianism which I have stated is more appropriate both to
contemporary and historical utopianism, and to the 'now' of contemporary feminism – more appropriate, that is, than what I have
called the 'standard' (or colloquial) view of utopianism.[1] Many
elements of this standard view are retained: utopianism, I have
suggested, can be best approached as a political phenomenon, containing political critique and engaged in contemporary debates. I have
rejected form as a useful point of approach, but have said that utopian
thought is often expressed in such a way as to give it the status (often
pejorative) of fiction because it does not claim to be real or true, and
also because of its wishful, imaginative and (sometimes) fantastic
nature. In making this assertion I have privileged an approach to
utopianism that combines consideration of function with that of
generic content. Linked to this is the tactic of estrangement that is
variously practised by utopian thinkers – the estranged texts of the
utopian genre have, I have suggested, various transformative and
oppositional functions.[2] Further hallmarks of utopian thought are its
critical function and, importantly, its creative function. Utopian
thought creates a space, previously non-existent and still 'unreal', in
which radically different speculation can take place, and in which
totally new ways of being can be envisaged. In this space transformative thinking can take place, and paradigmatic shifts in approach can
be undertaken. A newly formed and informed approach will enable
new conceptualization of the phenomenon and significance of utopianism. An important feature of my suggested approach to utopianism is that it does not include reference to perfection; or rather, it sees

the author's attitude to perfection as important. An imperfect utopia is still a utopia, and its very imperfection tells us something important about the politics and approach of its author(s).

My discussions in Part I, then, were intended to illustrate my claim that an approach that privileges the perfect content and blueprint function is not appropriate to the genre, because, amongst other things, it misrepresents not only the work of contemporary feminist thinkers, but also that of such people as Thomas More and William Morris. It is the intended function of this chapter to substantiate further my claim that the proposed approach to utopianism is more appropriate to the 'now' of contemporary feminism(s).

I shall be narrowing the focus of discussion in this chapter to the true subject of this book: contemporary feminist utopianism. I will be discussing late twentieth-century instances of this phenomenon from the context of feminist thought and theory/theories of the same period or moment. Within this context I shall be saying that feminism (or rather, the approach that I am taking towards feminism) sets the tone for a new utopianism – a new approach to utopianism that replaces the old 'standard' with something more flexible, more interesting and more appropriate.

It is fast becoming standard practice to open discussions of contemporary feminism(s) with a disclaimer: 'Any conclusions reached by this discussion are the responsibility of the reader.' Discussants claim to be more interested in posing pertinent questions and (the brave amongst them) in proposing to explore the implications of their questions than in reaching conclusions. There are a number of reasons for this reticence, and two of the more sustainable ones are pertinent to this book. Feminist theory of the 1990s is less self-assured than was that of the 1970s – few now claim to hold the universal solutions to patriarchal and perennial (universal) oppressions. Indeed, the concept of universal oppression has itself become suspect. This attitude is rooted for some (myself included) in a wariness of universalism that stems from a desire to return a verdict of 'not guilty' upon our methodology. The implications of a universalist approach to feminism will be explored at further length below. Briefly, though, a strong case can be and has been made, particularly by black feminist theorists, that universalist feminism is exclusive of those from a different sociological background: not all women experience the same oppression in the same ways, and so, the argument goes, no one solution can be posed.

The second relevant reason for this reticence has its roots in poststructuralist observations about the function of closure. The act of closing a debate or text is believed by those taking this approach (again, I include myself) to be a political act, the function of which is to impose a methodology that privileges sameness and oneness and favours self over other.[3] This position will be explained and explored in the discussions that follow.

Anne Phillips and Michèle Barrett link these two concerns in the introduction to their co-edited volume, *Destabilizing Theory: Contemporary Feminist Debates*:

> Feminists have long criticized the pretensions of 'grand', 'high', and 'general' theory and have demonstrated the difficulties that attend any such enterprise. Universal claims have all too frequently turned out to be very particular, supposed commonalities false, abstractions deceptive.... Here, in a sweeping attack on the falsely universalizing, over-generalizing and over-ambitious models of liberalism, humanism and Marxism, many feminists have joined sympathies with post-structuralist and post-modernist critical projects.
>
> (Barrett and Phillips, 1992: p. 1)

The kind of approach taken by this book to debates within feminist theory, and that results from reformulating our understandings of utopianism in the ways suggested above, is, indeed, symptomatic of a 'joining of sympathies' with some (namely Derridean) poststructuralism. Again, I find resonance in Barrett and Phillips's description of the kinds of feminism that result from this meeting of sympathies:

> In the context of these recognitions, many feminists have opted for an analysis of the local, specific and particular. Much of this work is 'deconstructive' in character, seeking to destabilize – challenge, subvert, reverse, overturn – some of the hierarchical binary oppositions (including those implicating sex and gender) of western culture. Thus we have a developing feminist theory whose intention is to destabilize.
>
> (1992: p. 1)

Whilst I shall be attempting to reach some conclusions, then, in this discussion, many of the questions raised are, I suggest, best left unanswered. Examples of questions of this nature are 'What is feminism?', 'What is (a) woman?', and even 'What do women want? What *is* the utopia of contemporary feminism?' I make this suggestion and these contextualizing points regarding my own approach at this juncture by way of making my own politically and intellectually informed disclaimer.

Both of these concerns will be explored further in the following discussion. Both can be connected in different ways to approaches to the concept of difference, and to different conceptualizations of difference.[4] In order to make the discussion of contemporary feminist thought manageable, I shall be focusing on two areas or issues that I shall be arguing are (1) related and (2) central to understanding the 'nature' of contemporary feminist theory and utopianism.

Over the past ten or so years feminism has become increasingly introspective. It has been concerned with a fundamental dilemma that relates to the tension between the needs, on the one hand, for what might be called integrationist thought in order that women might be able to articulate and act *as* women – that feminism, in other words, might mean something; and, on the other hand, to acknowledge and respect the differences amongst women so that feminism does not continue to mean or represent the silencing of the articulation of diversity. This fundamental tension is one of the two that structure the following discussion. The other is the approach taken by feminist theorists towards equality and/or difference. Taken together, these two areas of (irreconcilable?) tension represent the central preoccupations of contemporary feminism.

Whilst reading different feminist approaches to these areas, I shall be attempting to show why the utopianism proposed is important and relevant to these problematic debates. It is cautiously offered as one route away from the dilemma of contemporary feminism(s): namely, where do we (if there is a 'we') go from here? First, though, it is necessary to consider some of the more dominant and influential conceptualizations of difference upon which this book draws. These approaches to difference all come from outside feminist discourse.

CONCEPTUALIZING DIFFERENCE

Before proceeding further it is necessary to note some of the difficulties and complexities of this project of examining different differences. The word 'difference' is used (by individual theorists and by disciplinary and politically defined groups) to signify a variety of concepts, meanings and approaches to the world. Put simply, difference means different things to different people. I am interested in this fact, and also in the conceptualization of difference: in how the various and diverse meanings are constructed, and in what they signify in the larger sense of approach. What, in other words, do people's under-standings of the word 'difference' tell us about their intellectual and political approach to the world? This brief introduction to different differences goes some way towards indicating a response to this question, which is 'a lot'.

Where ambiguity is present between different approaches or meanings, I shall endeavour to untangle the web of difference by labelling or flagging the approach as sociological, poststructuralist, colloquial, patriarchal, etc. I accept the crudity of this approach and am conscious of the irony of one such as myself (who is committed to maintaining the porosity and transgression of boundaries) being forced into such a categorizing methodology. It seems, though, that this is the only route to clear and accessible introduction to the question of difference, and thereby to the larger questions with which this chapter is concerned – namely: (1) how contemporary feminist thinkers approach and 'deal with' the overriding question of differ-ence); and (2) why a flexible and openended approach to utopianism is particularly appropriate to contemporary feminist thought.

Colloquial understandings of difference are informed by and inform (or reinforce) the empiricist sociological approach described below. Briefly, to be different in this sense means to be unlike or recognizably dissimilar (non-identical). Two things – subjects or objects – which are different in this sense possess non-identical specific qualities. The assumption of the everyday approach to difference is that it is possible to perceive, count or enumerate these qualities. An example might be the differentiation of men from women according to a number of visually perceptible (enumerable) biological qualities such as genitalia, breasts and body hair. Another example could read sexual difference in terms of observably different behaviour that might be taken to characterize male and female actors.

The term 'sociological difference' is used in the broadest sense to refer to cognitive (perceptible) and often physical or manifested differences (in a colloquial sense) that are perceived to exist between different social groups. The sociological approach to difference seeks a 'scientific' or universally applicable formulaic schema by which explanation of these phenomena can be made. The term 'sociological difference' is therefore used in the sections below to refer to both physical ('concrete') differences such as the colour of one's skin or the sex of one's body, and to the sociological (empiricist/cognitive) approach which attempts to signify and encode these 'differences'.

Patriarchal approaches to difference are assumed by most feminist theorists to be the dominant or standard ones. Patriarchal conceptualizations rely on colloquial enumerable differences which are identifiable by reference to specific qualities. With regard to sexual difference, for example, patriarchal approaches construct the sexes by reference to one another. Woman is not-a-man – 'she' is different. The patriarchal approach is universalizing. It constructs or 'observes' two 'different' (opposite) concepts (man/woman) and ascribes to each construct universal features, functions and roles. Sociological approaches to patriarchal constructions of difference have developed the concept of gender, which attempts to differentiate physical differences from their socio-cultural significance (via socialization, for instance). The following discussions aim to extrapolate patriarchal constructions of difference further, and so I will leave this subject for now. First, though, I should like to introduce two further interpretations of difference which inform this book.

Poststructuralist and postmodernist differences are, in the first instance, manifold and varied and, in the second instance, complex and enmeshed in different theories and approaches to the world. Honi Fern Haber identifies what she calls 'a law of difference' at work in poststructuralist and postmodern accounts – she describes this as 'the inescapability of difference and the need for its recognition' (Haber, 1994: p. 113). Poststructuralism is, she says, 'metaphysically and ontologically committed' to this law, and postmodernism presupposes it (1994: p. 113). It seems to me that she is right – that although there are many different and often contradictory approaches to the concept and conceptualization of difference within these types of critique, the one thing that they share, and indeed which characterizes them as poststructuralist or postmodern, is this commitment to the importance of difference. This, however, is the only generalization that I believe can be made regarding poststructuralist and postmodern 'differences'. That said, I do use the terms as descriptive categories in this chapter.

In many cases, poststructuralist and postmodern theorists of difference insist on it as incommensurability or dissimilarity. This shared insistence does not, however, represent grounds for generalization, because different theorists make this assertion for different reasons. Three approaches that have particularly influenced my own are those of Jean-François Lyotard, Jacques Derrida and Emmanuel Levinas. *Différance* (Derrida) and 'alterity' (Levinas) are the subjects of Chapter 4, but some brief introduction to these concepts and to Lyotard's *différend* may be useful at this point. A *différend* is a moment of no common measure (Lechte, 1994). More than this, it is the silencing of a 'player' in a language game. When there is no way of expressing what is different in a 'language' or discourse (the difference can range in form from an idea to a grievance), then the player that is different (or aggrieved) is silenced:

> 'Society', as one says, is inhabited by differends. I would say that there is a differend between two parties when the 'settlement' of the conflict that opposes them is in the idiom of one of them while the tort from which the other suffers cannot signify itself in this idiom.

(Lyotard, 1993: p. 9)

The inability to articulate one's cause in the same idiom or language creates a *différend*. The injustice suffered by the different one is inexpressible – the 'differences' between the two parties remain unarticulated: difference is incommensurable.

Derridean conceptualizations of difference are made more explicit in the next chapter, when I privilege a certain interpretation of Derridean poststructuralism. Briefly, though, it should be stated at this point that references to 'poststructuralist differences' in this chapter signify Derridean poststructuralism and not, for instance, Foucauldian approaches. Derrida's writing can be considered as a search for *différance*. Derrida coined this phrase when working on Saussurian structuralism, and he uses it to refer to unconceptualizable difference. This concept does not feature until Chapter 4, and so I will not dwell upon it here. Lyotard's *différend* and Derrida's *différance* are not 'the same'. Both focus on language, both privilege what they interpret as difference, but *différend* is 'about' restrictions placed upon interacting parties by the language (games) in which they are situated, and *différance* is 'about' the constrictions and constructions of language itself.

Like *différance*, 'alterity' does not appear until Chapter 4, but again, a word or two of introduction may be useful at this point. Levinas's conception of alterity is informed by his work on phenomenology and by his readings of the Talmud and other research into Jewish theology. The presence of God is unusual in a poststructuralist text. Like Derrida and Lyotard, Levinas is interested in difference, or rather in the way that difference is conceptualized as 'otherness'. From phenomenology comes Levinas's belief in 'there is' – the givenness of embodied existence. Levinas links this to horror, but alterity as otherness takes the other as being 'there', prior to the self; and, as such, the other is greeted with awe and wonder. We do not desire to appropriate this wondrous other for ourselves: alterity does not suppress difference. I will expand on this in the next chapter but, for now, it is sufficient to note that alterity is a radically different conception of difference to those discussed above.

Other uses of the word 'difference' will, no doubt, occur during the following sections, but these mentioned are the primary informing ones from outside feminism. With this in mind, then, I shall turn now to the true 'subject' of this chapter: the nature of contemporary feminism and why an openended and radical approach to utopianism is of value when discussing feminist responses to its primary (current) concerns.

FEMINISM AS EQUALITY-VERSUS-DIFFERENCE?

Within political theory in general and feminist theory in particular, equality is commonly seen as standing in opposition to difference: equality and difference are perceived to be in direct (binary) opposition. Socialist desires for equality, for instance, are frequently criticized at a superficial level at least for failing to respect diversity, for desiring an equality of outcome which is read in these critiques as sameness. Socialist claims for equality are, in other words, read as suppressing difference (individuality).[5] Debates focusing on the (un)desirability of equality as a feminist goal are not new: most historical analyses of feminist thought begin their chronologies with an account of what is commonly called first-wave feminism, the theoretical bases of which are clearly discernible in modern liberal feminisms. Strands of feminism associated with liberalism are informed by a certain commitment to equality, which is manifested in demands for equal access to and representation in the public sphere. The theoretical roots of this position lie in the assertions that women are (potentially) capable of doing what men do; and that women are as capable of rationality and the exercise of reason as are men (reason and rationality being the values historically privileged in/by the public realm). With regard to sexual difference, a standard liberal feminist stance is that gender is (and should be) irrelevant in, for instance, the spheres of education and the law. The stress here is on individual choice and ability that is autonomous (which, in this context, translates as being unencumbered by the dictates of gender).

Radical feminism(s), these chronological analyses tell us, privilege (sociological) difference, criticizing liberal feminist notions of equality on the grounds of political and ethical naivety. Simplified, one line of argument runs thus: women are essentially (physically and meta-physically) different from men; struggles for material equality in-evitably involve the assimilation of male/masculine attributes. The desire for equality results in the shedding of female attributes and the acquisition of those male ones which are necessary to survive in patriarchal institutions. Examples are competitiveness, aggression and self-centredness. Equality, in this analysis, is identified with (that is, made identical to) sameness, to which difference is subsequently opposed.

What is comparatively new, however, is the move over the past ten years or so towards the translation of feminism into the terms of an equality-versus-difference polemic. Black feminist critiques of main-stream (white) feminism are, for instance, often considered from this perspective. Attention to the equality/difference debate is clearly necessary and important in the interests of intellectual and political rigour. The reduction of such debates to a single oppositional stance, however, is over-simplistic. Black feminisms *do* stress the differences between women, and the implications of this for the mainstream, historically dominant, white feminisms have been profound. For instance, black feminist critiques strip mainstream feminism of its universalist pretensions, laying bare an insidious cultural imperialism in the assumption by some women (non-coincidentally white, Wes-tern, often middle-class, frequently heterosexual) of the authoritative position of enunciation.[6] The view that assuming the authority of enunciation invokes closure and exclusion is explored further in the discussion below of the works of Jacques Derrida.

Black feminisms, however, consist of more than a polemical critique of the white women's movement(s). In the first place, the reduction of black feminist theories to a position of opposition to those of white women (corresponding to the difference/equal opposi-tion) implies a false homogeneity within the two groupings. The opposition 'black/white' needs to be looked at more carefully: black, in this instance, refers to all who are not white, thus the differences between[7] and within ethnically defined communities[8] are left un-noted and thus rendered invisible. Reading 'black' and 'white' feminisms as being in binary opposition also assumes a 'white' feminism and represents an absurd reduction of the diversity within this construct.

A further implication of the reduction of black feminism to a feminism of binary opposition is that the sole concern of black feminisms is a critique of mainstream (white) feminism. Black feminism consists of much more than this – black women theorists have, quite simply, more pressing concerns than the criticism and education of their white 'sisters'.

My point then is quite simple: the same/other, equality/difference debate, whilst informative and important, should not be the sole matrix through which contemporary feminist debates are read. By this I mean that we should not approach feminist theory as though its various branches and manifestations can be divided and categorized as desiring *either* equality *or* difference. Such a move is exclusive of other debates and I suggest is representative of a suppression of otherness (difference). It further leads to an oversimplification of the complex and multiple nature of the debates themselves. The 'camp' of difference, as stated, is more than one camp – difference is privileged and desired as a political goal in a number of different ways. A consistent theme of this book is the argument that an axis of binary opposition does not provide an adequate framework upon which to base coherent social or political theory. When feminism(s) is or are translated through such a theoretical framework, the subtle complexities of that/those movement(s) are oversimplified and misrepresented: equality-versus-difference is rarely embodied in a pure form.

This is not, however, to say that feminist scholars should cease debating the topics of equality and difference, as feminism has, I believe, reached a crux point at which consciousness of differences – and different readings of differences – amongst and between women appear to threaten the cohesiveness and perhaps existence of feminism itself. A different or other understanding of the relations between women and the relations between equality, sameness and difference needs to be advanced. This understanding needs to be transgressive of a binary conception of opposition. I shall be suggesting in the discussions that follow that this new relation can best be thought about inside a utopian speculative space. In this way feminism may perhaps remain in existence rather than self-destruct, and may reconstruct itself as a valid force of integrity and social relevance.

Feminist utopianism can, I suggest, be read as engaging in these and related debates on difference. Within feminist utopian literature these concerns are manifested as a tension between separatist eutopias and integrationist or multigendered worlds. This is a theme of Part III. Briefly, though, Sally Miller Gearhart's *Wanderground* (1979) can be taken to represent the separatist vision (a world of difference); Letty Cottin Pogrelin's 'Born Free: a Feminist Fable' (1974) as a eutopia without gender difference (a world of equality); Marge Piercy's *Woman on the Edge of Time* (1979) as representing an integrationist approach (a world of equality *and* difference); and Monique Wittig's *Les Guerillères* (1971) as a eutopian exploration of a third gender (a world of difference with a difference). Pogrelin's and Gearhart's contributions to the genre contain visions of a perfect or ideal society; they are stagnant, closed and 'finished' worlds. It is more common to find the questions of equality and difference being addressed in more subtle ways than this.

Within the field of feminist theory, the project of rethinking difference has been approached from a number of angles. I propose to focus the remaining discussion on those which resist the closure of liberal and radical feminisms (and of utopias of perfection), and then look at difference with what might be called a (poststructuralist) difference. It is here that I will be suggesting we can find approaches to theorizing and thinking that are utopian in the ways suggested in Chapter 2. The approaches focused on in this chapter reject a binary choice of either equality or difference, and create a new (utopian) conceptual and speculative space in which we can start to think creatively and differently about equality and difference. In this way, new or different paradigms can be imagined and established to guide and inform emancipatory thought.

Joan Scott's important and influential article 'Deconstructing Equality-versus-Difference' (1992) represents a clear example of a different discussion of difference. On the uses of poststructuralist theory for feminism, she writes the following:

> When equality and difference are paired dichotomously, they structure an impossible choice. If one opts for equality, one is forced to accept the notion that difference is antithetical to it. If one opts for difference, one admits that equality is unattainable.
>
> (Scott, 1992: p. 260)

Scott's response is similar to that made throughout this book. She rejects the dichotomy that is assumed between equality and difference in a double move, which consists first of an exposure of the power relations of the construction of the polemic and secondly (simultaneously) of a refusal of acceptance. The discourse of equality is shown to deny the articulation of difference. To phrase it in Lyotard's terminology: she declines the offer to play a (language) game, the rules of which she took no part in constructing, and the prescribed outcome of which is in conflict with her interests. Equality, says Scott, cannot be divorced from difference, as pretensions to equality involve ignoring difference. These concepts are not read by Scott as being situated in binary opposition; rather, they are interconnected. The framework of conceptualization is being shifted by Scott away from one of 'either/or', dualistic construction. In a subtle move, she makes the poststructuralist suggestion that to ignore something is (tacitly) to acknowledge its existence: 'Demands for equality have rested on implicit and usually unrecognized arguments from difference; if individuals or groups were identical or the same there would be no need to ask for equality' (Scott, 1992: p. 261). The relations between equality and difference are then, for Scott, characterized by inter-relationship rather than by mutual exclusion. Equality no longer negates difference, but rather is reliant upon this concept for its own meaning. Of central import to this issue, it seems to me, are the roles of equality and difference.

The function, or role, of the concept of difference in the here and now of patriarchy is far from emancipatory for those designated as actually being different. Charlotte Bunch makes the perceived situation clear in the following statement:

> Patriarchy has systematically utilized diversity as a tool of discrimination in which we learn in childhood that such things as sex and race bring differences in power and privilege, and that these are acceptable. . . . When power hierarchies are accepted as inevitable, people can be manipulated to fear that those who are different are a threat to their position and perhaps even to their survival.
>
> (Bunch, 1988: p. 288)

The function of difference under/in patriarchy, in this reading, has been a legitimation of fear and distrust of the Other, which in turn manifests itself as a competitive relation whose result is inequality, the nature of which is vaguely reminiscent of the Hobbesian nightmare of perpetual war grounded in fear. Patriarchal difference legitimizes treatment aimed at inequality. Likewise, treating people equally (the same) is tantamount to a certain blindness to differences which perpetuates unequal political, social and economic relations.[9] The patriarchal conceptualization of difference produces the concept of difference as deviance: difference as inferiority.

These functions or roles of the concept or conceptualization of difference, and of the way in which is it constructed in opposition to equality, go some way towards showing why these concepts need to be reapproached. This can, I suggest, be best done through a new conceptual space that is not confined by binarism and dualistic oppositionality – a new 'no place' that is, in both positive and negative senses of the word, utopian.

Taking what might be broadly described as a feminist/postmodern approach, Elizabeth Grosz also sees the concept of difference as having an insidious function in the (patriarchal/masculinist) conceptual present. She stresses that this is the outcome of a patriarchal input to the concept rather than an inherent quality of the concept itself:

> For patriarchs, difference is understood in terms of inequality, distinction, or opposition, a sexual difference modelled on negative, binary or oppositional structures within which only one of the two terms has any autonomy; the other is defined only by the negation of the first. Only sameness or identity can ensure equality.
>
> In the case of feminists of difference, however, difference is not seen as different *from* a pre-given norm, but as *pure difference*, difference in itself, difference with no identity. This kind of difference implies the autonomy of the terms between which the difference may be drawn and thus their radical incommensurability. Difference viewed as distinction implies the pre-evaluation of one of the terms, from which the difference of the other is drawn; pure difference refuses to privilege either term.
>
> (Grosz, 1990: pp. 339–40)

In this reading, difference is rethought as transformable and thus potentially emancipatory. Patriarchal constructs of difference imply a deviancy from a norm. Sexual difference therefore constructs 'woman' in many ways as other to or different from the (privileged) male point of reference.[10] A feminist politics of difference, however, denormalizes sameness, to which difference is no longer opposed. Difference is thus no longer deviant; rather it is representative of dissimilarity and non-identity – representative, in other words, of the impossibility of similarity or identity.[11]

Rosi Braidotti makes a similar point:

> In my understanding of the term, what distinguishes *feminist* theories of sexual difference is the need to recognize as factual and historical reality that there is no symmetry between the sexes and that this symmetry has been organized hierarchically.

Recognizing that difference has been turned into a mark of pejoration, the feminist project attempts to redefine it.

(Braidotti, 1989: pp. 90–1)

Again, the dissimilarity of the sexes is stressed, and, as a consequence, the field/space in which difference can be conceptualized is broadened and transformed. The (patriarchal) binary hierarchical model of difference is conceptually dispensed with. Stripping the historical and theoretical linkages and restrictions from these concepts creates a totally new field of play/work/thought. I shall be referring in further detail to Braidotti's work in a later chapter. For now, though, I introduce this rejection of the conceptual symmetry between the sexes as another example of the kind of approach that I am favouring.[12]

Braidotti further rejects the established (conceptual) dichotomy between equality and difference:

Far from separating the struggle for equality from the affirmation of difference I see them as complementary and part of a continuous historical evolution. The women's movement is the space where sexual difference becomes operational, through the strategy of fighting for the equality of the sexes in a cultural and economic order dominated by the masculine homo-social bond. What is at stake is the definition of woman as other-than a non-man.

(Braidotti, 1989: p. 91)

She is, in other words, undermining the conceptual system through which these concepts are given meaning. This is the kind of approach that results in the destabilization of theory mentioned above (Barrett and Phillips, 1992). It is also profoundly utopian. It has the effect, described here by bell hooks, of destroying the conceptualization process which makes possible domination and subordination: 'Our emphasis must be on cultural transformation: destroying dualism, eradicating systems of domination' (hooks, 1984: p. 163). The *dualism* of equality/difference has been challenged by these thinkers, and each concept has been reconceived as a result.

This, I suggest, is utopian thinking. It is a way of thinking that begins from dissatisfaction or disaffection with/in the political present as perceived and experienced by the writer concerned. It is critical of the present, destroys certainties, challenges dominant perceptions and, in the process, creates something new. It is therefore critical utopian thinking in the sense described by Tom Moylan. Transgressive thinking of this kind is transformative thinking.

It is this kind of utopian thought that allows Luce Irigaray to reach the following theoretical position:

> To demand equality as women is, it seems to me, a mistaken expression of a real objective. To demand to be equal presupposes a point of comparison. To whom or what do women want to be different? To men? To a salary? To a public office? To what standard? Why not be themselves?
>
> A rather more thorough analysis of the claims to equality shows that at the level of a superficial cultural critique, they are well founded, but that as a means of liberating women, they are utopian. Women's exploitation is based upon sexual difference; its solution will come only through sexual difference. . . .
>
> Equality between men and women cannot be achieved without a *theory of gender as sexed* and a rewriting of the rights and obligations of each sex *qua different*, in social rights and obligations.
>
> (Irigaray, 1993a: pp. 12–13)

The first passage above begins by sounding like a classically radical feminist assertion of sociological and psychological sexual difference, but Irigaray goes beyond this. She also goes beyond the liberal feminist quest for equality and proposes that an ethic of sexual difference should ground social relations: that difference, in other words, should be inscribed into cultural and actual law (Irigaray, 1993b). Echoes of Lyotard's regionalism or localism can be heard here. The importance of Irigaray's approach, for the purposes of the present discussion, is the fact that her conception of difference is not grounded in a dualistic understanding that places sexual difference as men-versus-women (woman as not-a-man). Difference here is the 'pure' (conceptually) separating kind proposed by Grosz.

The rejection of binary oppositional thought and the nature of the choices which it proffers are a central theme of this and subsequent chapters. This rejection, I assert, is one way in which systems of (linguistic and hence cultural) domination can be destroyed. Feminism, I suggest throughout these chapters, remains oppositional whilst transcending the limitations of patriarchal binary oppositionality. These new and transgressive approaches to the framework by which meaning is constructed are profoundly utopian in the sense described above. By addressing this trend in feminist thought, I suggest that we

77

can begin to see why an openended conception of feminism is necessary and why feminist utopian texts (of theory and fiction) tend to be marked by a resistance to closure.

I stated in the introduction to this chapter that I would be reading contemporary feminist thought through its attitudes towards the equality/difference (equality–difference) debate(s), and through the approaches taken by contemporary feminists to the question: 'What is feminism?', or rather, 'What should feminism look like and be in the historical now?' In other words, I said that I would be looking at the integration–dis-/anti-integration debate. Is the historical 'now' a space in which women can integrate into society on equal (unreconceived) terms with men – a 'now' of homogeneous utopianism? Or is it a 'now' defined by incommensurable differences – a 'now' for which perpetually heterogeneous utopianism is appropriate? My own preferred position is the latter, and it is this position that informs my remaining chapters. It is to these questions that I should like briefly to turn now. Differing approaches to the equality–difference debate result in differing approaches to questions about the nature and state of contemporary feminism. With regard to sociological differences, for instance, claims are made by some black feminists that the needs and experiences of black women are so different as to warrant a separate or different feminism. This is an example of what I am calling a disintegrationist approach.

Anti-integrationist approaches to feminism, in contrast, insist upon the conceptual (as 'opposed' to practical)[13] impossibility of integration within and between feminist thought. Approaches from this perspective are 'rooted' in a sympathetic relation to postmodernism and/or poststructuralism, and it is upon these anti-integrationist 'threats' to feminist coherence (integration) that I now propose to focus. These approaches are linked to those outlined above which approach difference as a conceptual phenomenon. They share a belief that feminism cannot and should not strive for coherence in the form of universal answers to universal oppressions, but rather that diversity is itself empowering and that closure to the debate on 'What is feminism?' should be resisted. They transgress dualistic thinking, and open new conceptual space in ways that I have suggested are representative of utopian thought.

Much work has been done by feminist scholars on the emancipatory potential of a marriage between feminism and postmodernism, and it is not my intention to rehearse these debates in any great depth. Rather, I shall be proposing a new (and utopian) way of approaching the possibility of a meeting of feminism and postmodernism, which is pursued to its limits in the next chapter. The approach taken in this chapter is broadly cautious. That of the next chapter is unrestricted by conceptual–structural restraints, and the result is a chaotic and transformative experiment in utopian thought.

Following through on the metaphor of marriage may help to explain my caution regarding the implications of a union between feminism and postmodernism: in the conventional (Anglo-American, Christian) marriage the female partner takes her husband's name. It is my contention that a marriage between feminism and postmodernism will address the 'problem' of difference with which feminism is concerned by legitimizing not just an exchange of one name for the other, but the loss of feminist identity. Anglo-American feminist critiques of marriage commonly point out that the name given up by the woman is that of her father (Rowbotham, 1973; Weitzman, 1981). The name 'feminism' can be thought of in these terms, and the suffix 'ism' situates it within the theoretical context of ideology. Much of the current concern about the survival of feminism can, I suggest, be read as a concern to preserve its status as an ideology. Ideology, within political theory, is conventionally considered as providing a coherent world view that critiques the present and offers programmatic visions of the good life (Goodwin, 1987). In this sense the traditional view of ideology is close to the conventional view of utopia. I am not, however, concerned to explore the relation between ideology and utopia, even though it is a provocative area of considerable interest. My point is that feminism, in seeking coherence, is striving to fit into an existing (and patriarchal) model of what an ideology is. Coherence in the form of a single voice is conflated with unity and oneness. This is the inheritance or baggage that comes with the name of the father.

Were feminism to exchange this name and its related baggage for that of the postmodern son, I contend that it would experience disintegrative dislocation. The disillusionment with its own construction that characterizes much contemporary feminist theory need not, I suggest, lead down that particular path. This much said, I propose in the following section to suggest that a relationship (one that is wary of assimilation and cautious of appropriation) between feminism and postmodernism is of some mutual benefit.

FEMINISM/POSTMODERNISM: COHERENCE/ DISINTEGRATION?

Nancy Fraser and Linda Nicholson provide a useful introduction to the uneasy relationship between feminism and postmodernism in their co-authored article 'Social Criticism without Philosophy: An Encounter between Feminism and Postmodernism' (1990). Both movements, they believe, offer deep critiques of the institution of philosophy and of its relation to culture.[14] Both, they find, seek to develop social criticism which is not dependent upon traditional philosophical underpinnings. Whereas the focus of postmodernism, however, is (almost) exclusively on philosophy, that of feminism is, they find, primarily on social criticism. The relative strengths and weaknesses of the two movements are summarized thus: 'Postmodernists offer sophisticated and persuasive criticisms of foundationalism and essentialism, but their conceptions of social criticism tend to be anaemic. Feminists offer robust conceptions of social criticism, but they tend at times to lapse into foundationalism and essentialism' (Fraser and Nicholson, 1990: p. 20).

This noted, however, Fraser and Nicholson proceed to make the important point that an encounter between feminism and postmodernism need not consist merely of an exchange of criticisms. Rather, they see to be at stake 'the prospect of a perspective which integrates their respective strengths whilst eliminating their respective weaknesses' (1990: p. 20). My interest in this and subsequent chapters is not in highlighting and extending debates which result in or take negative positions regarding this point. I do, however, argue later that one consequence of an encounter between feminism and postmodernism is a mutual cancelling in a move which represents a silencing of their respective voices. It is, none the less, the creative and constructive (and utopian) potential of such an exchange in which I am interested here. Looking at the equality–difference, coherence–disintegration debates in this way has two functions. First, exploration of the tensions between feminism and postmodernism and their respective influences on each other can help to explain why contemporary feminism (and feminist utopianism) is resistant to closure. Closure represents total commitment which, as suggested above, is potentially self-destructive to/for feminism.[15] Secondly, engagement in the space created by these tensions enables further elaboration of a new theory of utopia.

Postmodernism evades definition. One problem faced when attempting to introduce postmodernism is its resistance to explanation; or, rather, to simple reduction. Lyotard's account of the metanarrative, and the influence of this account, are illustrative of this resistance. Lyotard holds an 'incredulity towards metanarratives': there can be no universally applicable explanations of the world and our conduct within/towards it because, in part, the world is too complex, and, further, because truth is not transcendent (Lyotard, cited in Bertens, 1995: p. 124). Another problem facing anyone trying to explain postmodernism is illustrated well by Hans Bertens. His text *The Idea of the Postmodern* (1995) provides full and accessible introductions to postmodernisms. Bertens, in other words, tightens up the conceptual sloppiness with which the word 'postmodernism' is frequently used, and shows 'postmodernism' to be a truly multiple phenomenon.[16] Describing or answering the question 'what is it?' of something as self-consciously multifaceted as postmodernism is, then, a task with which I am (intellectually) uneasy.

Of relevance to feminist debates are postmodern (and other) responses to the rationalism of philosophical modernism. Modernist thought can be characterized by reference to post-Enlightenment political theory, which has tended towards a celebration of the rational capacities of mankind (sic). For John Locke, Thomas Hobbes and Jean-Jacques Rousseau, for instance, this is the primary building block for the constitution of the human subject. 'Man' may be installed in a state of nature, but the primary distinguishing human feature, even in this state, is taken to be the capacity to reason. Simply put: the rational being inhabits the realm of culture and humanity, and the irrational being is associated with nature and the animal realm.

Christine de Stefano (1990) has identified three forms of feminist response to the resultant sexism[17] of a society thus grounded, one of which she describes as feminist rationalism. A feminist rationalist, or modernist, approach to the world views sexism as profoundly irrational. This view is similar in emphasis to that described by Sandra Harding as feminist empiricism. Feminist empiricism says Harding, views sexism and androcentrism as a result of social bias or prejudice rather than as a problem of methodology. The solution, from this perspective, is therefore 'stricter adherence to the existing methodological norms of scientific enquiry' (Harding, 1990: p. 91). In other words, a *more* rational approach is advocated.

Feminist empiricism and feminist rationalism can be read as feminisms that take a traditional (restricted) approach to equality. Sexual difference is seen to be the root of oppression: this difference is understood in terms of binary opposition through which women are excluded (irrationally) from the public sphere. That is, the public sphere (locus of power and wealth) is the sphere of reason and thence is a male province; the private sphere (locus of familial and physical relations) is the sphere of emotion and thence is the female province. The grounds for this view of exclusion are well documented,[18] and the route to emancipation for feminists who take this perspective is the reduction of the sexual difference in whose name they are excluded. The importance of sexual difference is, therefore, minimalized by these critiques. Women, as creatures of equal rationality to men, the argument goes, should be treated as non-differentiated equals. Further parallels, were we seeking them, could be found between these strands of feminist theory and that of liberal feminism. This approach to feminism contains the potentially disintegrationist ingredient of individualism, but primarily it is a feminism of coherence. This desired coherence is rooted in beliefs about universal rationality.

The second response that de Stefano notes she describes as feminine anti-rationalism which, being more committed to sexual difference, criticizes the hierarchy of dualisms in which Enlightenment thought consists. In this critique, as in that above, rationality is linked to masculinity and irrationality to femininity; hence the exclusion of women from rationally grounded constructs. Rather than assert the rationality of women, however, anti-rationalist critiques, according to de Stefano, attempt to revalorize femininity. Hence the desire for a social order that accommodates women as different: 'Anti-rationalism celebrates the designated and feminized irrational, involving a strong notion of difference against the gender-neutral pretension of a rationalist culture that opposes itself to nature, the body, natural contingency, and intuition' (de Stefano, 1990: p. 67). In this critique, the validity of the historical valorization of rationality as a humanizing characteristic, one that is a precondition for participation in the truly human public realm, is seen to be based upon imperfect knowledge or incomplete information.

Sandra Harding identifies what she calls feminist standpoint theories as challenging modern scientific knowledge in a similar way. Of standpoint theories she writes:

> Knowledge, they observe, is supposed to be grounded in experience. But what has counted as knowledge in modern, Western cultures originates in and is tested against only a certain limited and distorted kind of social experience. The

experiences arising from the activities assigned to women, understood through feminist theory, provide a starting point for developing potentially more complete and less distorted knowledge claims than do men's experiences.

(Harding, 1990: p. 95)

Again, a certain affirmation of difference is observable: women's experiences of the world, it is suggested, are *different* from those of men. A writer whose stance exemplifies these ideas is Mary Daly, whose tactics result in a powerful (but essentializing) revalorization of all that is feminine (which, for Daly, translates as constitutive of women as a result of their experience of the world).

Feminisms which are informed or influenced by postmodernism are characterized by de Stefano and by Harding as the third response, and represent an unequivocal challenge to Enlightenment thought and its methods of enquiry. Postmodernism is informed by post-structuralist deconstructions of modernist thought. Previous strategies which focused on the conception of rationality as a paradigm are rejected. Postmodernism questions the validity of quests for universal truths. Universalism, from a postmodern perspective, is a highly suspect concept. This can, I believe, be partially explained by translation into a consideration of the equality/difference debate outlined above. Postmodern feminism asserts difference, and it also destroys the concept of difference as we know it. It transgresses the conceptualization of patriarchal difference and renders it redundant. It performs the same function on all dualistic conceptualization. I attempted to show how this transformation works in the discussion of feminism and difference above. To assert a truth of difference; to say 'this is where men and women differ' and to create a construct of universal woman; is, in this critique, profoundly exclusionary. Hence, de Stefano writes: 'A proliferation of differences is counterpoised to the single difference of gender, and suspicion is cast on difference as an artifact of the very system of domination to which it is ostensibly opposed' (1990: pp. 67–8). A postmodern critique of difference can thence interrogate the concept and show the ways in which, for instance, it is employed to serve the construct of sameness. It can further reassess and re-employ the concept by desimplifying it, and removing the vestiges of universalism (totalitarianism). This is clearly useful to a project which is concerned with an examination of contemporary feminism, as I now propose to illustrate by reference to the essentialism debate.[19]

A point at which conversations about feminism and postmodernism and those about equality and difference intersect is in debates which focus on essentialism. This is generally understood to refer to the attribution of a fixed essence to a subject, the subject/object in this case being woman: 'Essentialism entails that those characteristics defined as women's essence are shared in common by all women at all times: it implies a limit on the variations and possibilities of change' (Grosz, 1990a: p. 334). Grosz points out the connections between essentialism, thus understood, and biologism, naturalism and universalism. Briefly, biologism attributes an essence derived from women's biological capacities and limits. Hence, for instance, comes the idea that women's identity and nature are rooted in their reproductive capacities. Naturalism, says Grosz, takes its roots from theology or ontology. A naturalist reading may, for instance, view women's 'nature' as God-given. Universalism commonly mixes biologism with social categorization: 'It refers to the attributions of invariant social categories, functions and activities to which all women in all cultures are assigned' (Grosz, 1990a: p. 335). Universalism asserts similarities, buries differences and has a homogenizing function.

An example of a universalist feminist text which evokes biologism and essentialist conceptions of woman is Shulamith Firestone's *The Dialectic of Sex* (1971). This text is utopian in the traditional sense which blueprints the future. Firestone links women's oppression to reproduction and creates a universalist utopian theory of emancipation. Mary Daly's *Gyn/Ecology* (1987) could also be read in these terms. Women, in Daly's analysis, are oppressed the world over by what she calls the 'sado-ritual syndrome', through which she asserts that religion is able to colonize the bodies of women and to mutilate their minds and spirituality. To combat this oppression, Daly's utopian vision evokes a spiritual concept of woman. Whatever else this text represents, it is undoubtedly essentialist and (non-coincidentally) universalist.

Universalist utopian visions are invariably rooted in essentialist theories of human nature. If human nature can be defined in these terms, then this does not present any theoretical or political problems. However, as Grosz says, essentialism does limit both existing variations and possibilities of change. It suppresses difference (by ignoring or actively suppressing it) and it (consequently) restricts the range of possible alternatives. Both of these factors are problematic to a project that seeks inclusive visions of humanity and its utopias. The essentialist-universalist approach is clearly one with an exclusive and restrictive methodology which produces unnecessarily confined understandings of the world.

Essentialism and its cognates (Grosz, 1990a) are criticized along the following lines. Essentialist conceptions of women, it is argued, do not take into account the differences *amongst* women. These conceptions result, moreover, in a certain stasis: if women really are naturally more emotional than men (as is often asserted by advocates of biologism) then the implications for struggles to move into the public realm are quite profound. The public realm has, as noted above, historically been constructed around the artifice of rationality. Progress or change is thus limited and the status quo effectively justified; patriarchal values remain unchallenged. Further, it is alleged, they are not context-specific and thus do not take into account historical, cultural or social relations and variations.

Monique Wittig is wary of essentializing concepts:

Belonging to a natural order, these relationships [between the 'two' sexes] cannot be spoken of as social relationships. . . . The category of sex does not exist a priori, before all society. And as a category of dominance it cannot be a product of natural dominance but of the social dominance of women by men, for there is nothing but social dominance.

(Wittig, 1976/1982: p.5)

In this passage Wittig can be seen to be expressing a belief that difference, in patriarchy, functions to create domination. The belief that differences are natural can, therefore, legitimize this domination. Hers is a radical stance. She can, I believe, be read as profoundly distrustful of dualisms, and I return to this later in a discussion of Wittig's proposed 'third' sex, or position: the lesbian position.

From the perspective of egalitarian feminism the affirmation of women's difference is essentialist, reductive and representative of an ideological/theoretical justification of patriarchy. From a postmodern perspective, similar accusations follow; which is, at first glance, ironic because postmodernist feminism has, as noted, stressed difference. The difference of postmodernist difference, of course, lies in its incommensurability, and this approach is, I suggest, useful to contemporary feminist theorizing.

De Stefano, though, notes that postmodernism can be read as making any feminist politics impossible, and this is a concern that should be taken seriously. Derrida, for instance, dismisses feminism on the grounds that it upholds/supports Western binary oppositional thought. In identifying with the feminine, for instance, feminist anti-rationalists do not seriously challenge the mechanics of the (binary oppositional) construction of thought itself. In this sense, calls for equality can be described as naive and oversimplistic. Further, feminism should not be perceived as a coherent and monolithic body of opposition to patriarchy, as this assumes a position of dualistic and binary opposition which is both limited and limiting. Women associated with postmodernism are often read as dismissing feminism on similar grounds. Hélène Cixous, for instance, has stated that she is not a feminist. Her disclaimer is couched in similar terms to those used by Derrida. It is important, however, to note that the feminism to which she refers is that of a white, Western bourgeois movement aimed at getting equality (sameness) and power in the existing (patriarchal) system. Discussion appears to have come full circle to a critique of feminisms of equality in similar terms to those expressed above.

I propose to extend this discussion of essentialism and postmodernist feminism later in this chapter. Before moving on, though, I want to summarize the points at which feminism and postmodernism intersect and to focus upon those elements of postmodernism which can be viewed as useful to feminist projects of emancipation. This addresses the larger project in which this chapter is engaged, namely exploring the nature of contemporary feminism and its relation to utopian thinking. I cited Linda Nicholson and Nancy Fraser earlier in this chapter as providing general pointers in this direction. Elements commonly held to be of value to a feminist critique are the post-structuralist approach to language as a system which constitutes meaning; the notion of discourse as an historico-socially specific structure of statements which contain an equally specific set of beliefs; the function of difference; and the technique of deconstruction. More generally, postmodernism is seen to offer insight into women's marginal position (in the Lacanian symbolic, for instance), critiques of universalism and truth claims. In the discussion that follows I provide a reading of the works of Derrida which encompasses and illustrates some of these concepts. I also argue that, whilst offering invaluable insights, postmodernism/poststructuralism can result in an immobilizing nihilism. It is important also to note that this section is illustrative of one of the claims being made throughout this book: that the nature of the approach taken towards a debate, concept or exercise in theoretical thinking (in)forms the consequent outcome of the debate, conceptualization or theorizing. I shall, for the purposes of this illustrative discussion, restrict my approach to one constructed by binary and dualistic oppositional thought. In the discussion of the potentialities of Derridean poststructuralism in the following chapter, I shall attempt a more utopian approach.

A Derridean approach

In this section I intend, through a reading[20] of the work of Jacques Derrida, to suggest that universalism is a masculine construct in a libidinal–economic sense, and that the (universalist, blueprinting and perfectionist) utopianism created by some approaches is disempowering to all but those who constructed it. Again, this enquiry addresses the questions of the nature of feminism and of utopianism. In this reading, masculinity is not essentially gender-specific; it is not a sociological phenomenon, but it does characterize the dominant values and norms which can be found to advantage men over women. This I intend to illustrate with specific reference to the quest for a universalist concept of utopia.

Analysis of the thought of Derrida requires time and caution. The function of the following discussion is primarily one of extrapolation and appropriation of certain themes within his work. I shall first spend some time introducing these themes as, to an extent, they represent the theoretical underpinnings of my own approach in this and subsequent chapters. My discussion focuses indirectly (for the sideways glance is the best way to read Derrida) on his work on universality and masculinity within the context of a discussion of what he describes as the realms of the Proper and the Gift: the drives of cultural economics which, Derrida finds, both amount to the same thing – appropriation.

According to contemporary theories of binary oppositional thought, our understanding of the world is constructed by language in which meaning is referential rather than inherent. Nothing, in other words, has meaning *in itself*, but rather by reference to other words, concepts and ideas. Good, for instance, is good only in reference to bad. Similarly, the universal stands in an oppositional and referential relation to the particular, the objective to the subjective, and reason to desire. The relationship between binary oppositional pairs is hierarchical, one term being subordinate to the other. This subordination, in the Derridean critique, is not simple, because the first (dominant) term relies on the second (subordinate) for its meaning.

Further, Derrida stresses the logocentric nature of Western thought. This is rooted in its dependence on words to bring into symbolic presence things which are in reality absent. He invokes the notion of an 'onto-theological' language. Ontology is concerned with being and beginnings, with origins and essences: an onto-theology is a religion of origin and essence and thus absolute presence. The relevance of this notion to utopia is that, in the dominant colloquial reading, utopia blueprints the future. It is, therefore, often translated as a plan for action, a way in which dream can become reality or presence. In this sense, traditional utopias are logocentric. Derrida plays a deconstructive textual game. The term 'deconstruction' has come to be thought of as synonymous with the name 'Derrida' and is widely used and misused in discussions of his work. Deconstruction is most accessibly described as consisting of two 'parts' or elements.[21] The first involves inversion or reversal of the binary oppositions through which meaning is constructed in Western thought. The second involves the forging of new or different meanings. An effect of deconstruction is to uncover, expose and hold up for examination the phallo-logocentric system of language within which we function.

There is, therefore, no objectivity or neutrality possible in the Derridean text(ual game of deconstructive reading). All texts are locked into language, which silently speaks (in) its own doctrinal system. A text, therefore, carries within itself more than the author's intended meaning. This connection can, I believe, be further explained by reference to Derrida's suspicion of the term 'concept' and its connection to what he calls the Drive of the Proper:

> Essentially and lawfully, every concept is inscribed in a chain or system within which it refers to the other, to other concepts, by means of the systematic play of differences. Such a play, *différance*, is thus no longer simply a concept, but rather the possibility of conceptuality, of a conceptual process and system in general.
>
> (Derrida, 1972a: p. 36)[22]

It is the word 'concept' or 'conception' that I would in turn question in its relation to any essence which is rigorously or properly identifiable. . . . The concept of the concept, along with the entire system that attends it, belongs to a prescriptive order.

It is that order that a problematics of woman and a problematics
of difference, as sexual difference, should disrupt along the way.

(Derrida, 1982: p. 448)

Concepts, then, like words, are not representative of givens; rather
they inhabit a system, the function of which is the creation of meaning
(hence my insistence in earlier chapters that the approach taken has a
profound effect upon the actual concept produced by the process of
conceptualization). This codification of meaning is referred to by
Jacques Lacan as the Symbolic Order. The possibility of conceptuality
can be usefully linked to the Drive of the Proper.

Naming, for Derrida, is claiming. Naming, asking and deciding
'What is it?', is central to philosophical discourses and relies upon the
possibility of attaining the truth. It assumes the (possible) presence of
truth, hence logocentrism. This project for Derrida is corrupt, not a
neutral quest of enquiry, but rather an imposition of an order which is
normative and repressive. There is no such thing as a neutral quest of
enquiry, as the question itself ('What is it?') is phallo-logocentrically
loaded.

Derrida plays with the word 'Proper', from which the concepts of
'property' and 'appropriate' derive.[23] All meanings invoked by the
words 'proper', 'property' and 'appropriate' are conflated and condensed in Derrida's reading. They constitute this 'drive', the function
of which is deeply repressive of difference. The possibility of conceptuality is, according to this critique, a profound expression of the
possibility of naming, which is claiming, which is enclosing and
restricting.

Implications

How does all of this relate, then, to feminism and utopianism?

A Derridean approach shows that the conceptualization of a perfect
utopia represents a confinement or enclosure. Moreover, this conceptualization, thus understood, represents an apparently inescapable
move of exclusion. Once a definition is established, that which lies
outside of its boundaries can be read as 'not', not included, not that
thing defined. Many early models of utopia, for example, as pointed
out in earlier chapters, exclude feminist utopian texts. They can thus
be read as 'not' utopian, in the 'proper' sense. Whilst one remains
within a conceptual framework of binary opposition *something* must be
'not', or negative to the positive, present concept being defined. The

political implications of this are profound. We cannot, according to this logic, establish an inclusive definition of utopia because, as stated above, the process of conceptualization involves exclusion. There may, at first glance, be nothing problematic in this, for surely the aim of any project of definition or conceptualization is the establishment of boundaries of delimitation. Definitions traditionally *desire* closure: imposing closure is their function. The importance of Derrida's critique to utopianism reaches deeper than this. The excluded, in this case, consists of feminist utopian texts. This may or may not be coincidental: in chapters below I explore the ways in which binary oppositional thought has constructed 'woman' as Other by similar mechanics of exclusion. The point in this case is that we cannot risk erecting exclusive definitions.[24]

The view that naming is claiming can be further illustrated by reference to what Derrida calls the masculine gift: 'In giving his name, a name of his choice, in giving all names, the father [God] would be at the origin of language, and that power would belong by right to God the father' (Derrida, 1985: p. 246). In the beginning was the word and the word was God. As the root of all names, God, the omni-absent ultimate presence, owns the power of naming. Derrida can be read as preoccupied with the (im)possibility of 'real' and 'genuine' giving – his concern can be read as follows: if giving (a name) is taking (possession) in phallo-logocentric discourse, can there be a 'true' gift? This question can, I believe, be seen to underlie, or overlie (in the background and in the foreground), much of his work.

He asks in *Psyche* whether he can make an incorrupt gift (in this case to the work of Emmanuel Levinas):

> I would like to do it faultlessly (*sans faute*), with a 'faultlessness' ('*sans faute*') that no longer belongs to the time or logic of the rendezvous. Beyond any possible restitution, there would be need for my gesture to operate without any debt, in absolute ingratitude.
>
> (Derrida, 1987: p. 408)

Giving, he finds, belongs to a cultural economy, the character of which can be understood in terms of the Proper: the drive for appropriation. Giving has an economic return which is normally manifested as debt or gratitude. Derrida's 'faultless' gift does not escape this economic exchange, as giving thus can only be paying homage. Homage is given in an act for which the script is written; homage is an act which *requires* ingratitude. Ingratitude, in this economy, is the return of the gift. Hence, says Derrida, 'The gift is *not*' (1987: p. 410). It is *not* a gift, there is no such thing as a gift, 'gift' being euphemistic for investment.

On the one hand the application of Derridean techniques to the concept of utopia can, I believe, be enabling to a feminist critique. Deconstruction, from this perspective, strips the construct of utopia of its pretensions towards neutrality and universalism. Thus deprived, the blueprinting approach to utopia as perfection can be seen to be uncompromisingly exclusive.

A further consequence of the exercise, however, is one of profound disablement. If the Drive of the Proper motivates and (in)forms conceptualization, then utopia cannot be reconceived. This way leads to silence and impotence. It strikes me as ironic that impotence, with its double meaning of powerlessness and masculine flaccidity, should be a product of a critique of phallocentrism. Postmodernism would appear to take away with one hand what it offers with the other. For social movements, such as those represented by the various feminisms, such an approach empowers and disempowers simultaneously. Should it perhaps be rejected?

Possible strategies

Various strategies have been offered by feminist theorists to resolve this apparent dilemma. Some focus on essentialism (mentioned earlier) and some insist that a certain essentialism is necessary in order to move from this position of immobility. Elizabeth Grosz suggests that to read the feminism/postmodernism dilemma as a choice between two pure positions – political commitment (feminism) and intellectual rigour (postmodernism) – is a mistake. Feminism, she says, will always be implicated in patriarchy and should/can, therefore, work from within this system. This, I suggest, is itself a move of deconstruction from within the cultural text of patriarchy, and Grosz moves us away from a dualistic conception of choice or possibility:[25]

> in assuming that feminists take on essentialist or universalist assumptions (if they do, which is not always clear) in the same way as patriarchs, instead of attempting to understand the ways in which essentialism and its cognates can function as strategic terms, this silences and neutralizes the most powerful of feminist theoretical weapons – feminism's ability to use patriarchy and phallocratism against themselves, its ability to

91

take up positions ostensibly opposed to feminism and use them for feminist goals.

(Grosz, 1990a: p. 343)

The following statement is from Rosi Braidotti. It can, I believe, be read as addressing the dilemma outlined above in the brief discussion of Derrida:

> Feminist theory and practice at the end of this century is a double-edged project involving both the critique of existing definitions, representations, and theorizations of women and also the creation of new images for female subjectivity and suitable social representations of it.
>
> (Braidotti, 1989: p. 90)

The critique offered above in my reading of Derrida moves towards fulfilling the requirements of the first part of this statement. The problem which Grosz, Harding and Scott are cited as addressing concerns the second: the construction of alternatives (which is an essential function of utopianism – and, of course, of political theory: without utopianism, feminism will grind to a halt). For Braidotti this can be achieved politically through the assertion of the need for women (real, historical beings) in what she calls 'positions of discursive subjecthood' (1989: p. 90). Theoretically, she says, there is a need for the rejection of universal and neutral concepts of the subject in favour of an embodied and differentiated model. Hence, she says, we cannot afford not to be essentialist. Her position is written thus, and addresses the dilemma of coherence–dis-/anti-integration in terms of the female subject:

> In my reading, the thought of sexual difference argues the following: it is historically and politically urgent, in the *here and now* of the common world of women to bring about and act upon sexual difference.... 'We' women, the movement of the liberation of the 'I' of each and every woman, assert the following: 'I woman, think and therefore say that I, woman, am.' I am sexed female, my subjectivity is sexed female. As to *what* my 'self' or my 'I' actually is, that is a whole new question, dealing with identity. The affirmation of my subjectivity need not give a propositional content to my sense of identity: I do not have to define the signifier woman in order to assert it as the speaking

subject of my discourse. The speaking 'I' is not neutral or gender-free, but sexed.

(Braidotti, 1989: p. 100)

Hence Braidotti accommodates the differences between men's and women's experiences of the world with the differences between women and, on a deeper psychoanalytic level, the differences within us. She does not privilege *either* sociological difference *or* postmodern difference; rather, she rewrites the rules of conceptualization.

The following statement comes from Anna Yeatman. It is directed at postmodern feminism but I find that it applies with particular resonance to Braidotti's tactical positioning:

> The basic proposition is that if there is to be a vision of freedom which contests phallocentrism, it must admit the existence and the significance of the particularity of embodied subjects. This means admitting the differences between differently embodied subjects. These differences are not reducible to a simple diamorphic sex difference, nor are they without socio-cultural mediation.... Such admission depends on providing the discursive space in which differently embodied subjects can find their own voices regarding their differences as embodied subjects.
>
> (Yeatman, 1994: p. 24)

Her essentialism stops short of universalizing 'woman' whilst acting as a bond/bind between women. Thus feminism is theoretically possible.

The works of Susan Bordo and Elizabeth Spelman raise questions that return us to the debates and dilemmas introduced at the beginning of this chapter. Bordo addresses the relation between feminism and postmodernism. Spelman's work is situated outside these debates but also addresses questions of the meaning of difference within and for feminism. Bordo is ambivalent about the possibility of a relationship between feminism and postmodernism: 'To invoke the ideal of endless difference is for feminism to self-destruct or to finally accept an ontology of abstract individualism' (Bordo, 1990: p. 134). For her, then, postmodernism cannot solve the problem of difference for feminism. She recommends flirtation with postmodernism and poststructuralist reading techniques, as they may be useful, but marriage, she says, should be avoided:

> In the context of our specific history, assessing where we are now,

93

I believe that feminism stands less in danger of the 'totalizing' tendencies of feminists than of an increasingly paralysing anxiety over falling (from what grace?) into ethnocentrism or 'essentialism'.... Do we want to delegitimate a priori the exploration of experimental continuity and structural common ground among women?... If we wish to empower diverse voices, we would do better, I believe, to shift strategy from the methodological dictum that we forswear talk of 'male' and 'female' realities,... to the messier, more slippery, practical struggle to create institutions and communities that will not permit *some* groups of people to make determinations about reality for *all*.

(1990: p. 142)

I have highlighted this collection of responses to the feminism–postmodernism, unity–dis-/anti-integration debate because none of them wholeheartedly endorses one of two proffered options or pure theoretical positions. Their approaches both desire and enact a certain reworking of the framework in which the choice is couched, and it is in this sense (of clearing and creating a space for speculation) that this thinking is utopian. I mentioned Elizabeth Spelman earlier, and her work in this area is helpful. Spelman's proposal is a radical one, and her understanding of the nature of contemporary feminism is complex: she considers the idea that gender difference can be understood in a multiple sense, that, in other words, there are 'many kinds of women, many genders' (Spelman, 1990: p. 176). She is led to this conclusion by consideration of the history of feminist thought, which, she rightly says, has been one of exclusion – the exclusion of women who are different (deviant from the newly established norm of what it is to be 'a woman'). The desire and need to speak as women has, for Spelman, resulted in the creation by feminism of an essentialist, racist and classist understanding of what it is to be a woman. Speaking as a woman, she says, means speaking as a white, middle-class, Western woman: 'the real problem has been how feminist theory has confused the condition of one group with the condition of all' (1990: p. 4). The phrase 'as a woman' then, is, for Spelman, 'the Trojan Horse of feminist ethnocentrism' (1990: p. 13).[26]

Paradoxically, of course, the Trojan Horse *did* get through the city gates, and feminism *does* need to present a united front. Spelman does not suggest that feminism is defunct; rather she creates a new (and utopian) space within which feminist critiques and construction can occur:

> Moreover, it is not a threat to the coherence of feminism to recognize the existence of many kinds of women, many genders. It may in fact help us to be more willing to uncover the battles among women over what 'being a woman' means and about what 'women's issues' are. It may make us more ready to recognise that our engaging in these battles is a sign of our empowerment, not something that stands in the way of such empowerment. Yes, we may want and need to make a united case against a hostile world. But it is also necessary and hence a healthy sign that we battle over what that case should be, rather than relegating the making of it to the usual spokeswoman.
>
> (Spelman, 1990: p. 176)

I propose that we decline to accept a dilemma in which any choice between one of two alternatives is necessary (that is to say, acceptance or rejection of feminism *or* postmodernism, unity *or* diversity, equality *or* difference), and that we transgress the binary position of either/or and say both, neither and more. This chapter has evoked and employed a multiplicity of approaches to and understandings of the term 'difference'. In so doing I have hoped to illustrate my claim that the space of conceptualization that is shaped by binary opposition is redundant. We can, I suggest, simultaneously accept and reject, thus creating a new space beyond binary opposition in which something else (the unforeseeable) can be foreseen. Thus we neither (fully) accept nor (fully) reject, and either/or is no longer a meaningful position.[27] This further allows for *more*, a more which, in the chapter that follows, I characterize as 'feminine'. This new space, this new position, is profoundly utopian.

I should, perhaps, move towards concluding this discussion by noting that this position is also profoundly *unsafe*. Elizabeth Spelman suggests that we let go of the security of a simple (binary) theory of gender. Monique Wittig's creation of the third gender of the lesbian who is not a woman is similarly destabilizing (Wittig, 1981); and bell hooks says that to create what she calls oppositional thinking it is necessary to forgo the familiarity and stability of the present:

> The formation of an oppositional world view is necessary for feminist struggle. This means that the world we have most

intimately known, the world in which we feel 'safe', (even if such feelings are based on illusion) must be radically changed.

(hooks, 1984: p. 163)

Oppositional thinking of the utopian kind proposed in this book is particularly destabilizing, not only of that which is opposed but also of the ground on which the opposers stand. Oppositional thinking of this kind pulls the proverbial rug from under our own feet, for if, as has been suggested, feminist opposition is multiple, multifaceted and multidirectional, the question must be asked: does and can feminism actually exist? Is there any cohesion in the works of those concerned with the position(s) of women in society? Is there any common ground from which women *can* speak *as* women?

These are perhaps the risks that feminism must run in order to gain integrity. From a position of integrity, then (again perhaps), political efficacy can grow. I have suggested in this chapter that an open conception of feminism is the only valid one. Following Spelman I also insist that 'though all women are women, no woman is only a woman' (Spelman, 1990: p. 187). The question 'What is it?' should not be asked of woman.[28] Feminism is mistaken if it sees gender as the only site of oppression. It must then open its ears and widen its vision to other discourses of oppression if it is really to concern itself with the various positions of women in society(ies). An open conceptualization of feminism is receptive to these voices and realizes that the only people to whom race and class, religion and sexuality are irrelevant are those who have traditionally dominated its main stream.

CONCLUSION

The moves identified in this chapter away from the standard mechanisms of conceptualization and analysis are indicative of a perceivable shift towards an openended self-understanding within feminism. This shift informs and addresses the new utopianism advanced earlier in the book. The backdrop to this shift consists of a series of interactions between feminism and poststructuralism/postmodernism. There is less self-certainty and dogma in contemporary feminism than there was in that of, say, the 1970s, and more receptivity towards the validity of multiple readings and respect for diverse opinions. The multiplicity and openended nature of contemporary feminist utopianism are reflective of these concerns.

The following chapter is concerned to pursue these questions further, and attempts to do so through continued exploration of the relations between feminism and utopianism. Connections are made between deconstruction and utopia which represent the foreground to this relation. In the discussion above I suggested through a reading of Derrida that poststructuralism led to silence. This reading, however, was couched in terms of a simple (binary) choice which can be expressed in the following terms: should feminism accept poststructuralism (and postmodernism) or reject it? I have proposed that we reject the terms in which the question is framed and seek grounds upon which choice can be made in terms that transgress binarity.

These ideas are expanded in the next chapter in a consideration of a utopianism that operates in an alternative economy of social and cultural exchange. This economy is characterized as feminine, a somewhat problematic label drawn from the works of Hélène Cixous.[29] A feminine economy as depicted by Cixous is not characterized by appropriation and acquisition. Rather it represents an attempt to come to terms with and to go some way towards responding to the dilemma of naming introduced by Derrida. Cixous's approach is presented as *one* way in which the new utopianism can be read, not as the final interpretation. It is hoped that by leaving interpretation open we can perhaps name a feminism which is not universalizing or exclusive, and a utopianism that is not marked by closure and finality of end.

4

UTOPIA AS NO PLACE
The transgressive discourses of
deconstruction and libidinal femininity

INTRODUCTION

In Chapter 3 I proposed an understanding of the relations between feminism and postmodernism, feminism and utopianism, that is transgressive of the dualist position of either/or. The 'problem' of difference was identified as the central problematic with which contemporary feminism is preoccupied. The proposed response to this problem was similarly transgressive: the approach advocated was one that rejected the conventional frameworks on which thought (and theory) are structured. It was transgressive of dualist thought and binary oppositional thought and was identified as utopian in the sense outlined in earlier chapters – it created a new conceptual space and had a transformative function: it provoked a paradigm shift in consciousness. The utopianism of feminism (thus understood) is, I have suggested, its redeeming feature. A utopianism of this kind has the potential to transform feminism from a politics of exclusion to a politics that is open to difference.

The concern of this chapter is to pursue this line of thought further, and to pull together some of the divergent strands of thought explored in previous chapters. The new kind of utopianism that I have identified is critical and creative. It is critical of the political present,[1] and in this it remains constant to the standard (content-based) conception of utopianism. It is imaginative and sometimes takes a fictional form; it fully exploits the ambivalent status of fiction and produces an estranged commentary. The point at which this utopianism diverges from the colloquial view is in its approach to the creation of alternatives. I have argued that this difference consists in an avoidance of the blueprint and a resistance to closure. I have also suggested that most content-based and form-based approaches are not appropriate and that utopianism is best approached through discourses which are similarly transgressive and resistant to closure. In this way we can approach utopianism as a radical phenomenon and conceptualize a radical utopianism which is transformative. Approaching utopianism with the tools of radical and transgressive discourses, then, permits the reconceptualization of utopianism.

In the last chapter I expressed concerns about the intellectual void that may result from 'marrying' feminism to postmodernism. I suggested that Derridean deconstruction can silence and immobilize. All of this does not, however, preclude the existence of a relation between them. The first section of the discussion below expands upon this point and proposes that in refusing to accept a choice between either/or (feminism or postmodernism, acceptance or rejection), a new and utopian space for exploration can be created. This is undertaken by an examination of the potential of a new relation between the poststructuralist (Derridean) activity of deconstruction and an open-ended utopianism. This chapter takes a new approach which is not marked by a desire for closure, and in this context the work of Derrida is considered as offering useful insights.

The focus of the second section below is more specific. In a close reading of Hélène Cixous's theory of libidinal femininity, I propose to add a further dimension to the new approach to (and understanding of) utopianism for which I have been arguing. In suggesting that utopianism can be situated within an alternative economy of exchange, the discussion below can be said to be practising utopia on utopia. A utopian and transgressive reading of the genre or field of utopianism is undertaken, which is explored further in the thematic reading offered in Part III.

Utopianism, feminism, femininity and deconstruction, then, are placed in a special relation, the nature of which is presented as transgressive of and potentially subversive of dominant symbolic orders, thought structure and other systems of representation. As a consequence, the fields and ideas in question (utopianism, feminism and deconstruction) are reconceptualized. This proposed relation is not oppositional or hierarchical. The following readings of this relation attempt to show how these fields and ideas have what Tom Moylan calls a critical utopian function and effect on each other and themselves: how, in other words, they are mutually critiqued, destroyed and transformed (Moylan, 1986).

UTOPIANISM, UTOPIAS AND DECONSTRUCTION

'Deconstruction is ... an activity of thought which cannot be consistently acted on – that way madness lies – but which yet possesses an inescapable rigour of its own' (Norris, 1982: p. xii). Derrida's poststructuralism goes beyond conceptualization, structure and order to a new/no place that I will suggest has some bearing on (and bears some resemblance to) the understanding of utopianism that this book proposes. This utopianism is openended and forbids closure, and the discussion that follows suggests that Derrida's work has the same function/effect.

There are a number of difficulties involved in this project, the problematics of which must first be addressed. First, the dangers of assimilation should be noted. Christopher Norris's excellent book *Deconstruction: Theory and Practice* (1992) carries as a sub-theme a warning of these dangers. He identifies the ways in which radical thought and insight are assimilated into and defused by what he calls 'tame methodologies': 'Once a term is fixed within a given explanatory system, it becomes (like "structure") usable in ways that deny or suppress its radical insights' (Norris, 1982: pp. 31, 32). Again, we can see the importance of approach, and it is my intention to use deconstruction for my own purposes, which can only be described as situated within a logocentric methodology, without denying it its radicalness. This may indeed in Norris's strict sense be a corrupt project but is, I suggest, worth considering as an alternative to madness and silence.[2]

A second problem is that of the articulation or expression first of Derrida's ideas and subsequently of my own. The nature of the problem is aptly illustrated by the last sentence: to articulate is to speak; to express is to state definitely – it is a statement couched in terms of a logocentric vocabulary, assuming the presence and attainability of both truth and certainty that can, in turn, be understood and clearly and unambiguously presented. It further uses the vocabulary of speech, which (according to Derrida) is intimately related to the metaphysics of presence due to the assumed bond between sound and sense.

This is approaching the kind of paralysis of which I wrote earlier, and its effects cannot be overstressed. This way indeed madness lies. It may, of course, be possible to step back from Derrida's texts into scholarly objectivity and to present his texts in a disengaged manner. I doubt it. I would also doubt the authenticity of such a reading on grounds similar to those established by Norris.

From this emerges a further problematic area, that of the inaccessibility of Derrida's actual texts. Derrida works from *within* the texts of others. Reading Derrida 'properly' therefore requires a depth of understanding of such thinkers as Nietzsche and Saussure that exceeds the scope of this project. I therefore propose an 'improper' reading that focuses broadly on the theme of deconstruction, without engaging actively in his debates with other thinkers. Many Derridean scholars will object to this approach to his work, but Derrida himself might, I suspect, approve. In addition to difficulty of content we are confronted with a style in which meaning is self-consciously elusive. As this chapter progresses these problems will, I suspect, become more rather than less apparent – as perhaps they should. The following discussion attempts to engage with deconstruction and to engage it further in 'conversation' with an openended conception of utopianism.

Deconstruction works from inside the text. Text, in this context, may be read either in the narrow, conventional sense, or in the wider sense of a cultural text. Deconstruction's purpose, in Derrida's hands, is to unravel, expose and transform the text. This function is also performed by utopianism, which is rooted in and acknowledges complicity with the present. By employing various tactics of estrangement, utopian thought provokes a certain distance from the present which permits the creation of new conceptual space. These parallels between the operations of utopian and Derridean thought are expanded in the discussion that follows.

Deconstruction is not a theory or a concept. Nor can it be described as a system or a method, due to the implications of order invoked by these terms. It is best described as an activity of reading (Norris, 1982). That deconstruction is not external to the text is an important fact to grasp. It challenges the logocentrism or metaphysics of presence which Derrida perceives as dominating Western thought. This challenge cannot occur from outside the text, since such an attempt would be utopian in the negative sense of the word: impossible and ridiculous. In order to understand why deconstruction must inhabit the text upon which it works, it is necessary to present Derrida's approach to writing. This will be attempted through the roundabout route of looking at Derrida's critique of the structural linguistics of Ferdinand de Saussure.

Derrida's work, as mentioned in Chapter 3, has its roots in

structuralist critiques of language, hence poststructuralism. Saussure's structural linguistics explore the relation between language and meaning, perception and reality (Saussure, 1974). Saussure challenged the assumption that language provides a mirror of reality and that meaning is intrinsic to words. He identified an 'arbitrary' relationship between signifier and signified (word and thing); arbitrary because of the lack of inherent content in the signifier. Meaning is rather conveyed by a play of sameness and difference. Crudely put, 'bat' is not 'cat' because of the phonemes 'b' and 'c', which *sound* different. Saussure further identified a structure to language which, he showed, shapes perceptions of reality. Language, in other words, orders our experience of reality and gives it sense and meaning; and language for structuralist thinkers, following Saussure, consists of codes and convention. *Parole*, then, or speech utterance, is distinguished from and contextualized within *langue*, a system of articulate relations.

Through a close reading of Saussure, Derrida argues that his work can be located within the metaphysics of presence. In the first instance, Saussure privileges speech over writing. The voice, for Saussure, signifies or represents truth and authenticity: it is indicative of a present self, and this gives it a certain vibrancy which writing lacks. Derrida practises a deconstructive reading of Saussure in which the opposition 'speech/writing' is inverted and then displaced. The opposition is inverted by Derrida's assertion that writing is prior to speech because it is the precondition of language. This can only be grasped by extending 'writing' from its normal usage of graphic representation to a reading closer to that of inscription. Writing (graphics) is less self-aware than is speech in the sense outlined above; that is to say, the speaking present self is absent in the written text. It is also less self-aware in the sense of being less transparent (Saussure assumes there to be a bond between sound and sense).

In the following extracts, Norris describes Derrida's approach to the Saussurian text:

> Writing, for Derrida, is the 'free play' or element of undecidability within every system of communication. Writing is the endless displacement of meaning which both governs language and places it for ever beyond the reach of a stable, self-authenticating knowledge.
>
> To question that bond [between sound and sense] is to

102

venture into regions as yet uncharted, and requires a rigorous effort of conceptual desublimation or 'waking up'. Writing is that which exceeds – and has the power to dismantle – the whole traditional edifice of western attitudes to thought and language.

(Norris, 1982: pp. 28–9)

I cite these passages in the first instance by way of illustration of the points raised above, but primarily by way of introduction to the relation between deconstruction and utopianism. One 'result' or consequence of imagining a new relation along the lines to be suggested will be a new utopianism. Derrida's approach to writing, as described by Norris, acts as an element of order and structure in that it governs language (which in turn gives shape to our perceptions of the world). It is also, and more interestingly, representative of endless displacement: we can never fully 'capture' its meaning (nor, within the Derridean framework, should we want to). Utopianism (the new understanding of utopianism for which I have argued) can, I suggest, be represented as the endless displacement of possibility, of the possible, which can, in turn, be connected to Derrida's treatment of meaning and reality. Saussure showed that we cannot perceive reality in transparency. Derrida extends and explores 'meanings' and their construction. Deconstruction itself cannot be read as the full stop to analysis, as the final interpretative word. Nor, I have argued, can utopianism. Were deconstruction and utopianism to stop, to reach an end, then logocentrism would be embodied, the truth attained, and process completed. These ends are neither desirable nor 'possible'. In this sense, then, utopian thought and deconstruction address the same concerns and provoke similar effects. Norris's statements serve also to illustrate the utopianism of deconstruction itself. To venture into regions as yet uncharted and to dismantle the edifice of tradition is to practise utopian thinking. Tom Moylan's analysis of the critical utopia is of particular relevance to this – as mentioned in Chapter 2, it operates in the following way:

in the Enlightenment sense of *critique* – that is expressions of oppositional thought, unveiling, debunking, of both the genre itself and the historical situation. As well as 'critical' in the nuclear sense of the *critical mass* required to make the necessary explosive reaction.

(Moylan, 1986: p. 10)

A critical utopia is internally destructive and transformative, as, I suggest, is deconstruction (and, as I suggested in Chapter 3, so is feminism). This operates at two levels: a critical utopia works on itself (internally) and on the historical moment in which it is rooted (internally). Deconstruction differs from this; it is not a theory to be reconceived, but none the less can, I suggest, be read as operating in the same double-edged way:

> Deconstruction is...an activity performed by texts in which they have to acknowledge their complicity with what they denounce. The most rigorous reading it follows, is one that holds itself provisionally open to further deconstruction of its own operative contents.
>
> (Norris, 1982: p. 48)

I have described deconstruction as a reading which exposes logocentrism, or a desire for presence and truth, in the texts within which it works, and have argued that it is utopian and that it addresses utopianism. The reversal and displacement of binary oppositions is a deconstructive activity: by reversing the positions of dominance of the speech/writing opposition, for instance, and by displacing the opposition, thereby showing writing to be located within speech (in traditional Western thought), Derrida unravels Saussure's structuralism. Speech is shown to be dependent on writing within the conceptual system or text of logocentrism. The structure which erects speech as dominant to writing is not therefore a natural or given entity, but rather a construction that is historically organized:

> Deconstruction in this, its most rigorous form, acts as a constant reminder of the ways in which language deflects or complicates the philosopher's project. Above all, deconstruction works to undo the idea – according to Derrida, the ruling illusion of western metaphysics – that reason can somehow dispense with language and arrive at a pure, self-authenticating truth or method.
>
> (Norris, 1982: p. 18)

Deconstruction, then, like utopianism, does not just reverse an existing hierarchy; rather it subverts and undermines the system which constructs those hierarchical relations. Radical utopianism, I have suggested, following Cixous, seeks to *destroy the space of domination* (Cixous and Clement, 1986). Deconstruction does the same: both can be said, at a superficial level, to be profoundly destructive. This provokes the somewhat problematic question of what, if anything, deconstruction proposes instead: in what ways does it offer alternatives? Is it, in other words, utopian?

An initial and immediate response to this question is 'Yes, deconstruction is utopian, because it represents an alternative in itself.' Deconstruction as a process is profoundly creative. At its most obvious level this creation comes in the form of neologisms, the specifics of which will be discussed later. A less apparent, but equally important, creative act of deconstructive thought is the (utopian) space that it creates in which reconceptualization can occur. This is conceptual space (outopos), and its creation indicates that deconstruction is not just destructive.

I have already stated that deconstruction, like utopianism, operates from inside the text with which it is concerned. It is estranged from that text and this estrangement permits the deconstructive displacement of meaning to occur. Deconstruction, then, is a *process* that can never stop or cease; it is profoundly resistant to closure. It works like a critical utopia, and also like the transgressive utopianism identified in Chapter 2. In particular, it creates new conceptual exploratory space by resisting dualistic thought, thereby undermining the structure or system through which meaning is created.

In order to explore this question of deconstructive utopianism further, I am going to turn briefly now to Derrida's essay 'Structure, Sign and Play in the Discourses of the Human Sciences' (1978b). At one point in this essay, Derrida turns to look at the work of Claude Lévi-Strauss. (The larger project with which the essay is concerned is that of shaking totalities and showing them to be founded on that which they exclude, thereby containing the seeds of their own potential disruption or destruction.) He examines Lévi-Strauss's approach to the nature/culture opposition. This opposition, says Derrida, is 'congenital to philosophy' (1978b: pp. 282–3) and also informs the science of ethnology:

> since the statement of the opposition *physis/nomos, physis, techné,* it has been relayed to us by means of a whole historical chain which opposes 'nature' to law, to education, to art, to technics – but also to liberty, to the arbitrary, to history, to society, to the mind, and so on.
>
> (Derrida, 1978b: p. 283)

What makes Lévi-Strauss's approach interesting to Derrida is that, on the one hand, he begins with a traditional understanding of the relation between nature and culture, whilst, on the other, he subverts the (oppositional) relation between these two concepts by referring, right at the beginning of *Elementary Structures*, to a phenomenon which undermines the opposition. This phenomenon is the incest prohibition.

In Derrida's reading of Lévi-Strauss, the conventional understanding of the relation of nature to culture runs thus:

> that which is *universal* and spontaneous, and not dependent on any particular culture or on any determinate norm, belongs to nature. Inversely, that which depends on a system of *norms* regulating society and therefore is capable of *varying* from one social structure to another, belongs to culture.
>
> (Derrida, 1978b: p. 282)

The incest prohibition is both universal (and therefore natural, according to Lévi-Strauss's formula) and a prohibition: a norm or rule which, therefore, belongs to the cultural sphere. This reading of Lévi-Strauss is deconstructive: it looks for cracks, gaps and subversions in/of the dualistic construction of meaning from within a text. Because the incest prohibition is both natural and cultural, the nature/culture opposition is undermined, exceeded and rendered meaningless in this instance (in this moment of deconstruction). This reading of the incest prohibition, then, creates something which does not 'fit' into a scheme of thought ordered around the nature/culture opposition. This is the utopian moment of deconstruction – the double-edged sword which exposes and creates at the same instant:

> It could perhaps be said that the whole of philosophical conceptualization, which is systematic with the nature/culture opposition, is designed to leave in the domain of the unthinkable the very thing that makes this conceptualization possible: the origin of the prohibition of incest.
>
> (Derrida, 1978b: pp. 283–4)

The language of philosophy contains *within itself* the seeds of its own disruption: when what Derrida calls the 'structurality of structure' begins to be thought – when, in other words, the conceptualization of concepts is examined (thought: created) – then the subject or discipline is decentred. When it is realized that there is no centre (in this instance, the nature/culture opposition) and that the centre is a construct or function, then these subjects become what Derrida calls discourses. The relation between sign and signifier – subject and discourse – can then be examined by, for example, deconstructive readings. But, Derrida acknowledges, even the latter are caught in what he calls a trap, a circle, because, as the quotation above illustrates, all discourses (metaphysics, ethnology, social 'sciences'), even when approached in a self-consciously transgressive way, contain rules that have constituted them historically and that will continue to assure their existence. So, even whilst using a disruption of metaphysics to subvert the history of metaphysics, for example, we are still situated (trapped?) within the language (structure, rules, etc.) of metaphysics. But, says Derrida, not all ways of giving in to this 'irreducible fact' are the same. One can, for instance, look for things that escape or exceed the structure of a given discourse – hence the focus above on the incest taboo, which erases the nature/culture opposition, albeit only for a moment.

The utopianism of this can be seen by referring again to the quotation above. The deconstructive readings of Derrida intrude into the domain of the unthinkable as, I suggest, does the utopianism advocated by this book. Utopian thought 'foresees the unforeseeable' (to paraphrase Cixous, 1981a: p. 245); it thinks the unthinkable by approaching thinking in a new way – a paradigmatically new way: not via the old oppositional structure but by trying to resist, expose and resist again this structuring of thought (this conceptualization of concepts). With regard to approach: it is not the incest prohibition *per se* that is of importance, but rather the 'origin' of it: the way in which it is conceptualized or conceived. Likewise, the approach to utopianism supersedes utopias themselves, in this present work. Deconstruction and (transgressive) utopianism both privilege process over object.

Derrida evokes the notion of 'play' towards the end of the essay: language, he maintains, lacks a centre, an origin, and in this sense it is (somewhat perversely) finite. Were it to have a centre, language would be infinite: it could capture all meaning and reflect all objects, concepts and ideas. But, because of this lack it cannot, and so a centre is invented for it. 'Play' is Derrida's term for the disruption of presence: play – of the signifier – permits meaning.

He concludes the essay by stating that there are two (broad) approaches to the situation that he has evoked:

There are thus two interpretations of interpretation, of structure of sign, of play. The one seeks to decipher, dreams of deciphering a truth or an origin which escapes play and order of the sign, and which lives the necessity of interpretation as an exile. The other, which is no longer turned towards the origin, affirms play and tries to pass beyond man and humanism, the name of man being the name of that being who, throughout the history of metaphysics or ontotheology – in other words, throughout his entire history – has dreamed of full presence, the reassuring foundation, the origin and the end of play.

(Derrida, 1978b: p. 292)

This second position is that occupied by Derrida and again represents a utopian moment in his work: it passes beyond structure, metaphysics and their familiars, beyond binary oppositional thought, to a new space. Utopias of perfection can be positioned alongside Derrida's first outlined response, and especially with humanism as described above. Blueprinting utopias of perfection (and the approach which insists upon such a utopianism) also represent the end of play forever: the expression of a desire for full presence (perfect society). The new approach to utopianism, and the new utopianism which it conceptualizes, can be read as constantly affirming play, process and dynamism.

Staying for a moment longer with Derrida, I should like to look briefly at his conception of the term *différance*. Here again I will be drawing parallels between utopianism and deconstruction as radically creative activities. *Différance* is one of Derrida's neologisms and, as such, is a creation in itself. It subverts and operates in the gaps of binary oppositional thought.

The question of difference, its construction and operative function, is at the heart of deconstruction. I argued in Chapter 3 that these questions are also at the heart of contemporary feminist debates. Difference, then, is a particularly appropriate place from whence to address these narratives. Derrida starts from Saussure's conception of language as a play of difference and adds to it the idea of difference as deferred meaning. The term *différance* is both part of and a result of a deconstructive reading. It creates new 'meaning' and is itself new in that it does not 'fit' into a hierarchical or dualistic conception of language; strictly speaking, it is unconceptualizable. Derrida's 'conceptualization' of *différence* is representative of a creative and transgressive utopian moment in his work. The readings of feminism offered in Chapter 3 could be interpreted as moments of *différance*: by rejecting pure positions of simple binary opposition, new (utopian) spaces of possibility were created. *Différance* conveys both temporal and spatial distance and difference: '*Différance* as temporization, *différance* as spacing. How are they to be joined?' (Derrida, 1972a: p. 9).

Difference as spacing is explained by Saussure: meaning is made through explicit or implicit contrast. Any unitary concept (Derrida shows) must contain repressed or negated material; a positive definition rests on the negation of something represented as antithetical to it.[3] Hence the oppositions 'presence/absence', 'unity/diversity' and 'universality/specificity' are identified as grounding Western habits of ordering thought and meaning.

Difference as temporization is a somewhat more complex idea, which Derrida describes in *The Margins of Philosophy* by reference to the operations of the sign in language:

> Let us start, since we are already there, from the problematic of the sign and writing. The sign is usually said to be put in the place of the thing itself, the present thing, 'thing' here standing equally for meaning or referent. The sign represents the present in its absence. It takes the place of the present. When we cannot grasp or show the thing, state the present, the being-present, when the present cannot be presented, we signify, we go through the detour of the sign. We take or give signs. We signal. The sign, in this sense, is deferred presence.
>
> (Derrida, 1972: p. 61)

The sign then both signifies absence and compensates for absence by implying presence. In language, then (or as Derrida terms it, writing), there is only absence. For this reason he privileges the signifier because, according to this logic, everything (object, referent or meaning) *is* a signifier (of absence). This spatial and temporal play of difference that Derrida calls *différance* is what permits conceptuality, 'meaning' and, in a sense, sanity. It permits (and constructs) order from experience.

Différance as temporal spacing also refers to the construction of the meaning of one term in terms of its difference from others:

> each element appearing on the scene of presence, is related to something other than itself, thereby keeping within itself the mark of the past element, and already letting itself be

vitiated by the mark of its future element, this trace being related no less to what is called the future than to what is called the past.

(Derrida, 1972: pp. 65–6)

The temporal and spatial elements of *différance* cannot be neatly separated (as perhaps is illustrated by the meandering structure of this last section). It is this feature of *différance* that can, I suggest, be located within an alternative economy of exchange. *Différance* does not place or contain temporal and spatial differences in opposition; there is no either/or posited by the term. Rather it is both and perhaps neither, in their 'pure', discrete senses. The oppositional framework has ceased to exist, as has the concept of hierarchical relations. *Différance* defers meaning, but *deference* is not part of Derrida's neologism.[4]

This understanding of *différance* bears further resemblance to my approach to utopianism in that it 'works' only as an activity in the present – in the moment of engagement (either writing or reading). Utopias of process, I have suggested, following Whitford and Irigaray, are transformative of the present in that they evoke shifts in consciousness. The elusiveness of *différance* can perhaps be read as addressing the present in a similar manner: working from within a (cultural) text to create something new, a certain elusiveness or slipperiness is necessary in order to avoid being embroiled and embodied in that from which escape is desired:

> Essentially and lawfully, every concept is inscribed in a chain or a system within which it refers to the other, to other concepts, by means of the systematic play of differences. Such a play, *différance*, is thus no longer simply a concept, but rather the possibility of conceptuality, of a conceptual process and system in general. For the same reason, *différance*, which is not a concept, is not simply a word, that is, what is generally represented as the calm, present, and self-referential unity of concept and phonic material.

(Derrida, 1972: p. 36)[5]

The utopian text is an estranged text that has its roots in that which it criticizes. Deconstruction can be read in the same terms:

> Deconstructions, allowing ourselves this word for temporary convenience, are not critical overcomings of the texts, not summary executions, not *destructive* as such. They may indeed

110

kill off certain existing mortifying tendencies of reading. But deconstructive readings do not conquer from the sky, they do not bring to a text concerns alien to its production and its structuration.

(Wood, 1992: p. 2)

[Derrida] is not the eagle flying high over the landscape and mapping the terrain. Rather his thought is like some mischievous lubricant which circulates through the texts he examines, and searches through the cracks into places formerly unknown.

(Boyne, 1990: p. 91)

Feminist (feminine) utopianism also works from within the text in which it is situated. It further kills off the mortifying tendencies of blueprint utopianism:

Those who claimed that utopia was dead were, of course, in a structural sense right. In that sense, utopia has always been dead. Rather than describe a vital impulse toward change, utopia as it has been traditionally defined represents a static and, in the most literal sense, reactionary stance: a place in which, being 'perfect', does not need to – and will not – change.

(Bammer, 1991: p. 2)[6]

Derrida reads feminism as an oppositional (binary) entity, working in dualistic and dialectical opposition to patriarchy and thus perpetuating the dualism 'man/woman'. Content-based approaches to utopianism which stress perfection and blueprint, I suggest, read from a Derridean perspective, are typical of logocentric thought. This kind of approach to utopias is the ultimate expression of the belief that truth can be grasped and problems solved: amen.[7] I have attempted in the readings offered in this section to go some way towards a confrontation and refutation of these positions. In highlighting points of convergence and contact between utopianism and Derridean deconstruction, though, I am not attempting to suggest or promote a project of assimilation. Rather, the intent of these readings has been to question the oppositional relation between them. Some readings of poststructuralism see it as just destructive, and some readings of utopianism see it as purely creative. I should like to suggest that both deconstruction and utopianism destroy and create simultaneously, and that the one act cannot occur without the other. It is always easier to destroy the existing than to create the authentically new. Utopianism and deconstruction, as approached in this book, manage to do both.

In the following reading of the works of Cixous, this relation is explored further in the development of another facet of feminist utopianism: the libidinally feminine utopian perspective. I have just suggested that the 'new' utopianism and deconstructive poststructuralism are both transgressive in form and function, and I have offered a reading in which they are seen to inform and address each other. The next section proposes that the relation established is not oppositional, not hierarchical, and is provocative of a shift in consciousness; and that 'radical' utopianism itself can be usefully translated as operating in an alternative economy of exchange – alternative, that is, to the dominant economy in which current social relations take place. This economy is characterized as feminine in the sense developed by Cixous, and the readings and discussion that follow have the intended function of enabling us to understand why utopianism is best approached in this new way. In this sense, then, we are at the heart of the book, and the chapters that follow go some way towards testing this hypothesis.

The import of this section and the arguments that it proposes should not, however, be overstressed. I stated earlier that this chapter did not seek to conclude or foreclose the debate (and a characteristic of a feminine economy is that it resists closure). And, in Chapter 3, I have already offered one response to this question of why feminist utopianism is different from the standard model and why what I call the new and radical utopianism has emerged from feminism. So the following section is intended only to offer a (an *Other*, different) layer of interpretation.

HELENE CIXOUS AND LIBIDINAL FEMININITY

For Freud the libido is masculine. The concept of a feminine libido challenges this assumption, transgressing the existing boundaries of sexual and social relations. Cixous has worked with the concept of a libidinal femininity which, I suggest in this chapter, can usefully be linked to utopian theoretical attempts to challenge and change the patriarchal present. If, as has been suggested by Freud, the libido governs our relations to the other, then a libido governed by femininity shifts the focus from masculinity and can potentially move away from a conception of the world ordered along an axis of what can best be described as binarity, opposition and phallocentrism. It is with this in view that libidinal femininity is treated in this work as a utopian concept; it provokes a *paradigm* shift in consciousness.

Libidinal femininity is a phrase employed by Cixous within the context of a feminine 'economy'. Masculine and feminine libidinal economics are the subject of discussion later in this chapter. Cixous's understanding of femininity is rooted in Freudian psychoanalysis: 'The qualifier masculine or feminine which I use for better or worse comes from the Freudian territory' (Cixous, interviewed in Conley, 1984a: p. 129). Her work can be seen to have been strongly influenced by that of Derrida. It is, I suggest, important that the extent of this influence be noted. It is often neglected by commentators on Cixous's works and profoundly affects our readings. Cixous's work must be contextualized and read with Derridean tactics at the back of the mind. The concept of libidinal femininity itself is, I suggest, a reworking and deconstruction of existing theories of femininity. 'What I say has at least two sides and two aims: to break up and destroy; and to foresee the unforeseeable, to project' (Cixous, 1981a: p. 245): this statement is from the opening page of one of Cixous's better-known theoretical essays, 'The Laugh of the Medusa', and can be read as summarizing her entire project, spanning a writing life of over twenty years. Further, it is illustrative of the influence of Derrida upon her approach. It can, I suggest, be read as a description of deconstruction: to break up and destroy and to foresee the unforeseeable. It is profoundly utopian, both in the sense that as a whole the project aims at a shift in consciousness as well as being an apparently impossible task (impossible within the context of dominant understandings of the present).

As noted above, deconstruction can only function from within a text, for, according to Derrida, there is nothing which exists outside of language. Cixous proposes a deconstruction of the cultural text of masculinity:

> If woman has always functioned 'within' the discourse of man, a signifier that has always referred back to the opposite signifier which annihilates its specific energy and diminishes or shifts its very different sounds, it is time for her to dislocate this 'within', to explode it, turn it around, and seize it; to make it hers, containing it, taking it in her own mouth, biting that

tongue with her own teeth to invent for herself a language to get inside of.

(Cixous, 1981a: p. 257)

Cixous's work on femininity operates from within the prevalent understanding of femininity as theorized, for example, by Freud, Lacan and Derrida. These theories are accepted as descriptions of the present but rejected as prescriptions for the future. She shares, for instance, Freud's conviction that bisexuality is the innate sexual/social position of childhood: 'sexual difference develops out of bisexuality which is the original condition of every individual and which is subsequently displaced, transformed by culture' (Cixous, interviewed in Makward, 1976: p. 22). Likewise, she follows Freud and Lacan in considering castration, or rather the symbolic threat of castration, as fundamental to the creation of the cultural constructs 'man' and 'woman'. Associated themes of bisexuality, *jouissance* and difference can be found throughout her texts. Her work, however, is not that of an apostle; rather it challenges the inevitability of the existing order. She also appears to imply that these influential readings of the present are not the only valid ones:

> Now it has become rather urgent to question this solidarity between logocentrism and phallocentrism – bringing to light the fate dealt to woman, her burial – to threaten the stability of the masculine structure that passed itself as eternal-natural, by conjuring up from femininity the reflections and hypotheses that are necessarily ruinous for the stronghold still in possession of authority. What would happen to logocentrism, to the great philosophical systems, to the order of the world in general if the rock upon which they founded this church should crumble?

(Cixous and Clement, 1986: p. 65)

From femininity then, which has been theorized by men as that upon which masculinity is built, Cixous suggests that instability is conjured: a fundamental instability which can, she believes, shake the foundations of the entire system. Femininity is characterized by Freud as passivity, by Lacan as being 'not all' and excess, and by Derrida as an infinite multiplicity. These traits of cultural femininity Cixous turns on the system itself in a double move which consists partially of inversion and partially of invention. The traits are, for instance, celebrated in her texts, thus inverting the existing hierarchy of

114

binarity. Femininity, for example, is traditionally connected to the body; Lacan's work on feminine *jouissance* is illustrative of this. Cixous frequently introduces the body into the text in a move which privileges the corporeal whilst at the same time transgressing the mind/body divide. The passage cited above is illustrative of this practice: Cixous writes of taking man's discourse (or rather, of taking its structurality and conceptualizations) between our teeth, biting its tongue in a punning and lucid style that invites the body into the text. Traits of cultural femininity are transformed by Cixous through the invention of a system of social exchange which is not driven by the Proper but is rather marked by the desire to give. Only by giving, living and loving, according to Cixous, can the other be regarded differently.

In Chapter 7 I expand and explore Cixous's contributions to theories of self and other, and identify ways in which feminist utopian thinking attempts to transgress the dominant relation, which is grounded in hierarchy and dualistic opposition and which privileges sameness. For present purposes, though, this area of Cixous's work is presented as an illustration of a transgressive and radical utopian thinking in practice. By advancing a new and different system of cultural and social exchange, she creates a utopian space in which conceptualization can be undertaken differently – not, in other words, through a framework of binary opposition that is driven by the desire to appropriate and possess difference.

Phallo-logocentrism relies upon order, the symbolic order of language, as identified, for example, by Lacan and Derrida. Libidinal femininity challenges and subverts this order but does not replace it with an inverted version of the same:

> It is not a question of appropriating their instruments, their concepts, their places for oneself or of wishing oneself in their position of mastery. . . . Not taking possession to internalize or manipulate but to shoot through and smash the walls.
>
> (Cixous and Clement, 1986: p. 96)

The discussion that follows explores further the concepts of masculine and feminine economies, linking them to a writing practice that represents a fusion of utopianism and radical theory. It is the nature of this fusion which I suggest marks a break both from a standard view of utopia as blueprint and from feminist theory, traditionally understood.

A MASCULINE LIBIDINAL ECONOMIC ORDER

Cixous speaks explicitly in terms of libidinal economies, which, she suggests, stabilize and regularize our sexual and social relations. That within which we now operate in Western society she describes as being c/overtly masculine: it constitutes an economy of exchange which mediates this phenomenon of a masculine libidinal order from a number of directions. She makes 'sorties' into its territory using the conceptual vehicles and tools of psychology, myth, fairy tale and philosophy. In short, she uses any discourse at her disposal which will enable her to destroy this particular space of domination. I propose, in this section, to undertake a brief survey of some of her approaches to the construct of masculinity.

In the first instance, as stated above, she employs the concepts of Freudian analysis – she describes the concept of the libido, for instance, in the following terms:

> It is something which can be defined from the body, as the movement of a pulsion toward an object, and which is part of the discoveries of Freud *par excellence*. It allows us to know what at other times had been analyzed as the treaty of passions. This is what I refer to, and I believe that the word 'economy' is important. It is the regime of that which in the past used to be called the effect of desire, of love. It is the love of life, or the sexual life, which is lived consciously, and which can be described as economic metaphors with moments of investment in passion, love, disgust, or anything else, moments of disinvestment from subject to object.
>
> (Cixous, interviewed in Conley, 1984a: p. 130)

The libido is the sexual drive or urge felt by one person for another (the object of the first person's desire). This, for Cixous, is the primary relation to the other. Freud identified the libido as masculine in its activity. Cixous expands this and finds the entire economy upon which present libidinal relations are based to be masculine. She further finds this libidinal economy to be fundamental to all social and sexual relations. In much of her early theoretical work she searches, as Derrida does, for the possibility of a gift that has no return: a gift that *is*.

Translation, or rather, interpretation of the libidinous relation to the other in terms of economics introduces a rich metaphorical vocabulary. In an essay published in translation as 'Castration or Decapitation?' (1981b), Cixous relates the Chinese story of General

116

Sun Tse, which she reads as representing the friction between two economies: one masculine, the other (potentially) feminine. The general is instructed by his king to make soldiers of his (the king's) 180 wives. The women respond to Sun Tse's efforts to teach them the marching language of the drum by falling about laughing, failing to take the exercise seriously. The general's response, says Cixous, is to put his code to the test: 'It is said in this code that should women fall about laughing instead of becoming soldiers, their actions might be deemed mutinous, and the code has ordained that cases of mutiny call for the death penalty' (Cixous, 1981b: p. 42). Despite the protestations of the king, the two women commanders of the troop/troupe were subsequently beheaded. The code of the general was the Absolute Law: 'They were replaced and the exercise started again, and as if they had never done anything except practise the art of war, the women turned left, right, and about in silence and never with a single mistake' (1981b: p. 42).The Absolute Law which is the code is thus learnt, and the women are educated. The story is subject to rich interpretation and is used by Cixous as metaphor for the effect of the material history of women:

> Women have no choice other than to be decapitated, and in any case the moral is that if they don't actually lose their heads by the sword, *they only keep them on condition that they lose them* – lose them, that is, to complete silence, turned into automatons.
>
> (1981b: pp. 42–3)

Cixous's approach to the story can, I believe, be read as illustrative of many of her concerns. The women's laughter, for example, can on one level be read as a feminine disruption of the masculine regimental order. Femininity and masculinity, in this sense, are not essentially bound to the gender of the participants in the exercise, although the story can be read, as suggested above, as a metaphor of the experience of women. The silence of the marching women is symptomatic of their subsequent disempowerment. Their gain in this economic exchange is that of masculinity in the form of their eventual ability to be perfect soldiers. It is, however, of no profit to them, representing rather obedience and subordination to a rigid code. Nothing has actually been given to the women; they are automatons under the threat of death.

The story can (I find) also be read through the mind/body divide, which is the subject of Chapter 5: the laughter to which the women succumbed held their bodies in its convulsions; rendering them

117

unable to stand in straight lines. This laughter came from within the bodies of the women. The body of the soldier, conversely, embraces the military code as it mirrors the erect phallus in its rigidity. The code is imposed upon the women; it is not their property.

The code embodies power, and its 'proper' adherents, the soldiers, have a rightful place in that particular hierarchy of power. The use of violence is legitimated by the code. The alternative, for men, is the chaos of feminine disorder which, under the Symbolic, represents the threat of castration: the deepest experience of lack:

> It's a question of submitting feminine disorder, its laughter, its inability to take the drumbeats seriously, to the threat of decapitation. If man operates under the threat of castration, if masculinity is culturally ordered by the castration complex, it might be said that the backlash, the return, on women of this castration anxiety is its displacement as decapitation, execution, of woman, as loss of her head.
>
> (Cixous, 1981b: p. 43)

Loss of her head, loss of her mind; the women is thus bound to the realm of the body. The masculine code offers nothing to women. Already castrated in the Freudian/Lacanian analyses, the women march in a silence that marks their new state of living death.

The femininity to which Cixous refers in the story is connected to the bodies of the women. Woman, the construct of the Symbolic, has traditionally been defined and confined in/by terms of her biology. The little girl, in the Freudian text, lacks the penis, envies the penis and desires a penis. Woman in Lacan represents lack: she is lack, she is also the impossible site of unity as Other; she is the phallus but does not possess it.

The identification by Cixous of femininity with the (female) body has led to charges of regressive essentialism. The vocabulary of the body is that which has traditionally been used to denigrate woman, and the identification of woman with the body has served a similar function. I would suggest, however, that rather than echoing and enhancing the ways in which existing theories of femininity have served to perpetuate women's subordination, Cixous's work represents a manipulation of this attitude. The female body is privileged in her work in a move of inversion, but the concept is also transformed. It is, she says, because of her body that woman has been relegated to her subordinate position. Further, it is because of her identification with the body that woman has been effectively silenced. This position, however, is not one of pure negativity. Woman, says Cixous, inhabits her body: she knows it from the inside. This knowledge, for Cixous, leads to a certain approach to the world. It does not conform to masculine structures of power and communication that are based upon linearity, binarity and all other patterns that rest upon unitary perceptions of the world.

These ideas are pursued further in Chapter 5, which focuses on a discussion of the dichotomy of mind and body, and examines feminist utopian attempts to establish alternative readings of this dualistic relation. For the moment, though, this reading of Cixous serves to show how the utopianism of her approach functions to provide a radical and transformative analysis which is profoundly critical. The creative function of her utopianism is explored in the following section.

Similar concerns can be read in Cixous's treatment of the story of Sleeping Beauty. She refers to it in several works, linking it to the death drive of masculinity. This drive she reads as desiring and needing the 'death' of femininity. Femininity in this critique is seen to represent a threat to masculinity:[8]

> Woman, if you look for her, has a strong chance of being found in one position: in bed. In bed and asleep – 'laid (out)'. She is always to be found on or in a bed: Sleeping Beauty is lifted from her bed by a man because, as we all know, women don't wake up by themselves: man has to intervene, you understand. She is lifted up by the man who will lay her in her next bed so that she may be confined to bed ever after, just as the fairy tales say.
>
> (Cixous, 1981b: p. 43)

> Man's dream: I love her – absent, hence desirable, a dependent nonentity, hence adorable. Because she isn't there where she is. As long as she isn't where she is. How he looks at her then! When her eyes are closed, when he completely understands her, when he catches on and she is no more than this shape made for him: a body caught in his gaze.
>
> (Cixous and Clement, 1986: p. 67)

Taken together, these passages metaphorize the theory of phallo-logocentrism upon which Cixous builds. We can see that woman is presented as defined in negative terms as a nonentity, a non-presence, and in the ultimate position of passivity: laid out, as for the ritual of burial. The play on the phrase laid (out) is indicative of the nature of the prince's desire. This desire is, I suggest, essentially necrophilic, based on the lack of life that he perceives before him, on its (her) emptiness. Beauty's response in the tale, once 'awakened' by his kiss, is compliant, grateful and bewitched. She is awakened to a state of sleepwalk. The return for the prince's 'gift' of life is the rest of her life. The man who walks into the bedroom of a sleeping beauty and kisses her as she sleeps is thus rewarded.

Beauty was laid out: ready for burial or, perhaps more appropriately, for mummification. Beauty is laid: the vulgar vernacular for copulation in the missionary position. The missionary thus brings his gift of salvation that strips the indigenous populace of their own culture and fills the subsequent void with that of the new ruler. The void which is woman is filled with/by masculine desire. Beauty is laid; Beauty is out: Beauty is absent.

Femininity as potential subversion of order is written out of the tale; it is swallowed and absorbed into the body of masculinity, which, in turn, assumes the authority of representation. Beauty is absent; there is nothing of her there whilst she sleeps except her body. Man thus creates her; fills the void which he sees before him. She is named and claimed and feeds masculinity; loved and made love to for what she now is: a phallocentric creation. She is needed as a mirror whose function is to reflect back to the prince a return of masculinity.[9] There is, I suggest, an element of the vampire in the prince.

Reading Cixous in these terms provokes powerful analyses that are evocative of many of the debates with which contemporary feminist theory is preoccupied. Her work is, I have suggested, utopian: it is quite profoundly imaginative (and transgresses generic boundaries), it is critical of the political present, and it presents an analysis in a form which is both rooted in and estranged from the here and now. This section has attempted to illustrate the ways in which Cixous's work performs the first of Moylan's critical utopian functions: destruction (Moylan, 1986). Transformation and revival (the creative-critical functions) are the subject of the following discussion of an alternative economy of exchange.

A FEMININE LIBIDINAL ECONOMY

Within Cixous's works is a glimmer of something new, something different from that which is characterized in her analyses of the patriarchal present: a feminine economy of exchange. A feminine libidinal economy is not a simple inversion of the masculine order, nor is it essentially bound to gender. It does involve a re-evaluation of the same/different opposition in which difference is reconceptualized and privileged, but this is, I suggest, a tactical move rather than representative of a goal in itself.

Cixous's goal, if a single goal can be identified in her work, is the discovery or creation of a space in which radically different relations to the other can be conceived. This space is utopian and does not represent closure. A masculine economy is driven by the need to possess, name and appropriate. Traits of a feminine economy include a willingness to take risks: to let go. Cixous writes, for example, of a feminine economy operating within what she calls the Realm of the Gift, in which giving is not motivated by the desire for reciprocation, and investment is not made in anticipation of a due return:

> If I can speak in simple terms one has to learn how to live. At first one exists, but then one has to learn how to really live, that is to be attentive to life, enjoy it, preserve it, enlarge it. . . . What we have to learn really is the essential of life. How to give – which is extremely difficult: how to receive, which is even more difficult; how to lose, which is something extremely beneficial, and how to have.
>
> (Cixous, interviewed in Sellers, 1986: p. 22)

This can, I believe, usefully be linked to deconstructing the universalism of many content-based approaches to utopia. It has been suggested that a gift in the dominant masculine economy of exchange is *not* a gift (or rather, is a gift that takes – autonomy and identity). From this it follows that utopian universalism, if understood within the context of a masculine economy, does not offer the Good Life to all, because the claim to offer a gift of a universally applicable and beneficial vision of ultimate perfection is not tenable. Rather it can be seen to represent the end of change, struggle and difference. Assuming access to the truth in 'true' logocentric tradition, a universalist theory of utopia, whilst apparently giving an emancipatory vision, suppresses the very idea of dissent and the possibility of the existence of other subjective truths in this privileging of sameness. The gift (the blueprint) has to take something, to negate something, because it always operates within a hierarchical system of conceptualization which is grounded in turn in a hierarchical system of binary opposition. It names and claims the future: it offers a blueprint which possesses the unitary truth – the truth of its author. Feminist scholars of utopia have noted the consistency with which women are oppressed, ignored or negated in many historical (male-authored) utopias. Hilary Rose, for instance, suggests that men's utopias are women's dystopias (Rose, 1988).[10]

In the passage below, Cixous writes of the willingness to 'let go' which is one characteristic of a feminine economy:

> Now most of the time these differences in attitudes are assigned to differences in gender or sexuality. But this is oversimplistic. It's true that women will have less difficulty in, for instance, learning the wisdom of separation, but this is due to their cultural placing. It's because they've been at the school of separation all their lives. It doesn't mean it has anything to do with any kind of essence.
>
> (Cixous, interviewed in Sellers, 1986: p. 22)

I quote this passage for two reasons. First, it is illustrative of Cixous's attitude towards the connections between the body (gender or sexuality) and femininity. It is, she says, the cultural experience of the body, rather than the body itself, that brings women closer to femininity than are men. There are men whom she cites as having produced what she calls feminine writing (such as Kleist and Joyce). These men she finds to occupy a marginal and unstable relation to the system through which social relations are construed and constructed. The (masculine) Symbolic Order marginalizes these men because of their sexuality. A system built on dualism places (male) transgressors (homosexuals) on the side of femininity. In this sense, then, Cixous says that their cultural experience is close to that of women: exclusion, and oppression in the name of sameness.

Secondly, the passage speaks of a certain separation which is feminine (in this non-essentialist sense).[11] The separation to which Cixous refers is a fundamental letting go of the self and, to an extent, of the concept of sameness: 'The way to the other is less self and more other. . . . All this has to do with being interested in the stranger, in the strange, as well as in the stranger part of myself' (Cixous, interviewed in Sellers, 1986: p. 22). The process, which involves self-knowledge, consists of inhabiting the self whilst letting go of the notion that sameness is safe, bonding and relevant in human relations. It is an attitude of mind that is not patterned by dualistic thinking. It is, I suggest, a feminine process in that it does not seek to possess: it is not driven by the Drive of the Proper. Property, possession and appropriation are not characteristics of this process. Nor is it necessarily the property of women, although, as mentioned above, women, by virtue of their historico-cultural experience, have a closer relationship to a feminine libidinal economy:

> Thanks to their history, women today know (how to do and want) what men will be able to conceive of only much later. ... Unlike man, who holds so dearly his title and his titles, his pouches of value, his cap, his crown, and everything connected with his head, women couldn't care less about the fear of decapitation (or castration), adventuring, without the masculine territory, into anonymity, which she can merge with, without annihilating herself: because she's a giver.
>
> (Cixous, 1981a: pp. 258–9)

The economy of femininity supersedes the metaphors of economics: it displaces them. It is not safe – the story of General Sun Tse illustrates the dangers of living femininity in a masculine economy. The women in the story found that compliance was appropriate for survival in this economy. The fragility and ambiguities of adopting a feminine position can be further illustrated by reference to Cixous's treatment of hysteria, which she presents as femininity in total excess (Cixous, 1983).

Her work on the hysteric is centred on a reworking of one of Freud's cases, 'Fragment of an Analysis of a Case of Hysteria' (Freud, 1905).[12] The Dora Case concerns a young woman who, at the age of 18, was taken to Freud by her father to be 'brought to reason'. The case history involves a network of illicit sexual relations between Dora's father and a family friend, Frau K, and between Herr K and a number of his children's governesses. A brief synopsis of the story will be beneficial to its analysis.

Dora was apparently fond of the family friend Herr K and was particularly attached to his wife, looking after her children whilst Frau K and Dora's father were together. As such, she appeared to play the role of substitute mother or governess to the children. Herr K treated Dora attentively, sending her gifts and flowers. In view of his past relationships with his children's governesses, the image of Dora as mother/wife substitute is particularly poignant. She is a symbolic simulacrum: image or shadow.

When Dora was 14, Herr K embraced her and kissed her on the mouth. She pushed him away and ran off, telling no one until he again attempted to seduce her four years later. Her parents did not believe her. Her behaviour became increasingly confrontational and she was eventually taken to Freud, who diagnosed her a hysteric.

Cixous explores the figure of the hysteric. She finds it, at one level, to be the ultimate position of powerlessness. In this sense the hysteric can be seen to represent a 'feminized' victim. At another level Cixous finds hope in the position of the hysteric, who disrupts and challenges the status quo. Her presentation of the femininity of the hysteric is thus ambiguous. On the one hand, like the Sleeping Beauty, she is a totally masculine creation:

> So he *makes*, he makes (up) his woman, not without being himself seized up and drawn into the dialectical movement that this sort of thing sets into play. We might say that the Absolute Woman, in culture, the woman who really represents femininity most effectively... who is closest to femininity as *prey* to masculinity, is actually the hysteric... he makes the image for her!
>
> (Cixous, 1981b: pp. 46–7)

This image is reinforced by the fact that hysteria is the sole 'property' of women – a masculine gift if ever there was one! (Remember the Drive of the Proper?) Hysteria is etymologically rooted in the female body: the Greek word *husterikos* refers to the womb. The connection of hysteria to the body is reinforced again by Dora's aphonia: she communicates with her body. She is moreover presented by the adults in the story as seductress, as using classically Freudian 'feminine' wiles to disrupt a stable family situation.

Dora's position is ambiguous. She is treated as a child whose parents know what is best for her. She was, for instance, taken to Freud as an unwilling patient. Her parents speak for her, as does Freud in his presentation of the case. Her story is full of gaps and silences which he fills. Again, I suggest that Cixous can be read as presenting the hysteric as a metaphor for the cultural construct of 'woman'. Alienated from language and driven into the private realm of the body, 'woman' (Dora) is not a fully matured or functioning person (that is, man). Superimposed upon her role as recalcitrant child, though, is that of Dora as a woman. She takes responsibility, for example, for Herr K's children. Her father talks to her as an equal in age. Her complicity in the various affairs is that of an adult conspirator. She is, therefore, neither child nor woman but both.

In co-existence with Dora's powerlessness, Cixous finds potential strength: 'The hysteric is, to my eyes, the typical woman in all her force' (Cixous and Clement, 1986: p. 154). The hysteric has no identity other than that which is given to her, and so Cixous's statement that she is an empowered figure is somewhat problematic. The hysteric is a reflective figure because her identity is that of a mirror. The external forces that construct her identity are bounced back to their source. In this sense, then, examining the hysteric as a caricature of femininity in a masculine economy (culturally constructed 'woman') can be an informative and therefore empowering exercise. Whilst the approach, or process, may be viewed in this way, none of this makes the actual *figure* of the hysteric an empowered one. For Cixous, the power of the hysteric lies in desire:

> It is a force that was turned against Dora, but, if the scene changes and if woman begins to speak in other ways, it would be capable of demolishing those structures. . . . The source of Dora's strength is, despite everything, her desire. The hysteric is not just someone who has her words cut off, someone for whom the body speaks.
>
> (Cixous and Clement, 1986: p. 154)

Like Angela Carter, Cixous privileges desire as a transgressive force. And like Marge Piercy, she presents a view of receptivity that challenges the normal passive connotations of that term:

> It is true that a certain receptivity is 'feminine'. One can, of course, as History has always done, exploit feminine reception through alienation. A woman, by her opening up, is open to being 'possessed', which is to say, dispossessed of herself.
>
> (Cixous and Clement, 1986: p. 86)

The case of Dora can be read as a metaphor for this historical alienation of woman, representing the role and position of woman in a masculine order.

In relations to the other, Cixous finds this receptivity to be a route away from oppositional relations: 'As for passivity, in excess, it is partly bound up with death. But there is a nonclosure that is not submission but confidence and comprehension; that is not an opportunity for destruction but for wonderful expansion' (Cixous and Clement, 1986: p. 86). This non-closure is connected by Cixous to a feminine economy that can be characterized by new ways of giving and receiving which let go of the idea of a proper return. In language, this can be worked towards by moving away from the naming process outlined in Chapter 3, towards an open language: one in which the opacity of words, for example, is apparent and their potential multiplicity exploited. This is a theme of Part III, in which I further explore utopian texts which self-consciously play with language. Naming in such a way does not claim to impose a unitary truth. Rather it is openended, as are the texts themselves: they let go.

They let go also of the notion of a singular truth; thus truth is defetishized. Utopian texts which I describe as feminine are marked by the absence of the 'gift' of the blueprint. The gesture of giving a solution which is final and perfect and which therefore precludes any alternatives is not made by these texts. They transgress the rules and boundaries which constitute the present, constantly moving away from the axis of binarity and opposition; but their move towards multiplicity is openended and unrestrictive:

> A woman-text gets across a detachment, a kind of disengagement, not the detachment that is immediately taken back, but a real capacity to lose hold and let go. This takes the metaphorical form of wandering, excess, risk of the unreckonable: no reckoning, a feminine text can't be predicted, isn't predictable, isn't knowable and is therefore very disturbing. It can't be anticipated, and I believe femininity is written outside anticipation: it really is the text of the unforeseeable.
>
> (Cixous, 1981b: p. 53)

The feminine text which I call utopian is strange. It presents to the reader the strange, the stranger, the other, the self, without fetishization or the creation of a new cult of the same.[13]

CONCLUSION

In this chapter I have engaged an openended approach towards utopianism in conversation with an openended approach towards feminism. This has been undertaken by using Derridean reading techniques and by adapting Cixous's conception of a libidinal feminine economy. In the process each concept or set of ideas has undergone a transformation. Deconstruction has been shown to contain traits and traces of a radical utopianism. The blueprint approach to utopias has been deconstructed. By suggesting that these transformations might be read as operating within an alternative economy, the discussion above has, I believe, opened further utopian space for the practice of conceptualization and exploration. This in itself is, of course, a utopian project.

The ways in which this new approach leads to a merging and transgression of generic boundaries is explored at greater depth in

Chapter 7. For the present it is sufficient to note that the kinds of utopian reading offered and proposed by this book are quite disturbing. In Chapter 3 I argued for a non-restrictive concept of gender and of feminism. The proposition of an understanding of feminism that is truly open to difference destabilizes the movement and leaves open the meaning of feminism. This is clearly a dangerous game in political terms. None the less I have argued that the safety and security of a solid identity are worth leaving behind, and that once this illusion is shed then perhaps something new can be realized. This again is a utopian proposition in the terms outlined in this and other chapters: to realize is both to accomplish and to cause something to seem real. Utopian feminist responses to the question 'Where do we go from here?' are explored in the chapters below.[14] No single response can be said to characterize feminist utopianism. In this sense, then, that body of thought cannot be said to offer a blueprint for the future. Attention to this fact will, I hope, serve to reinforce my arguments for an open understanding of feminism.

The approach proposed and offered by this book is also disturbing in that it destabilizes conceptions of reality: shifts in consciousness do not only open the future but also affect perceptions of the present. The kinds of theoretical reading privileged by this book also transform the meaning of theoretical pursuit itself. This, of course, is likely to disturb political theorists. Deconstructive readings, as stated above, always remain open to further deconstruction. There is no moment of closure and the truth is never attained (or sought). Likewise what I have called utopianism does not present or desire a final solution.

In a short essay, Gail Stenstad (1989) has addressed concerns that are similar to mine. The essay is titled 'Anarchic Thinking: Breaking the Hold of Monotheistic Ideology on Feminist Philosophy' and, as the title suggests, is concerned to move away from a conception of theory that results in a single assertion of truth.

Stenstad says the following of the traditional meaning of theory:

> The practice of theory-building presupposes some philosophical notions that serve to validate the contents of theories: truth, reality and objectivity. A theory seeks to give an objectively true account of the domain of reality with which it is concerned. The best theory is that which most closely resembles the true and the real.
>
> (Stenstad, 1989: pp. 331–2)

At the root of these suppositions she locates the assumption that there is one truth and one reality, hence monotheism (hence, too, logocentrism):

> The true. Goodness as conformity to the true. Conformity: sameness. God the father. God the son and his priests. All the same. Women: those who are defined in terms of privation (lack of a penis). Difference as lack. Lacking: truth, reality, goodness.
>
> (1989: p. 332)

The play of sameness and difference in the construction of dominant relations to the other is the subject of Chapter 6. For Stenstad the route past this block on consciousness is via what she calls anarchic thinking. In ways similar to what I have called utopian thinking, anarchic thinking transgresses the rules of discourse and the boundaries of the conceivable:

> We need to do much more than confront patriarchal thinking in its own terms and by its own rules. We also need to think in ways that deliberately break the rules, ways that deny to patriarchy the right to set a standard for feminist thinking. . . . One of the most subversive things that feminists can do is to think anarchically and then to speak and act from this thinking.
>
> (1989: p. 332)

This mode of thought is characterized by what Stenstad calls its 'atheoretical' nature. Adhering to the literal meaning of the word anarchy, she says that anarchic thinking is without rule: 'it is thinking that does not work from, posit, or yield objective distance, suprahistorical truth, hierarchical orderings, or a unitary reality' (1989: pp. 332–3).

This unruly thinking clearly bears close resemblance to the approaches privileged above. It is open to a multiplicity of meanings and interpretations, styles and possibilities. It is marked by unresolved tensions and is therefore always moving, never stagnant. The characteristics of such thought are outlined below:

> Persistence in questioning, working and playing with ambiguities, being alert for the presence of the strange within the familiar, and allowing for concealment or unclarity in the midst of disclosure are elements of anarchic thinking that stand out as particularly significant.
>
> (Stenstad, 1989: p. 334)

In the same way as I have suggested that utopianism can be read through a matrix of deconstruction or/and femininity, I suggest now that it can be read through a conceptual framework (although 'framework' is not really an appropriate term) of anarchic thought. The central point of this chapter is that it does not matter which is adopted; that none of these propositions leads to *the* truth, but all create new conceptual space.

Part III

UTOPIANISM AND TRANSGRESSION

5

FEMINIST UTOPIAN
TRANSGRESSION OF THE
SPIRIT/MATTER RELATION

INTRODUCTION

This chapter focuses on the division of spirit and matter which is perceived by many feminist theorists to lie at the heart of the Western philosophical tradition. I am concerned here with an exploration and assessment of the various ways in which writers of feminist utopian fiction and theory have attempted to transgress and reconceptualize or re-present the historically dominant relation between spirit and matter, body and mind. These attempts are connected to contemporary debates within feminism regarding the tension between the needs, on the one hand, to develop a coherent position of enunciation and, on the other hand, to respect diversity.[1] First, though, it is necessary to survey briefly the ways in which the dichotomy of spirit and matter is said to inform the Western tradition.

First, in colloquial terms, spirit is (conceptually) opposed to matter. The *Shorter Oxford English Dictionary* gives a full column to the word 'spirit', a condensed version of which follows:

spirit, n. 1. Intelligent or immaterial part of man, soul.... 2. Person viewed as possessing this, esp. w. reference to particular mental or moral qualities, ... person of commanding intellect etc. 3. Rational or intelligent being not connected with material body, disembodied soul, incorporeal being, elf, fairy.... 4. Person's mental or moral nature or qualities.... 5. Courage, self-assertion, vivacity, energy, dash.... 6. Person viewed as supplying this.... 7. Mental or moral condition or attitude, mood.... 8. Real meaning opp. to verbal expression, have followed the ~ of his instructions. 9 Animating principle or influence, mental or moral tendency.... 10. (Formerly) immaterial principle governing vital phenomena, whence (mod.)

ANIMAL.... 11. Strong distilled liquor.... 12. Solution in alcohol... [ME, f. AF *spirit(e)*, OF *esperit*, or L *spiritus* breath, spirit, f. *spirare* breathe].

These, then, are the more or less common usages of the term 'spirit' and, more interestingly, the normal contexts for employment of that concept. Spirit is, as stated, defined immediately in direct opposition to matter: it is immaterial. It is further related to the intelligent and rational part of 'man' (whether or not this is a generic employment of that term is hard to ascertain: see the use of the non-gender-specific 'person' later in the passage). The concept of the spiritual conflates the mental with the moral, and associates the moral with the intellect, which transcends partiality or matter.

In everyday usage and within the contexts of Western philosophical and theological traditions, the establishment of a dichotomy between spirit and matter is related to other dualistic pairs: mind/body, deity/man, rationality/passion, transcendence/partiality, intellect/sensation and, finally, man/woman. As is the case with other dichotomous pairings discussed in this book, the relation is hierarchical.

It is argued that the Western tradition erects an edifice of the man of reason. Genevieve Lloyd, for instance, examines the history of this figure, the man of reason, and her analysis begins with Aristotle. Aristotle is cited as viewing woman 'as it were an impotent male, for it is through a certain incapacity that the female is female' (Lloyd, 1989: p. 114). That which the female lacks is the principle of soul. Soul is associated by Aristotle with rationality. The rational capacities of woman are described as weaker than are those of man. Being less rational, she (universal Woman) is less able than is he (universal Man) to make moral judgements.[2] For Aristotle Woman represents materiality. Her body is receptive to male semen, which, for Aristotle, is that which engenders life and soul.

Early Christian thinkers continued the now well-documented tradition of associating women with materiality, introducing the moralistic vocabulary of carnality. In the writings of the Christian Fathers, Woman, as represented by Eve, is commonly seen to be the embodiment of the privation or absence of spirit. Woman is pure (or rather, impure) matter. Some, like St Augustine, see Eve as evil. Sexual intercourse is not evil in itself for Augustine; rather it is Eve's sexual desire that makes her responsible for the original sin of lust. Woman is thus dangerous and must, by necessity, be made subject to man:

In her mind and her rational intelligence she has a nature the equal of man's, but in sex she is physically subject to him in the same way as our natural impulses need to be subjected to the reasoning power of the mind, in order that the actions to which they lead may be inspired by the principles of good conduct.

(Augustine, 1961: p. 334)

Other early Christian writers place Woman in a less active role in the 'occasion of sin'. None the less, she is generally represented in such texts as being either wholly devoid of or otherwise lacking in spiritual fortification against evil: 'As nature abhors a vacuum, so does spiritual deficiency invite the seduction of the Evil one' (Hein, 1989: p. 297). The lust and spiritual weakness of Eve were feared to be contagious. Women, as potential temptresses, spiritual voids, and hence potential receptors and transmitters of evil, were fitting objects of social control: 'They must be covered, shaved, disfigured, maimed, and locked away – not as a corrective for their own spiritual lack, for which they are in a sense blameless, but as a protection against men's spiritual fallibility' (Hein, 1989: p. 297). Matter and spirit, then, work in opposition. Woman is most closely associated with matter and hence, in this oppositional scheme of things, is furthest from spirit. Spirituality is associated with morality and the ability to make rational moral judgements. It is the spirit that differentiates Man from beast, as well as establishing a hierarchy within the category of humanity. The ability to transcend the partiality of the body brings Man closer to God, in whose image He was created. Conversely, Woman is closer to the body and further from the spirit or soul. Void or vessel, Woman occupies a low position in this dualistically constructed spiritual hierarchy. It further follows that Woman is closer to animality than is Man.

For Genevieve Lloyd this oppositional framework is most clearly observable in the philosophy of the seventeenth century. It is to this period, she claims, that we owe current perspectives on the relation between the spiritual, the corporeal, and the Man of Reason. The Cartesian view of knowledge and humanity is, Lloyd argues, grounded in a sharp distinction between mind and matter:'The absolute certainty that accompanies clear and distinct ideas derives from their purely mental character. . . . Cartesian method is essentially a matter of forming the "habit of distinguishing intellectual from corporeal matters" ' (Lloyd, 1989: p. 116, quoting Descartes). In this view, the physical, as manifested in sensation and emotion, is an impediment to clear thought. Against a historical background in which women were considered more emotional and less rational than men, Cartesian methodology sharpened existing distinctions and prejudices. Here we have a clear example of an approach (to the process of conceptualization) which has a distinctive product. The product of the dualistic Cartesian approach was a hierarchical conceptual system organized along lines of binary opposition: 'The conjunction of Cartesian down-grading of the sensuous with the use of mind–matter distinction to establish the discrete character of Cartesian ideas introduces possibilities of polarization that were not there before' (Lloyd, 1989: p. 116). Concepts, Lloyd is saying, became further dichotomized in the wake of Descartes. The hierarchy of sexual difference is mirrored in the hierarchy associated with the matter/spirit distinction. Rousseau's Emile, for instance, describes the training required to enable transcendence of the distractions of the physical. For a girl, however, this training appeared unnecessary. Less rational, more emotional, the girl should be trained to make her life complement that of the boy/man:[3]

> To be pleasing in his sight, to win his respect and love, to train him in childhood, to tend him in manhood, to counsel and console, to make his life pleasant and happy, these are the duties of woman for all time, and this is what she should be taught while she is young.
>
> (Rousseau, 1974: p. 328)

The ideal of the Man of Reason has not remained historically constant. Nineteenth-century Romanticism, for instance, exalted the passions. The dichotomy of the cluster of concepts associated with the mind and the cluster associated with the body has, however, remained constant, as has the association of Woman with the latter group and Man with the former. This clustering can be schematically represented thus:

(hu)man	animal
culture	nature
spirit	matter
mind	body
moral	carnal
rational	emotional
intellect	sensation
transcendence	partiality
Man	Woman

Feminist strategies that attempt to transgress what has been identified as the dominant (dualistic) relation between matter and spirit are quite diverse. Utopian feminist theory that focuses on religion or spirituality is the first area to be examined in the discussions that follow, and strategies that rely on tactics of simple reversal are rejected. Those which focus on the structure of language itself, on the actual construction of dichotomous thought, are the subject of the second section of discussion. Finally I propose to examine feminist utopian attempts to envisage societies in which the relation between spirit and matter is represented, conceptualized and enacted differently. In most of the texts under discussion, the dichotomy itself is challenged in some way, and the division dissolved. This is not to say that consensus exists as to the most sound theoretical way past the mind/body divide, and I shall identify a number of, sometimes opposing, approaches to this question.

RELIGION AND SPIRITUALITY

Susan Griffin and Charlene Spretnak both contribute to Judith Plant's *Healing the Wounds: The Promise of Ecofeminism* (1989). This book is interesting in terms of both its content and its form. *Healing the Wounds* is an exploratory text of poetry, fiction, political theory, theology and philosophy. Its form is transgressive of disciplinary borders. Its content is ecofeminist, and contains many utopian elements. Griffin and Spretnak both identify Western culture as being grounded in dualistic thought:

> We who are born into this civilisation have inherited a habit of mind. We are divided against ourselves.... To us the word *thought* means an activity separate from feeling, just as the word *mind* suggests a place apart from the body and from the rhythms of the earth.... Our word spirit rises in our imaginations above the earth as if we believed that holiness exists in an inverse proportion to gravity.... Through the words *masculine* and *feminine*, which we use to designate two alien and alienated poles of human behaviour, we make our sexuality a source of separation. We divide ourselves and all that we know along an invisible borderline between what we call Nature and what we believe is superior to Nature.
>
> (Griffin, 1989: pp. 7–8)

The fundamental mistake, for Griffin, in such thinking, is that of false dichotomization.[4] We humans, she says, are *part of* nature; the mind is *part of* the body. The dualisms upon which the Western tradition of conceptualization rest are falsely placed in opposition to one another. Spretnak adds to this that spiritual life is part of material life:

> The mind is made up of tissue and blood, of cells and atoms, and possesses all the knowledge of the cell, all the balance of the atom.
>
> (Griffin, 1989: p. 17)

> In truth, there is nothing 'mystical' or 'other worldly' about spirituality. The life of the spirit, or soul, refers merely to functions of the mind. Hence, spirituality is an intrinsic dimension of human consciousness and is not separate from the body. For example, the Greek concept of *pneuma* meant breath or spirit or soul, and *spirit* comes from the Latin root for 'to breathe'.
>
> (Spretnak, 1989: p. 27)

Griffin and Spretnak both take a holistic approach to the world, which is mirrored in their conceptualizations of the relations of humanity to nature, mind to body, and spirituality to materiality. This transgressive approach to the concept of spirituality is a recurrent theme in feminist utopian theory and fiction. It is, I suggest, utopian in its function because, by rendering previous conceptual structures, divisions and borders unnecessary, it creates the potential for new ways of conceptualizing and thinking. It transgresses, negates and creates new conceptual space. Dorothy Bryant's *The Kin of Ata are Waiting for You* (1971) is one of many pieces of utopian literature in which the boundaries between spiritual and material life have ceased to exist. Bryant's people of Ata believe their waking lives to be insignificant in comparison to the 'dreamtime' of sleep, which is presented as a highly spiritual experience. In one sense, this can be read as an inversion of the respective importance of daytime and dreamtime, of material and spiritual life; but Bryant presents the relation in a wholly new and different way. It is shifted, as are the boundaries between the two spheres. Spirituality is not external to the body, and there is no external deity. Work and 'prayer' are not separate, nor are the two activities designated appropriate spaces: the inhabitants of Ata dance in the fields while they work and recite the experiences of dreamtime in the tents in which they live. Spirituality in this utopian society is not external to everyday life; there are no churches, nor is the society hierarchical; there are no priests.

Ecofeminist conceptions of spirituality are characterized by a combination of a reverence for nature with a tendency towards what is termed 'Goddess religion':

> The only holistic approach that involves an anthropomorphized concept of deity is Goddess spirituality.... The revival of the Goddess has resonated with so many people because She symbolizes *the way things really are*: All forms of being are One, continually renewed in cyclic rhythms of birth, maturation, death.... She is *immanent* in our lives and our world. She contains both female and male, in the womb, as a male deity cannot; all beings are *part of her*, not distant creations.
>
> (Spretnak, 1989: p. 128)

Goddess religion, as presented by Charlene Spretnak, is profoundly inclusive. It is grounded in a methodology that identifies and stresses connections between concepts and things. It humanizes the deity, and embodies spirituality in a female form. It also revalues and privileges traditional 'feminine' (female) traits: 'She [the Goddess] also symbolizes the power of the female body/mind' (Spretnak, 1989: p. 128).

Politically and theoretically, this theme, commonly found in ecofeminist theory, is worrying. Charges of essentialism and regression are frequently, and I believe rightly, made regarding such claims. Ecofeminist theory tends to argue that Man and Woman are culturally constructed figures, and that the distribution of associated attributes to these figures serves patriarchal interests. Yet they slip into the practise of an inversion of the internal hierarchies of dualisms. Such strategies can be seen, for instance, in the revaluing of 'female' attributes, such as Spretnak's celebration of the womb above. Existing prejudices are reproduced: Woman is closer to nature than is Man. The oppositional structuring of value is not convincingly challenged:

> Perhaps the whole contextless abstraction of virtue and vice, good and evil, along with their attendant praise and blame, punishment and reward, damnation and redemption, are mere instances of simplistic patriarchal dichotomization. Little would be gained by a duplication of the list of simplifications.
>
> (Hein, 1989: p. 306)

The approach taken by Mary Daly has a certain resonance here. Daly's work on religion is quite anarchic and is disruptive of the mind/

body divide. It stops short, though, of being fully transgressive because Daly, in the last instance, remains within a dualistic conceptual framework. Her work is, none the less, provocative and disruptive of the mind/body divide. For Daly, patriarchal values are internalized by women in a process that she neatly describes as mental colonization. This is achieved largely through language, and particularly through the language of religion and morality. A sense of urgency and mission infiltrates her work. She describes the book *Gyn/ Ecology* in the following terms:

> this book is primarily concerned with the mind/spirit/body pollution inflicted through patriarchal myth and language on all levels.... Phallic myth and language generate, legitimate, and mask the material pollution that threatens to terminate all sentient life on this planet.
>
> (Daly, 1987: p. 9)

A recurrent theme of *Gyn/Ecology* is the concern to show how the colonization or pollution of women's minds, bodies and spirits are connected. Here we have a, now familiar, association of knowledge with power. Her arguments are particularly forceful when focused on world religions. She outlines a universal pattern of ritual, the function of which is the social control and spiritual deprivation of women. This pattern she calls the 'sado-ritual syndrome', which has seven identifying features: an obsession with purity; the erasure of responsibility; a tendency to catch on and spread; the use of women as scapegoats and token torturers; the fact that the orderliness and repetitiveness of ritual distract from the horror; the normalization of otherwise unacceptable behaviour; and legitimation by the rituals of objective scholarship.

Daly's analysis of the 'sado-ritual syndrome' connects mind, body and spirit. The obsession with purity, for instance, is connected by Daly to the association of women with carnality, the sexual and lust, and, consequently, to their physical mutilation or extinction. These themes were introduced in the discussion above. Daly's critique is radical: the association of women with sexual impurity, for her, serves to legitimate such historical practices as female circumcision and European witch-burning: 'This obsession legitimates the fact that the women who are the primary victims of the original rites are erased physically as well as spiritually' (Daly, 1987: p. 131). In societies where religious values inform the norms of social behaviour, Daly finds that women become the objects of violent (physical and/or symbolic) social control. This, she says, is because of their alleged spiritual inferiority and subsequent closeness to the body. Physicality is both at the root of their inferior spiritual status and the means by which such control is exercised. Circumcision, for instance, negates sexual pleasure for a woman; the subsequent likelihood of active seduction is thus minimalized. Daly finds this reasoning to be flawed, because Woman does not need actively to seduce in order to be dangerous: her physical presence is temptation enough, for the Christian Fathers at least.

Daly continues to connect mind, body and spirit in her construction of routes to emancipation. She also adheres to dualisms. Sexual difference is one dualism that she (and indeed many other feminists) wishes to maintain. For Daly, sexual difference constructs emancipatory identity: female characteristics ground (potential) female power. She therefore keeps an essentialist dualism between masculinity and femininity. She is, for instance, critical of utopias of androgyny and invokes the myth of Dionysus as an illusory vision of freedom. Dionysus incorporates masculine and feminine attributes; he is a sensuous figure. Whilst breaking the stereotypically rigid boundaries between the constructs of Man and Woman, Dionysus, says Daly, represents a loss of identity for women:

> Madness is the only ecstasy offered to women by the Dionysian 'way'. While the supermasculine Apollo overtly oppresses/ destroys with his contrived boundaries/hierarchies/rules/roles, the feminine Dionysus blurs the senses, seduces, confuses his victims – drugging them into complicity, offering his 'heart' as a love potion that poisons.
>
> (1987: pp. 66–7)

Androgyny, then, is not, for Daly, the solution: 'Experience has proved that this word, which we now recognise as expressing pseudowholeness in its combination of distorted gender description, failed and betrayed our thought' (1987: p. 387). Indeed, androgyny, the ideal of a complete state of being, is/was, for Daly, a trap. It was built on the false assumption that masculinity and femininity (as we now understand them) are real. In actuality, she says, they are patriarchal constructs of patriarchal language. This is an interesting position, and quite a problematic one. The figures of Man and Woman have been consistently treated in this book as constructions or myths. Attributes pertinent to these constructions correspond to masculinity and femininity, culturally understood. Thus when Freud, for instance,

141

speaks of the progression of the little girl through the routes to 'normal' sexual and social maturity, we can say that he conflates the ideal of Woman with that of the feminine. The girl, says Freud, uses feminine wiles (flirtation, coyness, etc.) to attract the attention of the father figure. The girl is thus playing a prescribed feminine role as she proceeds towards the status of Woman. Feminist theorists challenge the natural status of Woman, identifying her as a culturally specific social construct. Her feminine attributes must also be challenged thus. The models of 'libidinal' femininity and masculinity upon which I have drawn throughout this book do not correspond to these cultural constructs, yet neither are they concrete 'realities'. Daly can, perhaps, be read through this framework when stating that masculinity and femininity are not real, and that androgyny is a trap. And yet she maintains essential claims for female characteristics. For Daly, then, masculinity and femininity correspond with maleness and femaleness, and she appears to reject that which masculinity and femininity represent in patriarchal reality in favour of other, alternative representations which inhabit a utopian reality. This utopian reality is grounded in (essentialist) observations of the 'truth' of here and now.

Patriarchy, for Daly, is a system of universal oppression. *Gyn/Ecology* represents a vertiginous journey of what Daly perceives as an exorcism of patriarchal myth. Her emancipatory strategies also include a celebration of a woman-centred spirituality. We can see that, by making these two moves, she enacts both the critical and creative functions of utopianism. Her goal is clearly the creation of a shift in consciousness: she desires that woman-centred, 'gynocentric' vocabulary should occupy the place that male-centred vocabulary currently inhabits. In other words, her goal, in true radical feminist tradition, is the creation of feminist thought and perception.

Rosemary Radford Reuther has developed some interesting thoughts along similar lines. Reuther also identifies the existing structure of dualistic thought as grounding contemporary religious/ theological perspectives. Her approach is perhaps more ecological and less feminist than Daly's, at least at first glance:

> An ecological-feminist theology of nature must rethink the whole western tradition of the hierarchical chain of being and chain of command. This theology must question the hierarchy of human over nonhuman as a relationship of ontological and moral value.... It must unmask the structures of social

domination, male over female, owner over worker, that mediate this domination of nonhuman nature. Finally, it must question the model of hierarchy that starts with nonmaterial spirit (God) as the source of the chain of being and continues down to nonspiritual 'matter' as the bottom of the chain being the most inferior, valueless, and dominated point in the chain of command.

(Reuther, 1989: p. 145)

Reuther's perspective is somewhat broader than Daly's, but certain themes are recurrent. Central to all of the above critiques of patriarchal religion is the challenge to its hierarchical conceptual structure. The dichotomy between spirit and matter, for instance, is seen to underpin other clusters of paired concepts. A common response, as seen above, is to embody the spiritual conceptually. This has the effect of introducing the body to the cultural text of spirituality:[5]

The God/ess who is primal matrix, the ground of being-new, is neither stifling immanence nor rootless transcendence. Spirit and matter are not dichotomized but are the inside and outside of the same thing. . . . Matter itself dissolves into energy. Energy, organized in patterns of relationships, is the basis for what we experience as visible spiritual energy. It becomes impossible any more to dichotomize material and spiritual energy.

(Reuther, 1989: p. 145)

There are a number of related problems in these critiques of religion and conventional spirituality. The first has already been mentioned, but serves here as an introduction to the second. First, then, these ecofeminist critiques tend to stop their analyses at the point of inversion or reversal of dualistic and hierarchical constructions. This results in a final utopian position in which previously devalued 'feminine' values and attributes are dominant and found a new utopian (in the traditional sense of the word) ethic.

This presents a number of difficulties: the universality of the construct of Woman is not questioned, and hence another universal view of 'human' nature is created. This universalist approach can provoke the utopian function of shifting consciousness (changing the way that we think) but it cannot provoke truly *paradigmatic* shifts. True, replacing male-centred thought with female-centred thought is potentially transformative on a grand scale, and societies founded on this ethic would look very different to the patriarchal ones which they critique. But truly paradigmatic shifts that repattern our approach to the world must, I suggest, undermine the real grounds on which current (repressive) approaches are made. Paradigmatic shifts must, in other words, undermine the dualistic and oppositional structure of thought, language and perception. Replacing one signifier of value (Woman) for another (Man) does not destroy the space of domination; it merely inverts the given hierarchy. It is not the content of this view that causes problems, rather its form and its restricted function. Audre Lorde in her 'Open Letter to Mary Daly' (1984a) asks why black women are presented in *Gyn/Ecology* only in the role of victims, and concludes that Daly's eventual utopian vision is grounded in a value system that is appropriate only to white intellectual women. This returns us to the old problems of the universalist utopia and to the exclusionary nature of Western feminism. Racial chauvinism, for instance, can be related to the above mentioned clusters of mind/body, spirit/matter, reason/desire. In this context it is the white/black dualism that is laid over the framework to ground and legitimize the devaluing of one group by virtue of its association with nature and physicality. Black women, of course, occupy a place at the bottom of this particular pile. We might expect it to follow logically that they should occupy the top of a utopian hierarchy, but those examined so far neglect to make this particular inversion.

Stopping at the point of inversion does not challenge the hierarchical nature of dualistic thought itself. Nor does it provide a sophisticated enough analysis on which to ground a universalist utopian blueprint for the future. Indeed, any universalist vision will, I suggest, inevitably be based on an exclusionary ethic which paves the way for a legitimization of racism, sexism, classism or a set of related beliefs. To say 'this is what it is to speak as a woman' is, as Elizabeth Spelman points out (1990), really to say 'this is what it is to speak like me'; anyone who speaks in different terms is not a woman. And, of course, if Woman is at the top of the particular hierarchy of humanity, those who deviate from the model/ideal will be placed at an appropriately denigrated level. These approaches which operate by inversion do not provide thoroughgoing emancipatory visions and are not appropriate to the complexities of contemporary feminist utopianism.

LANGUAGE AND THE EXPRESSION OF ALTERNATIVES

Feminist theorists have attempted to transgress and disturb the perceived dichotomy between spirit and matter. The section above has established some of the reasons *why* this is seen to be necessary and has rejected simple inversions of the dichotomy. My concern in this section is broadly with 'how?' and identifies language, and writing in particular, as a mode of expressing different conceptual relations between the body and mind – different, that is, to the predominant and oppositional relation. Our focus here, then, is on transgressive utopianism that disrupts the dualism rather than inverting it.

As stated above, a common theme or tactic in feminist theological or spiritual creative theory is the embodiment of the deity or spirit. In many language-centred approaches to this question, the text is treated as having a special relation to the body. Embodiment is also a theme of this approach, which employs such terms as 'embodiment of the text', 'textualization of the body' and 'writing and reading the body'. Its aim is to challenge and subvert the universalist constructs 'Man' and 'Woman'. My focus, in much of the discussion below, is directed at the early works of Hélène Cixous, whose call on women to 'write their bodies' forms a useful background to the discussion of other approaches to this issue.

My discussion will begin with a necessarily brief rehearsal of why this move is attempted and a similarly condensed description or evocation of the process itself. This process is found to exemplify transgressive utopianism: it transgresses dualistic thought and thereby negates the binary oppositional structure of such thought. It further and consequently creates a new (utopian) space in which conceptualization of alternative relations can be undertaken. It is process-orientated and dynamic. Focus then turns to the politically interesting question of the nature of this new conception of the body: what does it look and feel like? Can we touch it? Is it, in other words, useful to a feminist project of utopian imagining? How does it address current debates and concerns within feminist theory? Is it enabling? No coherent answer can result from such questions. This is due, in part, to the opaque nature of Cixous's work. I suggest, however, that glimpses of ideas in utopian theory such as that of Cixous can be found in the more accessible utopian literature of someone like Michèle Roberts.[6]

Ecriture feminine: why?

Ecriture feminine translates roughly as feminine writing or writing in the feminine. It is rooted partly in the desire to challenge psycho-analytic assumptions that Woman is equatable with lack, and partly in Cixous's desire to reconstitute relations to the other. Cixous seeks a relation to the world that is not based on the exclusive love of the same – a place where desire makes fiction exist, the good place which is no place:

> There will be some elsewhere where the other will no longer be condemned to death. But has there ever been any elsewhere, is there any? While it is not yet 'here', it is there by now – in this place that disrupts social order, where desire makes fiction exist.
> (Cixous and Clement, 1986: p. 97)

Fundamental to this project is the establishment of what Rosi Braidotti calls 'an embodied female subjectivity' (Braidotti, 1991: p. 238). The rethinking, or restructuring, of the mind/body relation is an integral part of this. It is a profoundly utopian project:

> The style known as feminine, characterised by disruptions of syntax leading to the disturbance of meaning, tends to express the body understood as a cultural counter-text, in order to decode the blanks in language and to express sexual difference.
> (Braidotti, 1991: p. 239)

Defined historically in terms of their physicality (and physical lack), women have, says Cixous, been excluded from intimacy with and knowledge of their bodies. One function of her work in this area, then, is to expose the universal and essentialist figure of 'Woman' as a cultural construct. A second and related function is, as she says in her essay 'Castration or Decapitation?', to 'dephallocentricize the body', to discover what a female sexuality might be (1981b: p. 50). We can, then, begin to see the critical and creative functions of utopian thinking at work in Cixous's approach to the mind/body relation. She destroys and transforms the ways in which spirit and matter are perceived to be related and proceeds to revive the concepts themselves as new utopian constructs. Put another way: she transgresses and negates the boundaries of conceptualization and creates new utopian conceptual space:

> Woman must write herself: must write about women and bring women to writing, from which they have been driven away as

violently as from their bodies – for the same reasons, by the same law, with the same fatal goal.

(Cixous, 1981a: p. 245)

The call on women to write themselves into history is a familiar theme of many branches of radical feminism. Cixous, however, is saying more than this. In the first instance, in saying that 'woman' must write herself, Cixous is challenging the framework in which Woman is historically situated. *Women*, she is saying, are not as they have been written by men. Women's sexuality is more than an imperfect version of that of men, a complement to the penis/phallus. There is more which has to be discovered and/or created: 'Almost everything is yet to be written by women about femininity: about their sexuality, that is, its infinite and mobile complexity' (Cixous, 1981a: p. 256).

This is not to say that biology is destiny, Cixous does not attempt a rewrite of biological 'fact' which can serve as a natural grounding for a new or different social order. Here the difference between Cixous's approach and that of someone like Mary Daly is most apparent. Some theorists of religious Utopias seek to establish women/Woman as the root of a new concept of spirituality. Cixous is concerned to attack the dichotomies of body and mind, spirit and matter, but does not erect an embodied 'feminine/female' spirituality. Rather, she attempts to embody women themselves. In other words, she asks women to claim authorship of their bodies. The passage quoted above continues thus:

> about their eroticization, sudden turn-ons of a certain minuscule area of their bodies; *not about destiny*, but about an adventure of such and such a drive, about trips, crossings, trudges, abrupt and gradual awakenings, discoveries of a zone at one time timorous and soon to be forthright.

(Cixous, 1981a: p. 256; my emphasis)

A further and connected set of statements and beliefs is involved in the call on woman to write herself. These are related to what Rosi Braidotti describes as 'the post-structuralist notion that the textual is isomorphic with the psychic' (Braidotti, 1991: p. 239). Cixous is operating from within an intellectual tradition in which language is perceived as the primary structuring force: the textual and the psychic are both formed by language; they are isomorphic in that both are phallocentric – shaped after the phallus. She articulates, in other words, a belief that certain attitudes, beliefs and value-structures are inscribed (written) into the psyche. This is important. In the case of women, this is related to their historico-cultural relation to the body. Hence, partially at least, comes the need to (re)write the body, as the body is already inscribed as a cultural text. The body *is* a cultural text. As such, women's bodies can be said to contain a narrative; they embody the stories referred to in the section above of construction, alienation and subordination. The body can be *read* as metaphor for the story of the construct of Woman. Women, then, need to read and (re)write the stories of their bodies.

I have, rather roughly, identified two sets of implications of the statement that 'woman must write herself', both of which have a broadly critical function. Utopianism, however, I have constantly asserted also has a creative function. This can be seen in the next set of connections that Cixous makes between writing and the body: 'This is how I would describe a feminine textual body, as a *female libidinal economy*, a regime, energies, a system of spending not necessarily carved by culture' (Cixous, 1981b: p. 53).

Put crudely, Cixous's utopias are situated in a feminine economy, and it is this towards which so much of her work drives. The act of feminine writing is one of (1) reclaiming (of the body) and (2) inscribing (a new and previously precluded and utopian history). Hence, I suggest, comes Cixous's introduction of (women's) bodies to the written and cultural texts *and* the related (and subsequent) embodiment of these texts. Asked in an interview of 1984 what would be the strategic 'goal' of feminine writing, Cixous responded by speaking of a feminine libidinal economy:

> I think that, if you like, a feminine libidinal economy is an economy which has a more supple relation to property, which can stand separation and detachment, which signifies that it can also stand freedom – for instance, the other's freedom. . . . So how is this going to work in a literary text? You will have literary texts that tolerate all kinds of freedom . . . which are not texts that delimit themselves, are not texts of territory with neat borders, with chapters, with beginnings, endings, etc., and which are a little disquieting because you do not feel the arrest, the edge.
>
> (Cixous, interviewed in Conley, 1984a: p. 137)

Implied in this rather indirect response, I think, is that the strategic goal of a feminine writing is to inhabit a feminine libidinal economy which represents a new conceptual (and political-economic) space. A feminine libidinal economy is ('if you like') a shift in consciousness.

In these explorations of the function or purpose of *écriture feminine* I have, in part, indicated what a feminine text might look like. Its function is to disrupt, and is close in many ways to that of Derridean deconstructive readings. It is also creative in a radically and transgressively utopian way; it is shifting, elusive and hence difficult to pin down. At its core (perhaps 'heart' would be more apt) is the body, or rather a certain relation to the body, and it is this which I now intend to explore a little further.

Cixous's theoretical-poetic-literary texts are pieces of feminine writing. They expound, exemplify and illustrate her theoretical position. They challenge and negate boundaries between genres; they do not, as noted above, have 'neat borders'. They also invoke *and* inscribe the body – the term 'a feminine textual body' can be read both/either as referring to a piece of writing, written in a feminine style, and/or to a female body, culturally inscribed.[7] The body, then, is, to a profound extent, present in Cixous's texts, just as the text(ual) is present in her understanding of the body.

What body?

What, then, do these bodies look like? Involved in this question are wider debates within feminist theory, and those surrounding the issues of essentialism and universalism are of particular relevance. Cixous in particular, and advocates of *écriture feminine* in general, is/are occasionally accused of attempting to found a new biologism. Monique Wittig has created utopian theory and fiction and works in similar areas to Cixous, but takes a stand against attempts to create a feminine text. In the reading that follows I suggest that Wittig is closer to Cixous than may, at first glance, be apparent.

The theoretical starting point of Wittig's work is that sex is a class or social category. This is not to say, as Shulamith Firestone (1971) says, that *the* sexes represent two classes; Wittig's critique is more subtle. Women, by virtue of their association with physicality and their exclusion from other realms, are read by Wittig as being entrapped within the category of sex, the function of which is the continued existence of a dualistic, heterosexual society:

> For the category of sex is the category that sticks to women, for only they cannot be considered outside of it. Only *they* are sex, *the*

sex, and sex they have been made in their minds, bodies, acts, gestures; even their murders and beatings are sexual.

(Wittig, 1981: p. 8)

She rejects feminist tactics of reversal:

> By doing this, by admitting that there is a 'natural' division between women and men, we naturalize history, we assume that 'men' and 'women' have always existed and will always exist. Not only do we naturalize history, but also consequently we naturalize the social phenomena which express our oppression, making change impossible.

(1981: pp. 10–11)

Nor does she endorse the strategy or practice of psychoanalytic feminism, which she characterizes as universalist and, again, as serving to perpetuate a society which is divided 'naturally' along dualistic and hierarchical lines:

> Thus one speaks of *the* exchange of women, *the* Unconscious, Desire, *Jouissance*, Culture, History, giving absolute meaning to these concepts when they are really only categories founded upon heterosexuality, or thought which produces the difference between the sexes as a political philosophical dogma.

(Wittig, 1980a: pp. 27–8)

For Wittig, the terms 'masculine' and 'feminine', and those of 'male' and 'female', are categories or constructions whose function is 'to conceal the fact that social differences always belong to an economic, political, ideological order' (Wittig, 1976/1982: p. 2).[8] She seeks, on the one hand, to establish that women constitute a socially and economically constructed group, and, on the other, to locate or define a subjectivity for women in materialist terms. Wittig's tactic is that of denial: she denies that the construct of Woman is applicable to her as a political and social being:

> Our first task, it seems, is to always thoroughly dissociate 'women' (the class within which we fight) and 'woman', the myth.... For once one has acknowledged oppression, one needs to know and experience the fact that one can constitute oneself as a subject (as opposed to an object of oppression), that one can become *someone*, in spite of oppression, that one has an identity.

(Wittig, 1981a: pp. 15–16)

Because women have always been defined in terms of their relations with men, Wittig finds that she can state that lesbianism does not conform with the category of Woman: 'lesbianism is the only concept I know of which is beyond the categories of sex (Woman and Man), because the designated subject (lesbian) is *not* a woman, either economically, politically, or ideologically' (1981a: p. 20). This third (subjective) position of lesbianism is a utopian construct. It is the product of transgressive thinking that disturbs and negates the dualism man/woman and that creates a new space in which a non-dualistic subjectivity can be written.

Cixous can also be read as saying 'I am not (a) Woman.' Although most usually read as sharing no common ground, the theoretical works of these two women are not, I suggest, so divergent. The point at which they do part company is over the issue of difference. Cixous embraces (sexual) difference both strategically and ideologically, writing the female body into her texts. One might expect Wittig to do likewise; indeed, much of her utopian theoretical-fictional piece, *The Lesbian Body*, is dedicated to an exploration of the female body. *The Lesbian Body* is a disturbing text; if nothing else it is an inscription of the body:

> But *she*, most definitely, is on the side of feminine writing. With her, undoubtedly, the body is there! But it is a disturbed body, a body intoxicated with words because she is trying to conjure up the flesh, to evoke it with words: this body, in fact, is very absent. And her anxiety is truly the anxiety of hysteria. It is, indeed: 'Where are they, where are my organs?'
> (Cixous on Wittig, interviewed in Makward, 1976: p. 27)

For Wittig, however, feminisms of (sexual) difference naively function to reinstate the dualistic biases of heterosexual culture. It is this belief that leads to the following statement in her 1980 essay, 'The Point of View: Universal or Particular?':

> That there is no 'feminine writing' must be said at the outset, and one makes a mistake in using and giving currency to this expression. What is this 'feminine' in 'feminine writing'? It stands for Woman, thus merging a practice with a myth, the myth of Woman. 'Woman' cannot be associated with writing because 'Woman' is an imaginary formulation and not a concrete reality; it is that old branding by the enemy now flourished like a tattered flag refound and won in battle. 'Feminine writing' is

the naturalizing metaphor of the brutal political fact of the domination of women, and as such it enlarges the apparatus under which 'femininity' presents itself: that is Difference, Specificity, Female Body/Nature.

(Wittig, 1980b: pp. 59–60)

Underlying such statements are two related concerns. The first addresses concerns regarding the entrapment of women into the category of Woman. The second articulates the belief that feminist affirmations of difference essentialize women and (re)place them in the very category from which they have attempted to escape. Wittig is wary of essentialism and of the related practice of totemism. The women in *Les Guérillères* articulate this concern:

The women say that they perceive their bodies in their entirety. They say that they do not favour any of its parts on the grounds that it was formerly a forbidden object. *They say that they do not want to become prisoners of their own ideology.*

(Wittig, 1971: p. 57; my emphasis)

Cixous's concept of feminine writing is, as stated in Chapter 4, not necessarily gender-specific (although she points out that women do, by virtue of their shared historical experience of culture and society, have a closer relation to a non-possessive economy than do most men). Whilst Wittig is not attempting the same project as Cixous, there is some shared ground and both analyses are rooted in concerns regarding dualism and dualistic thought. There is a shared desire to transgress dualistically constructed social–cultural institutions. Further, both women attempt an articulation of sexuality and subjectivity, and both use tactics of embodiment. Their goals and motivating desires, however, are different, and whilst in the above reading I suggest that they are not necessarily in opposition, their works should not be reduced to symbiosis. Materialist lesbianism and *écriture feminine*, may, as I suggest, be able to co-exist happily but they are not synonymous.

An altogether different, yet again similar, approach to the relation between the body and the text comes from Luce Irigaray, whose theoretical work is radically utopian. Irigaray is responsible for the powerful image of 'two lips', an image which she mobilizes to challenge phallocentrism and the monolith of the penis as focus of and for sexual desire/pleasure. She reads Western culture as based on the pre-eminence of maleness and characterizes it as homosexual (rooted in the love of man). Like Cixous, Irigaray views the body as inscribed: culturally formed. She is more careful, however, than Cixous, to stress that her conception of the body is not entwined with the 'biology is destiny' school, and employs the term 'morphology' rather than that of biology. Morphology, in its biological sense, refers to the study of the form of animals and plants. It also carries a philological sense which refers to the study of the form of language, of words and systems of forms. Irigaray has worked in the fields of psychoanalysis and linguistics and conflates these meanings in her use of the term. To speak of a morphological body, then, is to condense poststructuralist analyses of language and culture with those of contemporary feminisms and to state that the experienced body is a social phenomenon. It is both a product of socialization, in that it reflects systems of values that favour the dominant cultural group, and an internalization of the coded value-system and social structure which are acquired through language.

The metaphor of the two lips stresses both vaginal and clitoral surfaces as loci for and of sexual pleasure. It also addresses the issue of authorship of the body by evoking an image of the speaking mouth. It does not, however, attempt to propose a/the 'truth' of female sexuality. Elizabeth Grosz provides an interesting reading of the function of Irigaray's metaphor:

> Its function is not referential but combative: it is an image to contest and counter dominant, phallomorphic representations. Its purpose is to reveal the implicit assumptions, and the sexual positions constituted and affirmed in dominant representations, and to ease their hold over the terrain, so that different representations may be possible. . . .
> As strategic, it makes no claim to be eternal, transhistorical or transgeographical truth (which, of course, is not to say that it is false either – it is neither true nor false, for it is not within the realm of truth at all). Her purpose is to displace male models rather than to accurately reflect what female sexuality *really* is.
>
> (Grosz, 1989: pp. 116–17)

Grosz, in this reading of Irigaray as tactician and strategist, leads us into what I have characterized in chapters above as a utopian mode of thinking that is, or can be, situated outside of a masculine economy of exchange. It goes thoroughly and self-consciously beyond (binary) opposition to a place where the concepts of truth and falsity are rendered meaningless, a place of flux and ambiguity. To return briefly to Irigaray, the intended function of stratagems such as the metaphoric imagery of the two lips is to critique and expose and, more than this, to explore (the possibility of) alternative forms of representing the embodied subject.

The discussion that follows pulls together themes and ideas that recur in utopian theory in a reading of Michèle Roberts's utopian novel *The Book of Mrs Noah* (1987). Some defence, perhaps, is necessary of my inclusion of *Mrs Noah* in the category of utopianism. It does not present itself as an overtly political piece and would not 'fit' into many characterizations of the genre of utopia; it provides no blueprint. It is, however, utopian in that it criticizes the present from a recognizably political perspective (feminism). It is an imaginative and (es)strange(d) piece of 'creative' writing. It is fictional in genre if not in aura; it presents a fictional present that is quite estranged from our own. The female characters, however, are recognizably contemporary. It can, furthermore, be characterized as a feminine text: its ending is open; it is a text of multiplicity in terms of subjectivity and narrative; the female body is written into the text (see below); and, I suggest, it represents an attempt to inscribe the contemporary experiences of women and to explore (utopian) alternative points of subjectivity.

Mrs Noah does not, superficially at least, appear to form a single narrative. It is divided into short and apparently unconnected stories in a narrative strategy similar to a Chaucerian collection of travellers' tales. All but one of the stories are told by women, the exception being that of the old man who is 'the Word of God', dubbed 'the Gaffer' by the women.[9] The fundamental area of the Ark is the library, which represents a catalogue of the lives of women: 'The Ark's bookstack, extending over many decks, contains all the varied clashing aspects of women's imagination expressed in books' (Roberts, 1987: p. 20).

It is worth, for the purposes of the present discussion, considering the nature or form of these texts, for they exceed normal expectations of a book:

> Writing materials on offer include knotted strings, circular seals, blackboards and chalk, wampum belts, message tallies, tablets of clay and ivory and wood, oracle bones, slabs of gold and silver and wax, shards of pottery, strips of cloth and papyrus and paper, sticks of bamboo, palm leaves, bits of birch bark, leather scrolls, rolls of parchment, copper plates, pen and ink, palettes

and paintbrushes, sticks and dust-trays, printing presses, type-writers, tape recorders, word processors, etc.

(Roberts, 1987: p. 20)

The books are indexed on 'Soft thick pages: rag paper, lovely to touch' (1987: p. 21). This profusion of writing materials is perhaps intended as a reminder of the multiplicity of women's cultural histories and experiences. It further produces texts of a certain tactility: these books are perceptible by touch. It is, therefore, interesting to note that the words 'text' and 'textile' are linked etymologically by the Latin 'text' meaning woven; these items described above are writing *materials*. A feminine text, Cixous and Irigaray say, is marked by its tactility and its affinity and openness to the body. Roberts goes further than this, weaving the body into the narratives of the travellers.

On several occasions this is done through use of the vehicle of food as metaphor for the sexual body. Eggs are an obvious choice:

She breaks egg yolks into a bowl, whips them with sugar and flour, boils them with milk. Beats and beats with her wooden spoon to remove lumps. Lumpy female bodies. Lumpy bellies and breasts. Eggs breaking and splattering, warm mess of sweetness on the sheets, warm flow of sweat and blood.

(1987: p. 26)

The egg reappears when one of the women, the Babble-On Sibyl, dresses a salmon for dinner with a home-made mayonnaise. The comparison is drawn between this ritual and that of the anointment of the body of her own miscarried child (1987: p. 28). The female body, birth, pain, death and sexuality are intertwined as recurrent and sometimes disturbing themes of this work.

Another recurrent image is that of water, used by Roberts to invoke the womb. At times this is explicit:

The window in the bathroom that she shares with the tenants downstairs is cut low, just beside the bath, so that she can turn her head and look out at the thrashing green branches of the maple tree through the open casement. Baby in a glass womb.

(1987: p. 35)

Less obvious is the fact that the entire book can be read as an exploration of motherhood. This theme can be found throughout the book, in, for instance, the references to feeding, and their

155

proximity to pain and love can, I suggest, be read thus. In the later stages of the book this imagery becomes explicit:

> Creation starts here in the Ark. Love actively shapes the work. My mother nourishes me with words, words of such power and richness that I grow, dance, leap. But the purpose of the Ark is to leave it. The purpose of the womb is to be born from it. So when I'm forced to go from her, when I lose her, I can call out after her, cry her name. I become myself, which means not-her; with blood and tears I become the not-mother.
>
> (1987: p. 274)

The images of water and the womb come together at this point. The Ark as mother is a benevolent figure. In earlier chapters some more disturbing images of the *possessive* mother are evoked. Mrs Noah, on one of her exploratory trips to shore, enters a city that is above ground level but underwater (another womb?). She passes through a room of metamorphoses, where chaos reigns and all rules are transgressed in an orgiastic and sensually described scene. In the middle of these descriptions comes this somewhat unexpected passage on writing and the construction of form:

> A narrative is simply a grid placed on chaos so that it can be read in descending lines from left to right, if that's what you want to do. Some writers prefer simply to record, rather than to interpret, the interlocking rooms and staircases and galleries of this place, this web of dream images that shift and turn like the radiant bits of glass in a kaleidoscope. Others like the Gaffer, make a clear design, slot incident onto a discernable thread.
>
> (1987: pp. 67–8)

This description of the narrative as order is followed by a feeling of claustrophobia and panic, a sense of loss of direction. The palace in which she is lost becomes the grasping mother:

> Is this the mother then, this horror? This hold? This great gloomy imprisoning embrace that hangs on, that won't let the child step out free? . . .
>
> How could I ever become a mother, let myself become that embodiment of possessive power, fortress jangling with locked gates, sealed windows? . . .
>
> Mothers are not free. A woman entering pregnancy is entering time, and history, process whirling her inexorably

toward the moment of giving birth, that long road of mother-
ing, her life altered irrevocably and utterly, no going back....
  To become a mother is to become unfree; tied down....
  To become a mother is to own up to having a female body and
the social consequences of that: invisibility....
  Therefore motherhood is a woman's mythical destiny, her
fulfilment puts her in touch with the rhythms of the cosmos, a
glory men cannot aspire to....
  Therefore mothers can't invent their own lives....
  Therefore to become a mother is to accept death.... Therefore it is better not. Therefore men preach the resurrection and
eternal life. Therefore women are not men. Therefore women
are not.

(1987: p. 68)

This possessive, fettering and fettered ideal/model whose biology is
her destiny is renounced by Roberts. This figure is reminiscent of
what Irigaray characterizes as the phallic mother, 'closed in upon the
jealous possession of its valuable product' (Irigaray, 1981b: p. 104).
Irigaray also uses the imagery of food. In the following passage, she
imagines being stifled by her mother's smothering love: 'You feed me/
yourself. But you feed me/yourself too much, as if you wanted to fill
me up completely with your offering. You put yourself into my mouth
and I suffocate' (1981a: p. 61). It is the mother's identity as well as her
milk that is being forced on to the imaginary child in this instance.
Irigaray is concerned to develop a maternal relation that does not
reproduce the phallic mother figure, who is an element of the
construct 'Woman'. In the above essay (1981a) she describes the
effects that this has on the mother as well as on the child, her desire is
that the mother has a life and identity outside of this construct: 'And
what I wanted from you, Mother, was this: that in giving me life, you
still remain alive' (1981b: p. 67).
  The fictional renunciate, Mrs Noah, completes her journey where it
began, in Venice, city of water, with her husband. She is determined,
despite his wishes to the contrary, to have a child, but not to become
this figure of mother. The book ends with a sense of personal
empowerment that has clear political implications.
  This text, *The Book of Mrs Noah*, is illustrative of the kind of
political/theoretical utopianism discussed above, and more. It is more
than this because it is itself a piece of creative theory – Roberts has, I
believe, used the form of the novel as a vehicle for an exploration of

157

feminist theory and as a mouthpiece for voicing the experiences of women. I state this at this juncture by way of addressing current debates within political theoretical circles about the 'use' of literature as illustration of theory.[10] The concern is rooted in the tendency amongst practitioners to select appropriate fiction, poetry or other forms of 'literature' regardless of context, to illustrate and reinforce an argument. This book, however, is structured around those themes within fictional texts which coincide with those in feminist political theory, and particularly utopian theory.

The fragmented narratives of *Mrs Noah*, then, in this reading are argued to form part of a whole which is an exploration of the roles and functions of the female body in patriarchal society (and an allusion to alternatives). This 'whole', though, is not complete, as the text is resistant to closure. It can, I believe, be situated within a feminine economy of textualization. Each character, except the Gaffer, has been invited on the journey by Mrs Noah; each, to an extent, is a caricature of facets of women's experience.[11] Roberts acknowledges cultural differences whilst constructing a sense of cohesiveness 'as women'. In so doing, she can be seen to address the dilemma introduced in Chapter 3: that the feminist need for cohesiveness works in tension with the need to represent diversity. None of Roberts's characters expresses the concerns of women of cultural and ethnic groups other than white, but within this category considerable diversity is introduced. She can then be read as addressing Elizabeth Spelman's assertion that 'though all women are women, no women is only a woman' (Spelman, 1990: p. 187). Further, the introduction of this diversity to *one* form of womanness (the white Western kind) shows the universal construct of Woman (as not man) to be inadequate and redundant.

The common 'message' of the works of Cixous, Wittig, Irigaray and Roberts is that biology is not (necessarily) destiny; not, at least, in social and political terms. As such these diverse and, in many senses, divergent works also form part of a more or less cohesive whole. In this restricted sense, these works may correspond to what Tom Moylan (1986) calls the 'critical mass' of a 'new historic bloc of opposition'. I stated in an earlier chapter that Moylan was overly optimistic when referring to feminism in this way, but, with the qualifier that the opposition is not along the lines of a cohesive dialectic, feminist opposition to the mind/body divide can, I believe, be said to be of this 'critical' nature.

In order to stress the multiplicity of this opposition and to explore contemporary feminist utopian thought on this subject further, I propose, in the following discussion, to enquire into some visions of society based on or informed by the expression of a new relation between body and mind, spirit and matter.

ENVISAGED ALTERNATIVES

I propose, in this section, to examine ways in which feminist utopian theorists and novelists have envisaged societies in which the relations between mind and body, spirit and matter, are alternatively conceived and enacted. The focus of this section is somewhat broader than that above, as its function is to explore the implications of the related set of clusters identified in the introduction to this chapter:

(hu)man	animal
culture	nature
spirit	matter
mind	body
moral	carnal
rational	emotional
intellect	sensation
transcendence	partiality
Man	Woman

In these imagined and envisaged societies this cluster of oppositions is disrupted and rearranged, and the dualistic structuring is undermined: biology is not conflated with psychology and consequently is not destiny – not, at least, as presently devised. Of these societies I ask the following questions: what conceptual or concrete steps are necessary in order to imagine them? And what might such societies look like?

Rosi Braidotti addresses questions of conceptual stepping stones in her work in this area. In order for women to be able to create a (feminist) position from which to act and articulate, Braidotti adopts a theoretical creation of Irigaray's, that of the conditional mode. Women must, she says in her essay 'The Politics of Ontological Difference' (1989), project their desire for cohesion and coherence as a group onto a project of (and for) political action:

> It is the philosophy of *as if*: in order to enunciate a feminist epistemological position the feminist woman must proceed as if a common ground of enunciation existed amongst women. As if

the subjectivity of all was at stake in the enunciative patterns of each one. In this respect, feminist theory rests on another double negative: it proceeds as if it were possible to negate a history of negation, to reverse the practice, a centuries-old history of disqualification and exclusion of women.

(Braidotti, 1989: p. 103)

The tone of this statement is echoed in the title of Braidotti's book *Patterns of Dissonance* (1991), which implies that when establishing patterns of enunciation as women, dissonance should ring through, thereby audibly signifying, if not actually articulating, our differences. Women can, in my reading of Braidotti, speak as women without erecting a new artifice of 'Woman'. She places this in a present that she calls conditional because she wants to challenge the inevitability, naturalness and even 'reality' of the present. It is conditional on acts and attitudes of the past and of the here and now: the future is not determinate:

The conscious political realization of our being already present, however, in a system that has turned a blind eye/I to the fact of what we are and that we are, instead of becoming a statement of defeat, could pave the way for a new ethical and political project aimed at affirming the positivity of the difference we embody. Beyond the fantasy of feminine power and the illusion of a pure female species, the project of sexual difference and the ethical passion that sustains it may well be the last utopia of our dying century.

(Braidotti, 1989: p. 104)

There are utopian projections of a society in which attempts are made to make culturally manifest and valuable the difference that women embody. More common, however, in contemporary texts is the projection of a society in which sexual difference, as presently conceived and embodied, is absent. Both forms are transgressive of dominant trends, albeit in different ways. I propose now to explore these phenomena briefly through fairly close reference to three utopian texts: Suzy McKee Charnas's dystopian *Walk to the End of the World* (1979) and its sequel, *Motherlines* (1980), and Marge Piercy's utopia/dystopia *Woman on the Edge of Time* (1979).

Suzy McKee Charnas's *Walk* and *Motherlines* follow the (physical and spiritual) journeys of the character Alldera. Alldera is a 'fem', which is to say a female, and as such she lives in the world of Holdfast as a slave. Fems, women in this society, are defined purely in terms of their bodies. The following passages provide a man's perspective on a fem:

> They had no souls, only inner cores of animating darkness shaped from the void beyond the stars. Their deaths had no significance. Some men believed that the same shadows returned again and again in successive fem-bodies in order to contest for the world with the souls of men, which came from light.
>
> (Charnas, 1979: p. 55)

> There was a theory that a man's soul was a fragment of eternal energy that had been split off from the soul of his father and fixed inside his dam's body by the act of intercourse. Being alien to everything that the soul represented, the fem's body surrounded the foreign element with a physical frame, by means of which the soul could be expelled. Seen from that perspective, a man's life could be regarded as the struggle of the flesh-caged soul not to be seduced and extinguished by the meaningless concerns of the brute-body.
>
> (1979: pp. 102-3)

There are strands of thought in Charnas's construction of this (dystopian) society reminiscent of those discussed in the introductory section above. Femininity (femaleness) is associated with the body and thus with dark forces by virtue of their lack of a spiritual element. These women are considered to be spiritual voids: 'The spiral was the sign of the void, of fems, of everything inimical to the straight line of manly, rational thought and will' (1979: p. 117). Non-white men ('Dirties') are considered in a similar light but constitute less of a threat, as some vestiges of the soul are attributed to them. The purpose or mission of the men is 'the Reconquest of the whole world in the name of light, reason and order' (1979: p. 57). Women, in this dystopian society, are bred to be physically and mentally weak, controlled entirely by force because of the threat which they embody. (Alldera is unusual as she has been secretly trained as a runner and is of higher than average intelligence.) This is a dystopian projection of the logical extreme of the ways in which spirit and matter are currently conceptualized. The similarities between the founding logic of Holdfast and the Western tradition referred to in the last section of this chapter are quite striking.

The society of men is also characterized by control, being rigidly hierarchical. Sexual relations between men are the norm but are strictly contained within age rank. Familial ties have been broken, partly to avoid the Freudian scenario of 'the fated enmity of fathers and sons' and partly in evasion of the mythical overthrow of the father by the son: 'To know your father's identity would be to feel, however far off, the chill wind of death' (1979: p. 22). All of these various controlling mechanisms and structures implicitly acknowledge a 'natural' tendency towards aggression, compounded by the association of the body with weakness: 'It had, however, become a habit of thought to consider himself split into opposites, particularly after he had realized that it was through the body-brute that the will of others could be inflicted on him' (1979: p. 103).

The function of most fems in Holdfast is the performance of physical labour. Some, however, perform other acts of labour that are associated with the body: the 'pet-fems', for instance, tattooed and heavily adorned, provide their owners with sexual services whilst others, 'dams', are breeders. It is interesting to note that Charnas's dystopia is transgressive of the dominant norms of sexual behaviour of our present: pet-fems are universally despised because they perform 'perverted' (heterosexual) services in a culture in which the (physical and mental) bonding of men is the norm. Heterosexual penetrative intercourse is despised even by most pet-fems. These women are reduced to physicality, made into perverse sexual objects and despised for just that. This society could, perhaps, be said to operate within a super-masculine economy.[12]

Alldera's mission is to seek the mythical free fems said to live in the wilderness beyond Holdfast: the Wild. The sequel to *Walk*, *Motherlines*, finds her initially in the company of women who are not free fems but who also live in the Wild. A central theme of this book is, I suggest, concerned with the (initially and historically hostile) relations between two groups of women: those who find Alldera (the Riding Women, indigenous to the plains) and the free fems whom she sought. When she first enters a free fem camp Alldera finds that relations between the fems are the same as they were in Holdfast: fundamentally aggressive, mistrustful and hostile, and formed by the concept of possession. The character Daya, for instance, bred as a pet-fem, is still 'kept' (now by a woman) as a sexual object. Charnas's depiction of the relations between and within these two groups can, I believe, be seen to address current and historical debates within feminist theory. The book finishes with an uneasy but potentially happy 'ending' (or beginning) as, through increasing contact with each another, the two groups begin to learn about each other, despite concerns regarding the dilution of their respective cultures. What is particularly interesting about these cultures is that they are not dependent upon skin colour. The Riding Women are multiracial in this sense, the genetic features of a woman being passed to others in her motherline. Culture is derived from shared life experience. Again, I suggest, this addresses debates within feminism, as biology is in no sense destiny in *Motherlines*.

Another, related, theme of *Motherlines* is that of a non-possessive relation between mother and child. Alldera gives birth to a daughter in the Riding Women's camp. When she moves to live with the free fems she leaves the child in the care of her two 'share mothers'. The child reaches the age at which Riding Women celebrate the end of childhood, and at the naming ceremony Alldera is pushed by the fems to select a femmish name. She declines to impose her own cultural identity on her child:

> This cub is nothing to do with them. . . . That's the man's disease, thinking they're so important that everything connects to them and their schemes and desires. How I hate that mixture of the worst in both men and fems – cowardice and conceit together!
>
> (Charnas, 1980: pp. 225–6)

She does name the child, but not according to any cultural convention. Whilst proposing the absence of cultural imposition, Charnas does not advocate cultural ignorance. The child (Sorrel) lives as and with the Riding Women but learns of her cultural heritage through the old slave songs of the fems.

I suggested, in the first section of this chapter, that the hierarchical relation between the natural and the cultural is connected to the cluster of oppositions surrounding mind and body, spirit and matter. The culture of the Riding Women is significantly transgressive of the norms of this relation. Their culture has, on the one hand, a close relation to the environment. But both *Motherlines* and *Walk* are set in a post-apocalyptic, post-nuclear world. This is a common device of contemporary utopianism, but in Charnas's work the setting can be read as providing a starting point for challenging the realms of the established 'natural'. Even the environment is not natural in the strict sense; rather it is the consequence of the actions of mankind (sic).

The women's reproductive (previously 'natural') abilities were enhanced by scientific experiments before 'the Wasting' (the

163

ecological disaster that pre-dates Holdfast society). They need only a generative fluid in order to start the reproductive process, and this they acquire from the horses with whom they live. Even the human/animal hierarchy and dualism is disrupted here. Elaborate and symbolic ritual attends these procedures; mutual trust is established between human and animal by an elaborate and dangerous dance:

> We do have a bond, of our bodies and theirs. The balance of all things includes us and acts on us, and animals . . . are our links with the balance. We celebrate it every year at the Gather of all camps, where the young women mate.
>
> (1980: p. 102)

Balance and respect characterize this new and strange relation between the natural that is not, and the cultural which is derived from it. Similar themes appear in Marge Piercy's *Woman on the Edge of Time*. This is a more widely read text and the following analysis will, therefore, be less explanatory of the narrative.

Ecologically, the utopian community of Mattapoissett is close to the environment, relations being characterized by respect and an awareness of scarcity. One figure on the council of each township is, for instance, the Earth Advocate, while another acts as the Animal Advocate.

The theme of non-possessive parenting is also explored and Connie, at the end of the book, gives her child (symbolically, at least, she is a ward of state and not 'Connie's' to give) to the care of Luciente and the others. Perhaps more interesting is Piercy's presentation of the transgression of the natural with the aid of technology. Conception and gestation in Mattapoissett are extra-uterine:

> It was part of the women's long revolution. When we were breaking all the old hierarchies. Finally there was one thing we had to give up too, the only power we ever had, in return for no more power for anyone. The original production: the power to give birth. Cause as long as we were biologically enchained, we'd never be equal. And males would never be humanized to be loving and tender. So we're all mothers.
>
> (Piercy, 1979: p. 105)

Strong echoes of Shulamith Firestone's (1971) utopian political theory resonate throughout *Woman on the Edge*. In Firestone's reading, women's biology, before the advent of birth control, rendered them physically and economically dependent on men. Firestone's utopian

164

goal, as presented in *The Dialectic of Sex*, is the elimination of the cultural significance of biology:

> the end of feminist revolution must be, unlike that of the feminist movement, not just the elimination of male *privilege*, but of the sex *distinction* itself; genital differences between human beings would no longer matter culturally.
>
> (Firestone, 1971: pp. 11–12)

Artificial reproduction and the elimination of the biological family are/were, for Firestone, the routes to such a state. Other demands that she makes of a feminist revolution are the abolition of wage labour, the freeing of sexuality for women and children, and their full integration into society.

Piercy's utopian society can, I suggest, be read as a fictional exploration and extension of Firestone's theory. Unpleasant, repetitive work is automated; education is broad and liberal; work is fulfilling where possible and that which cannot be automated is performed by rota; communities are self-regulating and democratic in the participatory sense. It is a veritable 'paradise on earth' (Firestone, 1971: p. 274).

Firestone makes ambiguous reference to the end of racial distinction. It is possible that she means this in the same sense as that in which she refers to the end of sex distinction (see above). Considering her general insensitivity towards race, it is more likely that she has the image of the cultural melting pot in mind. Piercy presents culture as important and precious but not biologically or racially defined:

> But we broke the bond between genes and culture, broke it forever. We want there to be no chance of racism again. But we don't want the melting pot where everyone ends up with thin gruel. We want diversity, for strangeness breeds richness.
>
> (Piercy, 1979: p. 104)

The maintenance of and respect for diversity and richness are themes of both ecological and feminist thought today. Connie lives in a present recognizable as contemporary with our own. Her personal history has, in a sense, been closely related to questions of mind and body. Connie has a history of institutionalization in the state mental health system. Sectioned as violent, she has no autonomy. She is prescribed drugs that impair her mental and physical faculties: to refuse them is to be seen to behave irrationally, to take them is to be incapacitated. Her experience of technology is that of oppression and violation. Piercy describes, or perhaps imagines, the experience of ECT: 'A little brain damage to jolt you into behaving right' (1979: p. 81). This, I suggest, comes close to a physical manifestation of the situation Hélène Cixous depicts in her essay 'Castration or Decapitation?' (1981b), in which women are 'disciplined' to the state of automata.[13]

The third 'world' visited by Connie is an alternative future/present which is highly technological. The woman that Connie meets is a sexual object, heavily adorned. Her body has been artificially enhanced to represent 'a cartoon of femininity' (Piercy, 1979: p. 288). The purpose of her life is to give pleasure to men. Drugs simulate emotions and the 'Sensall' machine simulates sensory experience. The themes of the Sensall are those of sexual violence. This woman is a physical being with no mental autonomy: thoughts are 'read' by the security forces via an implant in the brain. This is a highly regulated society with no room for dissent. Implied in these two contrasting views of the role of technology is a common theme in feminist science fiction, namely the articulation of the belief that technology itself is a neutral tool. In the eutopia, women participated in its construction and control, and in the dystopia technology is a tool by which women are themselves controlled.

In Mattapoissett, communication by telepathy is practised. Connie is, apparently, unusually receptive: 'A catcher is a person whose mind and nervous system are open, receptive, to an unusual extent. . . . In our culture you would be much admired' (Piercy, 1979: p. 42). Connie, however is not flattered by this news, reading receptivity through the matrix of her own culture: 'Receptive. Like passive. The Mexican woman Consuelo the meek, dressed in black with her eyes downcast, never speaking unless addressed' (1979: p. 45). She further associates communication by telepathy with the mind control via technology (ECT and implantation) that she experiences in her own world.

Another book recently published by Piercy, *Body of Glass*, also mimics or enacts elements of feminist political theory. It is interesting as it is clearly influenced by Donna Haraway's 'Manifesto for Cyborgs' (1990). Haraway's 'Manifesto' is a piece of creative theory and is highly imaginative. It is most accessibly read as an attempt to explore and create an axis for postmodernist theories of society and those of feminism. The cyborg is a transgressive creation, a violator of the distinctions between the physical and the non-physical, organism and machine, animal and human. It is a utopian creation which functions

THE SPIRIT/MATTER RELATION

as a metaphor for the present. Haraway's argument is that these boundaries are already transgressed by science. The cyborg, then, is fact and fiction; it functions, in part at least, to challenge the distinctions between these two genres. As such, it is a metaphor for the undermining of binary oppositional thought.

On what is perhaps a less explicitly utopian level, Alison Jagger proposes a transgression of the divide between emotion and reason (body and mind). Her work is situated within the genre of political theory. Rather than the traditional view of emotion as subversive of knowledge, Jagger proposes an alternative epistemological model that accepts the indispensability of emotions to knowledge and vice versa. She identifies a number of historical and cultural functions of emotion as it is presently conceived. The first lies in the dualistic construction of thought:

> Typically, although not invariably, the rational has been contrasted with the emotional and this contrasted pair has been linked with other dichotomies. Not only has reason been contrasted with emotion, but it has also been associated with the mental, the universal, the public and the male, whereas emotion has been associated with the irrational, the physical, the natural, the particular, the private, and of course, the female.
>
> (Jagger, 1989: p. 129)

Emotions are further identified as belonging to the socialization process in that children learn the appropriate responses in given situations. In this sense emotions are culturally variable: fear of strangers, for instance, is appropriate to a certain form of society. In this sense, says Jagger, emotions involve judgements and are ways of recognizing and making sense of the world. These judgements she finds to be facilitated by concepts: 'For this reason, emotions simultaneously are made possible and limited by the conceptual and linguistic rescouses of a society' (1989: p. 135).

For Jagger, emotions are not passive or involuntary responses: 'Rather, they are ways in which we engage actively and even construct the world' (1989: p. 136). For this reason they have an intrinsic and instrumental value – they enable us to act appropriately, and to give meaning to life. Given that the dominant values of a society reflect the interests of the dominant groups, Jagger proposes that our theoretical vision can be widened by acknowledging what she calls outlaw emotions:

The dominant values are implicit in responses taken to be precultural or acultural, or so-called gut responses ... in short, they blind us to the possibility of alternate ways of living.

By constituting the basis for a ... subculture, outlaw emotions may be politically (because epistemologically) subversive.

(1989: p. 144)

CONCLUSION

The theories and novels discussed in this chapter have been found to be surprisingly similar in their shared desire to revoke the standing norm which conceptually divides mind from body, spirit from matter, and reason from desire. More or less integrationist, and more or less transgressive, these women attempt to varying degrees an introduction of the body (in)to the cultural text, and a reconceptualization of the relation of matter and spirit. Reading and writing the inscribed body are processes of this transgressive utopian approach. And, more or less successfully, they contribute a new conceptual space to the dilemma of contemporary feminism over the 'Woman' problem.

In this chapter I have illustrated how an openended conception of utopianism and an openended reading of feminism can be profitably engaged in consideration of the problems which currently preoccupy intellectual feminism. This engagement is, I suggest, profitable, but not within the terms of what was earlier identified as a masculine economy: the 'return' is perhaps, in these terms, not worth the investment of time and space, as no conclusive answer to the problems has been reached. Rather, an alternative approach to the world has been suggested and illustrated. This approach is transgressive utopianism; it transgresses, negates and creates new conceptual spaces from which to reapproach the world in a non-dualistic way that is not driven by the desire to possess. Considered within an alternative ('feminine') economy, though, the profit does not consist in the possession of truth, but rather in the opening of further alternatives and possibilities. Certain diverse conceptual shifts have been explored that transgress dominant and restrictive ways of construing the world. This, then, is utopianism of process.

6

FEMINIST UTOPIAN TRANSGRESSION OF THE SELF/OTHER RELATION

INTRODUCTION

I indicated in Chapter 3 that conceptualizations of difference can be theorized as partially constitutive of relations of domination, and that a new approach to difference has formed part of utopian feminist projects of emancipation. The approach that conceptualizes difference as deviance from an established norm was portrayed as repressive, being one that relied on dualistic thought which posits an either/or choice. Within the context of Chapter 3, this way of conceiving difference was related to the opposition of difference to equality.

This chapter represents a thorough extension of these ideas as read through the Self/Other relation in feminist utopian theory and fiction. Within this context, difference can be read as Otherness.[1] The discussions below begin with a summary connection of debates detailed above to those concerning the construction of subjectivity and Otherness, and I suggest that we can read feminist utopian theory and fiction as containing this as a central theme. The first section of discussion, then, is concerned to read and analyse the Self/Other relation through utopian fictions and theories of sexual difference. This section lays the ground for an 'other' reading of the concept of otherness from the utopian perspective of estrangement.

Various attempts to reconstruct or reconceptualize the relation between Self and Other are examined in the following sections. Some favour a new, homogenizing relation, and others advocate a heterogeneous approach. The argument is offered that (some) feminist utopian literature and theory can be read as profoundly transgressive of the binary opposition of Self to Other. The suggestion is made that this transgression can usefully be read in terms of what Hélène Cixous calls a feminine libidinal economy.

ANALYSES OF THE SELF/OTHER RELATION

A number of diverse theoretical perspectives can be found to address the question of identity, a fundamental element of which is the Self/Other relation. Those considered in the discussion that follows include political theory, philosophy (particularly ethical philosophy and theories of epistemology and ontology), psychoanalytic analyses and theories of language (particularly poststructuralist critiques). Feminist scholars from all of these disciplines can, I suggest, be read as reaching the same broad conclusions, namely, that the Self/Other relation is constructed through binary opposition and that this is a contributory factor to the subordination (variously expressed and manifested) of Woman to Man, women to men, femininity to masculinity – sameness to O/otherness and like to different.

Otherness as difference can be understood only if sameness and difference are seen as placed in an oppositional relation, and can be related to the cluster of oppositions mentioned above. Luce Irigaray is one utopian theorist on whom I focused in Chapter 5. In the abstract that follows, she condenses these ideas of Otherness and difference in a consideration of the construction of sexual difference:

> 'Sexual difference' is a derivation of the problematics of sameness, it is, now and forever, determined within the project, the projection, the sphere of representation, of the same. The 'differentiation' into two sexes derives from the a priori assumption of the same, since the little man that the girl is, must become a man minus certain attributes whose paradigm is morphological – attributes capable of determining, of assuring, the reproduction–specularization of the same. A man minus the possibility of (re)presenting oneself as a man = normal reason.
>
> (Irigaray, 1981b: pp. 26–7)

Irigaray refers in this passage to the Freudian account of sexuality, which takes the development of the boy child as its point of reference from which that of the girl is deviant. The progression of the girl is not the same as that of the boy; it is this difference that marks it as 'abnormal'. Feminine sexuality is defined only in terms of its difference from masculine sexuality. Masculinity is thus equated in such accounts with normality and sameness. Difference is always difference from, never autonomous.

Monique Wittig takes up the theme of sexual difference as

construct and explores its political implications for women in the utopian text *Les Guérillères*:

> The women say, the men have kept you at a distance, they have supported you, they have put you on a pedestal, constructed an essential difference. They say, men in their way have adored you like a goddess or burned you at their stakes or else relegated you to their service in their backyards. They say, in so doing they have always in their speech dragged you in the dirt. They say, in speaking they have possessed violated taken subdued humiliated you to their hearts' content. They say, oddly enough what they have exalted in their words as an essential difference is a biological variation. They say, they have described you as they described the races they called inferior.
>
> (Wittig, 1971: pp. 100, 102)

The function of sexual difference, currently defined in masculine terms is, for Wittig, the subordination of women. Femininity, in these analyses, is created from a masculine (male) point of view. The effect is a devaluation of the status and value of what it means to be a woman and a corresponding enhancement of what it is to be a man.

Moreover, the assumption of sexual difference itself as natural is, for Wittig, the foundation stone of patriarchal heterosexist society. Women, she states, are a class, a political and economic category, not a natural group. The construct of Woman is an oppressive myth (as Wittig says in a passage already cited in Chapter 5):

> Our first task, it seems, is to always thoroughly dissociate 'women' (the class within which we fight) and 'woman', the myth. For 'woman' does not exist for us: it is only an imaginary formation, whilst 'women' is the product of a social relationship.
>
> (Wittig, 1981: p. 15)

Woman, the mythical construct, is defined solely in relation to men. In making this observation Wittig is not disagreeing with those feminist analyses discussed above. The originality of her work lies in its subversion of the two mutually dependent yet hierarchically arranged categories of sex. The extract that follows was also cited in Chapter 5, and is illustrative of the reasoning behind Wittig's controversial statement that 'the lesbian is not a woman':

> Lesbianism is the only concept I know of which is beyond the categories of sex (woman and man), because the designated

subject (lesbian) is *not* a woman, either economically, or politically, or ideologically. For what makes a woman is a specific social relation to a man, a relation that we have previously called servitude, a relation which implies personal and physical obligation as well as economic obligation ('forced residence', domestic corvee, conjugal duties, unlimited production of children, etc.), a relation which lesbians escape by refusing to become or stay heterosexual.

(1981: p. 20)

The lesbian position is, for Wittig, substantially different to that of Woman in patriarchal (heterosexual) society by virtue of its autonomy. The lesbian position is neither reliant on nor connected to Man or men. As such, lesbian women are self-defined, with no need for the hierarchical/complementary construct of Otherness outlined above. This subjective position is a transgressive and utopian conception.

Wittig's analysis can, on an explanatory level, be read as a play of binary oppositions, hierarchically arranged so that the privilege of one corresponds to the subordination of the other. In this sense it can be said to enact one element of the critical utopian function as identified by Moylan: it destroys something that exists and is perceived to be natural and inevitable (Moylan, 1986). In addition to this destructive function, Wittig's creation of the conceptually autonomous position of lesbianism is a transformation and subsequently a revival of the concept(ualization) of sexual difference. This text can also be seen to provoke what Whitford calls a paradigm shift in consciousness: paradigm because the patterns and structures through which consciousness of the given situation/concept are perceived are subverted and transformed.

A further reading of the construction of sexual difference as a play of sameness and difference is that of poststructuralist deconstruction. The following extract is the much-quoted section from 'Sorties' in which Hélène Cixous provokes meditation of binary oppositional thought as a hierarchical structuring of meaning, at the base of which she locates the constructs of man/woman:

Where is she?
Activity/Passivity
Sun/Moon
Culture/Nature
Day/Night

172

Father/Mother
Head/Heart
Intelligible/Palpable
Logos/Pathos
Form, convex, step, advance,
semen, progress
Matter, concave, ground – where
steps are taken, holding- and
dumping-ground.
Man

———————————

Woman
(Cixous and Clement, 1986: p. 63)

The relations between these oppositional pairs is complex. In the first instance they are part of a hierarchy; power and status being located within the masculine concepts of activity, culture and the mind. Further, these concepts, rather than existing autonomously or carrying inherent meaning, are part of a referential system in which they are placed as couples. Cixous highlights this point in the following passage: 'Everywhere (where) ordering intervenes, a law organizes what is thinkable by oppositions (dual, irreconcilable; or sublatable, dialectical). And all these pairs of oppositions are *couples*' (Cixous and Clement, 1986: pp. 63–4). The political importance of this structuring cannot be overstressed. The structuring of oppositional concepts as couples naturalizes and obscures the hierarchical nature of the relation between them: the couple is a unit, a whole in itself. Hence the interdependencies of this relation are obscured: the 'master' signifiers or concepts need a corresponding 'slave' in order for the hierarchy to have meaning.

In this reading, the construct of Woman and, indeed, living historical women are excluded from intimate relations with power because they (women, Woman) correspond to the points of negativity by which masculinity and that which corresponds to it are deemed to be positive. There can, however, be no positivity without negativity. This is often explained in philosophical terms by the 'A: not-A' equation (Grosz, 1989). Woman, for example, is 'not-man'; the little girl, in Freudian terms, is 'not-boy'. In a masculine economy, as represented by patriarchy, 'A', the initial point of reference, is always possessed of 'masculine' characteristics. This economy or tradition is phallocentric.

173

These constructions are satirically illustrated by reversal in the following extract from Michèle Roberts's *The Book of Mrs Noah.*[2] The Gaffer, whose predicament is portrayed here, is introduced as the Word of God, truth incarnate, author of a once best-selling Book, the Bible. He finds himself in a library of the thoughts of women:

> He strokes his chin. First of all, some research. How to define men's writing? What do men write about? What is this thing the sibyls keep banging on about called masculinity? He could start here, in the Reading Room. A man is: not-a-woman. Scan all these female texts, discover what they leave out, then plunge into that blank space and explore.
>
> (Roberts, 1987: p. 235)

Hélène Cixous takes this idea a step further: not only is woman defined by a logic of negation, but also, in her position of subservience, props up the entire conceptual system: 'Night to his day, that has forever been the fantasy, Black to his White. Shut out of his system's space, she is the repressed that ensures the system's functioning' (Cixous and Clement, 1986: p. 67).

It is common, in feminist utopian literature, to find expression of this covert dependency depicted in concrete terms. Josephine Saxton's short story 'Gordon's Women' (1986d), for instance, presents a dystopian society in which women are both the concrete and symbolic Other of men. Gordon, the patriarch, assumes that women have no value or identity. The function of Gordon's women (they are literally his possessions) is to serve him. The story begins at the end of a busy day: 'He had organized the picking of a fruit crop and purified a dam, all without leaving his rooms. He had also exterminated two surplus women, whose serial numbers indicated that they were over-aged' (Saxton, 1986d: p. 111).

These women are vessels, vassals of and for his will. Essential to the smooth running of Gordon's world, they are denied humanity. The story contains a twist, as at the end it becomes apparent that these are not real women at all but robots programmed by an underground society of real women. Gordon, however, is unaware of this and the points made above regarding the construction of Woman from a male point of view are, I believe, well illustrated by this story. Human relations are constructed in this text by reference to the concept of property. Gordon has ownership of these women; they are pro-grammed to give him sensual pleasure and to labour for him. Like the women in Hélène Cixous's version of the story of Sun Tse

174

(examined in Chapter 4), these caricatures of Woman are denied autonomy. And like the Sleeping Beauty, these women awaken, smile and desire to please. They can then, I suggest, be read as internalizing (and externalizing) the role of Woman in a masculine economy – this economy characterized by the (masculine) desire to possess, control and appropriate difference. A masculine gift of identity is the creation of this kind of Otherness: Woman is 'not-Man', hence the exaggerated characteristics of 'femininity' which the man Gordon 'possesses' through ownership of the women.

A further illustration can be found in Suzy McKee Charnas's dystopian novel *Walk to the End of the World* (1979). 'Fems' and 'Dirties' function in this society to perform the manual labour that ensures the system's material functioning.[3] Further, they are considered to be subhuman, and exist as an underclass without rights or access to political power. Their exclusion from power is an illustration of the kind of apartheid that can result from making hierarchical what it is to be human.

This introductory reading of the Self/Other relation through utopian theories and fictions of sexual difference has thus far raised a number of complexly related points. To summarize: the Self/Other relation can be found to correspond to that of same/difference and should be firmly located within the phallo-logocentric symbolic order of meaning and language. Logocentrism seeks and privileges unity and absolute access to the presence of truth. Phallocentrism gives to the phallus the function of the logos – the word which is presence. From the perspective of sexual difference theory, the constructs of femininity and masculinity underwrite the hierarchical structuring of binary oppositional thought. This structure, it is argued, is fundamentally oppositional yet simultaneously involves a certain interdependence, the benefits of which are not equally distributed.

I suggest that this schema can be usefully reinterpreted in terms of the Self/Other relation, and argue that it is this, rather than Man/Woman, which underwrites the system. 'A' needs 'not-A' to confirm its own existence. This is partially achieved by defining 'not-A' in terms of negative difference or Otherness. This can be applied to the Man/Woman couple as follows: Woman is outside (O/other) in terms of access and power, but inside (O/other) in terms of her supporting function:

Phallocentrism is a subtle and not always easily identifiable representational system. It has three distinct forms, which, if

175

taken together, describe the historically varied positions that have been socially acknowledged for women in patriarchal cultures: whenever the two sexes are conceived as *identical*, as *opposites* or as *complements*, one of the two terms defines the position of the other.

(Grosz, 1989: p. 105)

I have, thus far, focused on the oppositional and/or complementary positioning of women in relation to men. The conception of women as identical to men is located in critiques which are characterizable by their affection for sameness. Ann Ferguson (1989) identifies three models of the self, one of which she terms the Rational Maximizer.[4] The Rational Maximizer is essentially a creature of liberalism and is assumed to be a unified, rational, thinking subject who is possessed of free will and the ability to choose and attain goals in the absence of external constraints. This theory of self is non-differentiated in terms of gender: 'On the Rational Maximizer view of self, women do not differ from men in terms of personal identity and the human ability to choose reasonable goals and means to them' (Ferguson, 1989: p. 93).

Letty Cottin Pogrebin (1974), in a short depiction of a perfect utopian society, sketches an ideal of non-gender-differentiated sub-jectivity. The story is that of a child, Milleny, born in the year 2000 into an egalitarian society with no gendered role models. This is an individualistic culture in which freedom of choice is privileged. There is, for instance, free choice with regard to where and how to give birth, to educate children; resources appear to be infinite. There is sexual equality in politics, education and business, and men and women have equal earning power. The story is trite and tedious, as is often the case with Utopias of perfection.[5]

The subject can, however, in such a setting, act as a fully rationally maximizing being. Sexual difference, in such models, is merely external: men and women are essentially the same. Such accounts fail to historicize why social and/or cultural differences along the lines of, for instance, gender, race, class and ethnicity both exist and can be transformed. They also place no value in these differences.

The assumption of rationality as the defining human characteristic has traditionally been treated with suspicion by feminist scholars. The work of Iris Marion Young provides a thorough exploration of the effects of such an approach. Her article 'Impartiality and the Civic Public' (1986) offers a deconstructive reading of the related concepts of impartiality and reason, desire and affectivity. Modern political and ethical theory, she argues, assume a rational and impartial political actor, and hence value the universal over the particular. This rational actor, she finds, is assumed able to transcend his (the actor of this type is assumed to be possessed of universally 'masculine' characteristics) particularity of context in order to evaluate dispassionately and judge the universal truth of a given situation or position. Young finds this ideal of transcendental reason, and the masculine figure who embodies the ideal, to be dependent upon a devaluation of desire, the body and affectivity. The political implications of such a move are that those people with whom these latter attributes are closely associated are effectively excluded from the ideal and hence from the political arena. For instance, all women, and men of colour, have been historically represented as emotional and close to the body. We/they are therefore constructed as representative of and objects of desire, and are left outside in the political cold.

The Rational Maximizer theory of self can, I suggest, be read in such terms: the assumption that women are outside the public realm because they choose to be so assumes, in the first instance, an unrealistically level field of play. Further, such a choice surely is not rational, as it is in the political-public realm that status and economic power lie: to choose to remain outside is to choose impotence and exclusion. Ironically, then, this model re-emphasizes the supposed irrationality of women.

Young reinforces her own arguments with regard to the exclusionary effects of such model in the article 'The Ideal of Community and the Politics of Difference':

> Any move to define an identity, a closed totality, always depends on excluding some elements, separating the pure from the impure. Bringing particular things under a universal essence, for example, depends on determining some attributes of particulars as accidental, lying outside the essence. Any definition or category creates an inside/outside distinction, and the logic of identity seeks to keep these borders firmly drawn.
>
> (Young, 1990: p. 303)

Young's position here is close to that of Jacques Derrida, discussed in Chapters 3 and 4, in that she expresses similar concerns regarding the activities of defining or categorizing. On the Self/Other relation, this extract returns us to the point made earlier regarding the dependent nature of binary oppositions: 'A' needs to define 'not-A' as such in order to reinforce its own substance and uniqueness.

One obvious consequence of such a move which has not yet been discussed is the positioning of 'not-A' as outsider: O/other. Hélène Cixous expresses this facet of the self/other relation by writing self-consciously from the position of O/other as an Algerian Jew. A passage from 'Sorties', subtitled 'Murder of the Other', combines biographical detail of this experience with a theorization of Otherness. Of her childhood, for instance, she says:

> Already I knew all about the 'reality' that supports History's progress: everything throughout the centuries depends upon the distinction between the Selfsame, the ownself (– what is mine, hence what is good) and that which limits it: so now what menaces my-own-good (good never being anything other than what is good-for-me) is the 'other'.
>
> The paradox of otherness is that, of course, at no moment in History is it tolerated as such. The other is there only to be reappropriated, recaptured, and destroyed as other. Even the exclusion is not an exclusion. Algeria was not France, but it was 'French'.
>
> (Cixous and Clement, 1986: pp. 70–1)

Maria Lugones explores similar themes in an article 'Playfulness – "World"-Traveling, and Loving Perception'. She stresses the need for flexibility when positioned as an outsider who shifts in and out of mainstream life. This movement she calls world travelling. She suggests that the Other, or different, is positioned as outsider by what Marilyn Frye calls arrogant perception:

> I am particularly interested here in the many cases in which white/Anglo women do one or more of the following to women of color: they ignore us, ostracise us, render us invisible, stereotype us, leave us completely alone, interpret us as crazy.
>
> (Lugones, 1989: p. 279)

Arrogant perception contributes to what Patricia Hill Collins (1990) has called controlling images of women of colour. The parallels between these perceptions of what it is to be Other and those of the theorists discussed above are clear. So too are the differences: from Lugones's perspective it is white women who create their Other in this way. These divergent perspectives can, I suggest (cautiously), be read from within a matrix of non-essentialist matrices of masculinity and femininity.[8] I refer here to the function and definition of femininity in a masculine libidinal and material economy. Controlling images, I suggest, emerge from the arrogant perception of difference as inferior, (dangerous) and hence Other. The Other is the stranger, the strange, and thereby becomes the estranged.

A Utopia and the genre of utopia are particularly appropriate places from which to explore relations of O/otherness and estrangement. Estrangement has, historically, played a fundamental role in utopian literature. Content-based and form-based approaches to utopianism often identify one convention of utopian thought to be the presence of a visitor who is temporarily estranged from her/his own environment (for example, Kumar, 1991). The experience of this visitor can, I suggest, be read as world-travelling in the sense outlined above. Lugones refers to travelling between concrete worlds, but the visitor to a Utopia also shifts in and out of different cultures and frequently experiences corresponding shifts of identity and behaviour: 'The shift of being one person to being a different person is what I call "travel"' (Lugones, 1989: p. 283). This is further compatible with the internal/external play described above, and numerous examples of world travelling can be found in recent feminist utopias. The effect of such travelling on visitors to utopia is usually that of an enhanced awareness of their own present. The character Cendri, for instance, who visits Marion Zimmer Bradley's Amazonian world of Isis (1980), begins, in this new context, to question the nature of her relationship with her husband Dal. She has hitherto perceived this as equal. The marriage emerges, however, as being based upon the giving up, by Cendri, of personal ambitions and her bending of her desires to those of her husband. The marriage survives, in other words, because she comes to complement and enhance his position as a scholarly genius.

Joanna Russ's *The Female Man* (1986), to which I refer in some detail later in this chapter, is exemplary of the complex internal/external play involved in the construction of identity (self) and relations to O/other(s). The book is narrated throughout in the first person singular. The speaker, however, is not one person, but five: Jeannie, Janet, Jane, Jaelle and, at one point, Joanna Russ herself. All of these women inhabit different worlds. The narration can be read as the expression of internal thoughts and perceptions regarding the self and others, and as external perceptions of each of the characters *by* the others. *The Female Man* is a difficult read: the shifting identity of the 'I' is further complicated by the changing natures of the characters as they are affected and infected by the presence of the others.

Tom Moylan connects the convention of estrangement to the subversive function of utopia:

Estrangement, the mechanism of the utopian text whereby it focuses on the given situation but in a displaced manner to create a fresh view, is identified as central to the subversive quality of the genre – and indeed of its cousins in the fantastic mode in general.

(Moylan, 1986: p. 33)

Moylan's understanding of estrangement is more conventional than that of *The Female Man*, in which the reader is also estranged from the text and characters by Russ's narrative technique. Further, because this text focuses on the characters over and above the setting, we read their worlds through the characters themselves. There is, then, a certain estrangement from the worlds inhabited by the four fictional 'I's. And again, on a deeper level of personal identity, the characters are seen to be estranged from themselves – not until close to the end of the book does the idea emerge that these 'I's might all be the same person as manifested in different worlds:

[Jaelle] It came to me several months ago that I might find my other selves out there in the great, gray might-have-been, so I undertook – for reasons partly personal and partly political, of which more later, to get hold of the three of you.

[Jaelle] Do you remember the old story of the Doppelganger? This is the double you recognise instantly, with whom you feel a mysterious kinship. An instant sympathy, that informs you at once that the other is really your own self. The truth is that people don't recognize themselves except in mirrors, and sometimes not even then.

(Russ, 1986: pp. 160–2)

It is worth noting that the recognition of sameness here is equated with affinity. What is frequently absent, however, in the utopian context is the conventional equation of difference with a negative Otherness. Not only are women constructed by phallocentric discourse as Other in negative terms, but this negativity is, according to some critiques, internalized and manifested as self-hate:

– Not only is she the portion of strangeness – *inside* his universe where she receives his restlessness and desire. Within his economy, she is the strangeness he likes to appropriate. Moreover, the 'dark continent' trick has been pulled on her: she has been kept at a distance from herself, she has been made to see

(= not-see) woman on the basis of what man wants to see of her, which is to say, almost nothing. . . .

One can teach her, as soon as she begins to speak, at the same time as she is taught her name, that hers is the dark region: because you are Africa, you are black. Your continent is dark. Dark is dangerous. You can't see anything in the dark, you are afraid. Don't move, you might fall. Above all, don't go into the forest. And we have internalized this fear of the dark. . . . Woman is disgusted by woman and fears her. . . .

They have committed an anti-narcissism in her! A narcissism that only loves itself if it makes itself loved for what is lacking. They have created the loathsome logic of antilove.

(Cixous and Clement, 1986: p. 68)

The construction of Woman as Man's Other by a binary system of hierarchical opposition is, in this reading, doubly divisive. In the first instance, women internalize the hierarchy and the structuring and distribution of values, and thus find themselves inferior, contemptible. Further, individual women are alienated from others (other women). A commonplace illustration of this operation in processes in the real world can be found in prevalent attitudes towards the female body and its adornment. This has been well documented and researched and I have neither the time nor space to rehearse the arguments fully. Briefly, a certain ideal shape and size are established, and clothing which is fashionable suits that particular shape. Most women cannot meet the ideals of the advertising world, and the resultant effects usually range from low self-esteem to severe psychiatric disturbance, anorexia, bulimia *et al.*

This, for Cixous, is the masculine economy in operation. The gift, as discussed in Chapters 3–5 above, in the masculine economy is not free in any sense. To give something an identity (a category or definition to which to belong) is, in this reading, to restrict its autonomy and to deny it the authority to name itself. This critique, applied to the issue of Self/Other–Man/Woman relations, has considerable force. To name, I stated above, is, in a masculine economy, to claim. Thus Woman has been named and claimed as Other. Thus further, by means of the dark continent trick, women internalize the loathsome construct of woman. 'Hate them more than you hate yourself, and you'll stay free!' says Connie in *Woman on the Edge of Time*, in a statement which, rather than being an inversion of misogyny, reaches beyond binary opposition to challenge the ways in which this self-hate is structured and functions (Piercy, 1979: p. 366). Connie, in her present world, is treated in the psychiatric system as subhuman. Her refusal to internalize this perception is predicative of her survival. Transgressive utopianism which negates dualistic and restrictive conceptualizations can, it seems, be politically efficacious.

Vincent Geoghegan makes an interesting point regarding utopian estrangement and O/otherness. He refers, in the following statement, to the classical utopian form, but I find his point relevant to modern works:

> The classical utopia anticipates and criticizes. Its alternative fundamentally interrogates the present, piercing through existing societies' defensive mechanism – common sense, realism, positivism and scientism. Its unabashed and flagrant otherness gives it a power which is lacking in other analytical devices. By playing fast and loose with time and space, logic and morality and by thinking the unthinkable, a utopia asks the most awkward, the most embarrassing questions.
>
> (Geoghegan, 1987: pp. 1–2)

Geoghegan can be seen here to posit an *other* otherness: a utopia, by virtue of its otherness, estranged nature, or profound distance from the present, exists 'outside'. One receives a different perspective when looking in than from being in. This Tom Moylan expresses in terms of 'a dialogue between the world as we know it and the better world that is not yet', which, he claims, constitutes a manifesto of otherness: 'This manifesto of otherness, with its particular systems that mark the uniqueness of each utopian text and carry out the ideological contest in diverse forms, is the commonly accepted *raison d'être* of the utopian narrative' (Moylan, 1986: p. 37). Women, feminist political and social theorists state, subsist on the exterior of patriarchal structures of power and status, be they economic, political or socio-cultural. Woman, psychoanalytic theorists say, is Other, perpetually and by necessity the outsider, despite and because of her position inside the systems by which the masculine self is constructed. Women, woman and femininity as constructed by a masculine economy are outside, 'not-A': not:

> Patriarchy is the practice, phallologocentrism the theory; both coincide, however, in producing an economy, material as well as libidinal, where the law is upheld by a phallic symbol that

operates by constructing differences and organizing them hierarchically. A dialectic of one/other is thus established, which organizes the sexes in a power relation. Through such a dualistic grip on the question of difference, patriarchal thought has associated woman with nurture, the body, the physical, as matter to be tamed and domesticated. This stigmatization of woman turns her into an outside, or rather, the borderline image, pointing to the outside of the cultural and symbolic order.

(Braidotti, 1991: p. 213)

In my reading, then, utopian estrangement can be linked to the positioning of Woman/women in (Western) patriarchal culture and society. This can be related to my arguments in chapters above regarding the femininity of utopianism. Fundamentally, though, this critique not only expresses women's Otherness but also, by connecting it to utopian tactics of estrangement, gestures towards routes of emancipation. If a woman is outsi'e, and her perception is different from that of the One, or masculine Self, then she can be said to have a different knowledge of reality. This is not a transcendent perspective, but one that is outside the masculine sphere of control/knowledge. Not all women will have the same experiences or perspectives. But perhaps by making Sorties into the mainstream, or by world-travelling, we need not abandon a sense of self but rather can create an-other self/other relation not grounded in arrogant perception, fear of difference, or other manifestations of the adherence to cultural superiority.

In the sections that follow, I propose to explore further feminist (utopian) alternatives to the oppositional Self/Other–same/different relations. Discussion will be broadly divided into those which propose a homogenizing view of the self/other relation and those which promote a heterogeneous view.

HOMOGENIZING VIEWS OF THE SELF/OTHER RELATION

Homogenizing theories of the self/other relation promote a unifying conception. This self is encouraged to view the other as an equal. This is frequently accompanied by a (problematic) association of equality with sameness. Key terms in these critiques are those of affinity, empathy and intimacy.

The work of Carol Pearson provides a useful point of entry into this debate. Pearson's work has already been discussed in Chapter 2. Briefly, though, she indicates a number of common themes in feminist utopian fiction. One of these is a concern with the nature of woman: '[These] novels challenge and correct biases about female "nature". They counter stereotypes by emphasizing women's strength, courage and intelligence' (Pearson, 1981: p. 64). Another, related, theme concerns the relation to the mother: 'In these novels, reclaiming the self is often associated with coming home to mother' (1981: p. 65). She suggests that projected societies in which human relations are thus conceived maintain order by feminine tactics of persuasion rather than force: 'Coming home to the self, then, is based upon an organic, anarchic ethics of growth rather than a dualistic pattern of ownership, denial and repression' (1981: p. 68).

In Chapter 2 I provided a critique of Pearson's analysis in which I questioned its accuracy and found it to be generally overly simplistic. Whilst she does, correctly I believe, identify dualistic relations as providing the basis of oppressive relations between Self and Other, her approach is dangerously essentializing. Further, it relies upon a logocentric notion of the presence or 'reality' of a true feminine/female self that awaits discovery. Mary Daly's work is similarly essentializing and universalist and is, perhaps, exemplary of this approach. Daly seeks in *Gyn/Ecology* (1987) a true, wild, Woman's self, which she perceives to be dormant in women, temporarily pacified by patriarchal systems of domination. The dangers of essentializing 'Woman' were outlined in Chapter 3 above. Briefly, however, essentializing theories are considered to be politically and ideologically dangerous in that a supposedly universal woman's 'nature' is what has traditionally served as a legitimizing strategy for placing women in nurturing, passive roles in the private realm. Banal clichés regarding cavemen and the natural strength (hence superiority) of men are common amongst such discussions of women's 'lib'. Essentializing theories are further perceived as oversimplifying the 'reality' of oppression; they deny the social and cultural inputs to the construction of the self.

Pearson seeks a female subjectivity that is independent of a male point of view/reference. Sally Miller Gearhart takes a similar approach in her utopia: *The Wanderground: Stories of the Hill Women*. Gearhart proposes a society in which contact between men and women is minimal. Women, in *Wanderground*, are defined completely without reference to masculinity. Indeed, men are no longer considered to be of the same species as women (Gearhart, 1979: p. 125). Relations between women in this imaginary society cannot, in accuracy, be expressed in terms of S/self and O/other, as there is no real differentiation between them. The women are intimately connected through telepathy, and one therefore knows the other as one knows oneself: this is the Utopia of Gearhart's utopia. There is no trace of individualism in this society.

The issues of intimacy and knowledge are raised by Iris Marion Young in her critique of the ideal of community and can usefully be applied to Gearhart's world of Wanderground. Community, says Young, privileges face-to-face relations which are not mediated by time and space. Whereas this face-to-face relation may be projectable in a society such as that imagined by Gearhart, it is not representative of contemporary relations between the self and others.

A further point made by Young concerns a certain logocentrism and affinity for unity which are promoted by the ideal of community: 'The ideal of community, I suggest in this chapter, privileges unity over difference, immediacy over mediation, sympathy over recognition of the limits of one's understanding of others from their point of view' (Young, 1990: p. 300). The political implications of this are a suppression of difference and an exclusion of those with whom identification is not possible, and in Chapter 3 I explored the implications of such a move for the feminist movement. Young's analysis is comprehensive and persuasive, linking dualistic hierarchical oppositions to theories of logocentrism. Community, in this critique, is perceived as being opposed, by its advocates, to individualism. The binary nature of such positioning effectively denies the (potential) existence of any other alternatives. Again, I suggest that 'either/or' is not a neutral position. Young finds the communitarian ideal to be totalizing in two further ways. First, it seeks to 'realize the unity of the general will and individual subjectivity', and secondly, it is presented as a telos (or (blueprint) utopia), 'an end to the conflict and violence of human interaction' (Young, 1990: p. 308).

Sally Miller Gearhart's *Wanderground* can, I suggest, be read in these terms. The privileging of face-to-face relations and the assumption of a transparent other and a self-knowing self are, in this setting, not unrealistic, but they work only because of the lack of differentiation between the women. These women have all grown up in the same environment and know no other; there are no significant others who are different. Men and Gentles (men who have forsworn sexual contact with women) are considered a different and inferior species. Hierarchy and exclusion can then be seen to underwrite this apparently egalitarian society. Further, it is possible to argue that these women are *not* actually defined in independence to men. Gearhart's imaginary subjectivity is not the result of a considered analysis of current relations. The position that she imagines has no grounding; there is no such position available, either in conceptual or in material terms. Far better, I suggest, to write from the estranged perspective of the margins than falsely to imagine oneself truly outside, free of culturally determined structuring.[7]

Pearson's essay 'Coming Home' (1981) locates the relation to the mother as a fundamental factor in the unification of the self and other. This is a theme of Caroline Whitbeck's theory of subjectivity. Whitbeck attempts both to challenge and to transgress binary opposition: 'This ontology has at its core a conception of the self–other *relation* that is significantly different from the self–other *opposition* that underlines much of so-called "western thought" ' (Whitbeck, 1989: p. 151). Like Young and others cited above, Whitbeck locates dualistic thought as the source of oppressive relations between Self and Other. Her critique is provocative and interesting, structured initially along lines similar to my own. She locates the Self/Other relation as central to a cluster of binary pairs amongst which are such concepts as theory/practice, culture/nature, spirit/matter, knower/known (Whitbeck, 1989: p. 151). Women, she suggests, have historically been defined in relation to men; masculinity being the point of reference that is endowed with those attributes associated with the conscious and rational (hence human) self. Her aim is to develop a non-dualistic, non-oppositional conception of the subject. She attempts, in other words, to provoke a paradigm shift in our consciousness of this relation that can be said to be utopian.

A point of divergence between Whitbeck's approach and my own is located in her attempt to move towards this new conception though privileging a certain type of practice which she describes as 'the (mutual) realization of people' (1989: p. 52). This mutual realization she locates in what has traditionally been women's work, such as child-rearing, and is based on an affinity for sameness.

Whitbeck stresses relationship over opposition and develops an ethics of responsibility which contrasts with the individualistic ethics of rights advocated by liberalism.[8] (This privileging and contrasting of one view over/to another does not, however, escape a methodology of binary opposition.) The development of a sense of self is, according to Whitbeck, dependent on one's relations with others:

What I call the 'responsibilities view' of ethics takes the moral responsibilities arising out of a relationship as the fundamental moral notion, and regards people as beings who can (among other things) act for moral reasons and who come to this status through relationships with other people.

Since the fulfilment of the responsibilities for the welfare of others attends one's relationships to them it is essential to the maintenance of moral integrity, each person's moral integrity is integrally related to the maintenance of the moral integrity of others. Thus, on this view, their self interest is not something that can be neatly separated from the interests of others.

(Whitbeck, 1989: pp. 66, 67)

The central weakness of Whitbeck's thesis is not her adherence to the ideal of community, although the article could be effectively criticized in such terms. Rather, it lies in her redefinition of the self/other relation in terms of an affinity that is rooted in sameness:

The ontology is based on an understanding of the relation of self and other as a relation between analogous beings. The nature and extent of the analogy is something to be determined in each case. Therefore, the distinction between the self and an other does not turn on construing the other as opposite; another distinct being may, and usually does, possess some of the same characteristics as the self.

(Whitbeck, 1989: p. 68)

This, I suggest, is not so very different from the Self/Other relation that Whitbeck is trying to subvert. Affinity or recognition of similarity is at the base of present relations. Whitbeck stresses relation over opposition, but what of those to whom the One or self bears no resemblance?

Further, by what criteria is such resemblance to be judged? The most obvious criterion is that of physical appearance. The following passage would appear to bear out this assumption in a rather slippery re-reading of Freud:

I read the girl's development as follows: girls form their self-concepts in large part through identification with their first significant other(s) who share the same socially defined possibilities of a female body. As a result, the self–other distinction is neither symbolised by a distinction between the sexes, nor does it involve the assumption that the self and other possess opposing characteristics.

(Whitbeck, 1989: p. 62)

The latter half of this assertion is grounded in Whitbeck's belief that 'gender is neither taken to be, nor to be symbolic of, an important ontological difference' (1989: p. 51). Even so, I do not find the statement regarding the girl's affinity to a female sexed other and that regarding a gender-free distinction to be coherently connected. I would suggest rather that even if this reading of Freud is accepted as accurate, the self/other distinction must still be symbolized by a distinction between the sexes. If, as Whitbeck states, the little girl finds her significant others to be analogous beings by virtue of their femininity (female body, socially defined), then the self/other relation is indeed gendered, albeit on the basis of an affinity to sameness.

For all the problems in her approach, Whitbeck is, I believe attempting to create a female-centred sense of subjectivity, one that does not rely upon a masculine point of reference. A utopian theorist with a similar goal is Mary Daly, whose work was mentioned above. Daly proposes that the way to escape patriarchal colonization of our (female) minds is through a woman-centred journey of introspection:

> Journeying centerward is Self-centering movement in all directions. It erases implanted pseudodichotomies between the self and 'other' reality, while it unmasks the unreality of both 'self' and 'world' as these are portrayed, betrayed, in the language of the father's foreground.

(Daly, 1987: p. 6)

For Daly the perceived self is a social and patriarchal construct. In challenging the 'reality' of the world (internal and external), she is attempting to unmask other realities, possibilities and perceptions; attempting, in other words, to provoke a profoundly utopian shift in consciousness.

An element of this process, this progress towards the self, is attention to the other in such a way as to challenge the Self/Other dichotomy. The following extracts are illustrative of Daly's proposals regarding a new unity of self and other. She begins by outlining how, in her analysis, a uniform identity is externally imposed and internalized on to women:

> The daughter is turned against her mother, the pseudosister is the re-sister of her Sister, standing against her. As her re-sister

188

she is a reversed imitation, a mirror image, her 'life-like' reproduction. She covers and re-covers the Sister until she can no longer find her Self, having forgotten to search for her Self. Trapped into re-searching she finds only the re-sister.

(Daly, 1987: p. 338)

Competitive or hostile relations between women, then, for Daly constitute the right conditions for the patriarchal 'reprogramming' of self-perceptions. It runs something like this: the daughter is confronted with the mother, a woman, whose identity she, the daughter, rejects but eventually absorbs. The *real* innate self or subjectivity of the daughter and mother are buried in this process. Daly continues the above passage thus:

In order to search for the Sister it is necessary to see the dis-membered Sister within, the Sister Self, and to re-member her, coming into touch with the original intuition of integrity. Once mindful of the Sister, the Self need no longer resist her, her mind is full of her. She IS her. She is her Self. Re-membering is the remedy.

(1987: p. 338)

In ways that are reminiscent of Sally Miller Gearhart's *Wander-ground*, the women of Mary Daly's utopian vision know each other, literally, inside out. Intimacy, affinity and identity are the keywords here. These women are essentially the same, knowable to the extent of identity. There is, within Daly's vision, an underlying assumption that the self is immanent, dormant and awaiting recovery. Her work is quite flamboyantly essentialist and, as such, universalizes the Nature of Woman. Regardless of the dubious desirability of such intimacy or melding of identities, it is unlikely, given the complexities of modern life, that the Self we may find awaiting us in the other is one with which we feel identity and affinity. Affinity based upon identity can only, I suggest, be divisive along the lines of sameness and difference discussed above.

As they stand, the analyses of Whitbeck and Daly are divisive along lines of gender: this O/other (who is the same) to which they refer may be related to in a non-competitive, non-dualistic fashion, but what of those who are different? The dangers of analyses grounded in biolo-gism were touched upon in Chapter 3, and if nothing else, they can be argued to pave the way for a racially divided society. These schemas are eventually hierarchical and dualistic, even if the loading of values is shifted to favour feminine principles. They fail, in other words, to transgress and undermine the framework through which these concepts and relations are constructed.

Whitbeck attempts, unsuccessfully, to distinguish between difference and differentiation. Her failure can be accounted for partly by the fact that she does not explore the historico-cultural functions of the same/difference dualism, and hence she adheres to the desire for a relation based on recognition of sameness. In Chapter 3 I introduced feminist debates regarding a conception of difference that does not rest upon binarity. It is at this point that some discussion of the theorization of heterogeneous relations of self to other becomes pertinent.

HETEROGENEOUS SELF/OTHER RELATIONS

I have described in previous chapters the discernible move in the utopianism of contemporary feminism towards a more open and shifting conception of the future. A central tactic and theme of this is, I have argued, a certain attitude towards difference and binarity. Whitbeck's work is exemplary of an unsuccessful attempt to move beyond opposition; unsuccessful because of its affinity to sameness. The bulk of the utopian literature and theory researched for this book focuses on and celebrates difference in a more radical and successful way that is multiple, non-restrictive and, as suggested in Chapters 3 and 4, feminine in a non-essentialist way. I shall be suggesting that heterogeneous approaches to the self/other relation are representative of the transgressive utopianism formulated in earlier chapters.

The oppositional Self/Other relation is, I have argued, fundamental to Woman's constitution as Other and to women's exclusion from access to political power. In the discussion that follows, I explore suggested routes to emancipation which favour a heterogeneous relation between self and other. An approach which favours heterogeneity is linked in the discussions that follow to those in earlier chapters regarding Hélène Cixous's conception of an alternative feminine economy.

Relations to the other in this utopian economy of cultural and social exchange are characterized by a non-possessive attitude: a letting go of the notion of property and the desire to possess; a shift from the position in which naming is claiming; which, I have argued, can be found in those utopian texts which do not blueprint (name/claim) the future. In the first instance, then, this section represents further interpretation and expansion of Cixous's ideas.

On my own reading of Cixous, she places the Self/Other relation in a central position regarding other pairs of binary oppositions. This is a contestable reading, as Cixous is more normally read as placing man/ woman in the centre.[9] However, not, I suggest, until the self/other relation is reconciled in some way can the oppositional relations between other concepts such as Man/Woman, masculine/feminine and black/white be transgressed and repositioned. The oppositional Self/ Other relation underlies all oppositional human relations:[10]

Other Love. – In the beginning are our differences. The new love dares for the other, wants the other, makes dizzying, precipitous flights between knowledge and invention. The woman arriving over and over again does not stand still; she's everywhere, she exchanges, she is the desire-that-gives. (Not enclosed in the paradox of the gift that takes nor under the illusion of unitary fusion. We're past that.) She comes in, comes-in-between herself and me and you, between the other me where one is always infinitely more than one and more than me, without the fear of ever reaching a limit; she cuts through defensive loves, motherages, and devourations: beyond selfish narcissism, in the moving, open, transitional space, she runs her risks.

(Cixous, 1981a: pp. 263–4)

Her starting point, then, is that of difference; of 'our differences', she says, which, thus phrased, does not limit difference to externality and the other but can also, I believe, be read as incorporating our internalized differences: the differences within the self. This self is not transparent, all-knowing or intimate. Loving the other is a vertiginous and never-ending *process*, knowledge is never fully acquired; possession of the other is never achieved because knowledge is not equated with possession and naming is not claiming. The concept of possession does not inform this economy. The process is openended. Cixous makes a particularly dense reference in parentheses here to the gift in the masculine economy, and to the construction by such mechanisms of the logocentric fusion of, for instance, Self and Other into a couple (Man/Woman). This woman that is coming (another pun for readers of the English translation, conveying process, progress, potential arrival, and corporeality and sexual pleasure) is the Newly Born Woman of the title of the book (Cixous and Clement 1986) who is coming, or rather comes in the present tense, in an embodiment of Margaret Whitford's conception of the utopia of process:

Feminist utopian visions, then, are mostly of the dynamic rather than the programmatic kind; they do not seek to offer blueprints of an ideal future, still less of the steps to attaining it. They are intended more to bring about shifts in consciousness (paradigm shifts).

(Whitford, 1991a: p. 20)

The Newly Born Woman is constantly (be)coming:

To love, to watch-think-seek the other in the other, to despecularize, to unhoard. Does this seem difficult? It's not impossible, and this is what nourishes life – a love that has no commerce with the apprehensive desire that provides against the lack and stultifies the strange; a love that rejoices in the exchange that multiplies. Wherever history still unfolds as the history of death, she does not tread. Opposition, hierarchizing exchange, the struggle for mastery which can end only in at least one death (one master – one slave, or two nonmaster =/ two dead) – all that comes from a period in time governed by phallocentric values.

(Cixous and Clement, 1986: p. 64)

Here Cixous juxtaposes two ways of thinking, the first of which is her proposed alternative to the second, which, interestingly, she locates in the past tense. The second represents a severely condensed description of a poststructuralist perspective on the structuring of language and the subject/object–Self/Other relation(s). She refers by analogy to the Hegelian dialectic and to dualistic struggles for mastery. Cixous's preferred approach loves without possessing. This economy does not operate in terms of investment, ownership and interest, hence 'unhoard'. This is linked by the term 'despecularize' to a Derridean critique of classification.[11] The desire or love for the other(s) in this economy is overwhelming in its voracity but does not consume. Rather it gives:

She gives more, with no assurance that she'll get back some unexpected profit from what she puts out. She gives that there may be life, thought, transformation. This is an 'economy' that can no longer be put in economic terms.

(Cixous and Clement, 1986: p. 64)

Cixous puts these ideas forward more coherently (with less opacity) in her essay which is translated as 'Castration or Decapitation?':

Women have it in them to organize this regeneration, this vitalization of the other, of otherness in its entirety. They have it in them to affirm their difference, *their* difference, such that nothing can destroy that difference, rather that it might be affirmed, affirmed to the point of strangeness. So much so that when sexual difference, when the preservation or dissolution of sexual difference, is touched upon, the whole problem of destroying the strange, destroying all forms of racism, all exclusions, all those instances of outlaw and genocide that recur throughout history, is also touched on.

(Cixous, 1981b: p. 50)

Some cautious points of clarification need to be made regarding this passage. Women, for instance, are said to have the capacity to accomplish this new relation not because of any innate superiority to men, or because of any essentializing valorization of women such as that undertaken by Mary Daly. Rather it is because, Cixous asserts, women, by virtue of their historical exclusion from the power to possess, have a closer relation to libidinal femininity than do most men.

This may, then, be non-essentialist in terms of sexual gender, but Cixous does appear at points like this to verge on a universalist (hence essentializing?) reading. She suggests that women have a common experience of exclusion (from access to the power to possess). This could easily and logically lead to a position similar to that taken by Whitbeck: a position in which the category of women depends on recognition of sameness. But libidinal femininity is, in part, characterized by a willingness to let go, to take risks and to play fast and loose with security. I believe that Cixous, understood in these terms, can be seen to express a position similar to that proposed in Chapter 3: that women should and can *let go* of the desire to classify and to categorize. The words chosen by Cixous to describe this new relation, those of regeneration and vitalization, are words of life and energy, and they contrast with the masculine relation, which thrives on death and stagnation.

That which is destroyed in Cixous's reconceptualization of the relation is not the strange as such, not the stranger or different one. Rather it is the category or construct of strangeness and its accompanying baggage of fear, threat and danger, as embodied in xenophobia; hence the reference to racism. Cixous should not, I suggest, be read as affirming that sexual difference is the root of all oppression, as does, for example, Shulamith Firestone (1971) in her extension of the concept of sex–class. Rather, I suggest, it is the nature of the Self/Other relation – same and different, known and strange – which constructs hierarchies of inclusion/exclusion:

> Finally, each would take the risk of *other*, of difference, without feeling threatened by the existence of an otherness, rather, delighting to increase through the unknown that there is to discover, to respect, to favour, to cherish.
>
> (Cixous and Clement, 1986: p. 78)

Cixous places an intrinsic value on difference which can and should, she suggests, be recognized as such, loved as such, and learnt from.

Cixous's work on the Self/Other–self/other relations is profoundly utopian in all senses, and it is with these ideas in mind that I now return to Iris Marion Young's vision of the ideal city. Young's picture is hopeful, optimistic and rooted in historical givens: it aims at 'making something good from many elements of the given' (Young, 1990: p. 317). The good which she sees in the contemporary city is its 'energy, cultural diversity, technological complexity and the multiplicity of its activities' (1990: p. 317).[12] The city also provides anonymity for those deemed deviant, such as lesbian women and gay men.

The preconditions assumed by Young in her search for the unoppressive city are a level of productivity capable of meeting everyone's needs and a clean urban environment. She further assumes meaningful work for those who can work and dignity for those who cannot. Within this setting (again, utopian in all senses), Young projects a new relationship between people(s). The city, she says, already embodies inexhaustible difference in both its structure and its populace. It is a place of strangeness and of strangers in which 'Otherness' is *o*therness: 'They are externally related, they experience each other as other, different, from different groups, histories, professions, cultures, which they do not understand' (1990: p. 318). The potential for the kind of inexhaustible relation to the other to which Cixous refers is embodied in Young's ideal of the city: 'The unoppressive city is thus defined as openness to unassimilated otherness' (1990: p. 319).

For Young, public spaces such as city parks are places in which one can observe the other and remain a stranger. She is aware that the city park is at present the site of violent relations to the other: 'Of course, we do not have such openness to difference in our current social relations. I am asserting an ideal, which consists in a politics of difference' (1990: p. 319). The way to a politics of difference which embodies justice, respect and the absence of oppression is, for Young, possible first through giving political representation to group interests and secondly through celebrating the distinctive cultures and characteristics of these groups.

Young's work is interesting and provocative and has much common ground with that of Cixous. In order not to oppress the other, for example, we must greet it *as* other and learn to know it, not to assimilate it. This approach to the other is non-possessive. The relation is not grounded in sameness: neither Young nor Cixous assumes a transparent, self-knowing Self or Other. It is rooted rather in a new attitude towards difference, similar, I think, to that towards which Caroline Whitbeck attempts to work.

A further, but less complex, example of a heterogeneous approach to the Self/Other–self/other relation that is linked to the conception of an opaque self is Ann Ferguson's (1989) Aspect Theory. Ferguson rejects theories of difference on the grounds that they are static and essentialist. She refers, however, in her analysis to the Anglo-American radical feminist theoreticians of difference of the 1970s rather than to those presently under discussion. The Aspect Theory rejects a static model of subjectivity and a unified notion of consciousness, focusing rather on progress and change. She says, for instance, of gender determinism:

> If the self is seen as having many aspects, then it cannot be determined universally which are prior, most fundamental, or more or less authentic. Rather, aspects of our selves are developed by participating in social practices that insist on certain skills and values. Furthermore the *contents* of masculinity and femininity vary with the social practices they are connected to.
>
> (Ferguson, 1989: pp. 101–2)

Ferguson's imagery is evocative of that of Maria Lugones's (1989) 'world travelling' (discussed above), in which the self is transformed according to its environment. Further, it bears some resemblance to Elizabeth Spelman's notion of multiple genders (Spelman, 1990). Ferguson, though, is quite explicit about her goal, which is to 'degenderize' every aspect of social life. Only then, she believes, can personal empowerment be dissociated from gender-bound expectations: 'Only this can empower women to develop our potentials as unique individuals not constrained by social definition that sees our essential nature to be to serve men' (Ferguson, 1989: p. 104).

This reads like a manifesto for androgyny or sameness, but can also, I suggest, be read as a manifesto for difference. Ferguson's own intent is not clear and either interpretation is, I believe, viable. Marge Piercy's *Woman on the Edge of Time* (1979), for instance, degenderizes social and biological activities. In this world, men can have breast implants to enable them to breast-feed children. Mattapoissett is still, however, a society of difference. Whilst men and women are people, the pronouns 'he' and 'she' being replaced by the universally applicable 'per', they are also still men and women, distinct from each other as such in physical terms. Are they then the same or different? Both, I suggest, and neither and more. Binarity is transgressed.

In a way that can cautiously be said to be similar, Hélène Cixous advocates bisexuality as a route through the mind/body divide. This position of bisexuality is not, however, dyadic. Bisexuality in Cixous's reading cannot be reduced to either a state of physical androgyny or a particular sexual preference. Rather it is a state of body *and* of mind which allows visitation of the other:

> And it's this being 'neither out nor in', being 'beyond the outside/inside opposition' that permits the play of 'bisexuality'. Female sexuality is always at some point bisexual. Bisexual doesn't mean, as many people think, that she can make love with both a man and a woman, it doesn't mean that she has two partners, even if it at times means this. Bisexuality on an unconscious level is the possibility of extending into the other, of being in such a relation with the other that *I* move into the other without destroying the other: that I will look for the other where s/he is without trying to bring everything back to myself.
>
> (Cixous, 1981b: p. 54)

For Luce Irigaray, too, feminine sexuality is always multiple. She perceives there to be at least two sets of interests in culture: one of which, the masculine, dominates the O/other by assuming the authority of representation. She seeks autonomy for the feminine. The scope of her project is described succinctly here by Elizabeth Grosz:

> For women to be accorded autonomy as women, the entire social fabric requires major reorganisation: only *half* the possibilities, the alternatives, world-views, interests (at best) gain social

expression or recognition. Half of heaven, half of earth, half of creativity and history is yet to be developed.

(Grosz, 1989: p. 179)

Like Cixous, Irigaray seeks a space in which to imagine and express that which is excluded and silenced by phallocentric practices. She too seeks a utopian space. The area of Irigaray's work which addresses the concerns of this chapter is related to the conception of an ethics of alterity.

The concept of alterity upon which Irigaray works is rooted in the work of the Judaic scholar Emmanuel Levinas. The term 'alterity' has its etymological roots in the Latin 'alter', meaning other. Grosz defines alterity thus:

> A form of otherness irreducible to and unable to be modelled on any form of projection of or identification with the subject. The term refers to a notion of the other outside the binary opposition between self and other, an independent and autonomous other with its own qualities and attributes. The other is outside of, unpredictable by and ontologically prior to the subject.
>
> (Grosz, 1989: p. xiv)

This conception of the other is autonomous, independent of the subject, the One. Further, it is embodied. An other not constructed by reference to sameness, as prior to the subject, is alterity embodied: 'The alterity of the Other does not depend on any quality that would distinguish him from me, for a distinction of this nature would precisely imply between us that community of genus which already nullifies alterity' (Levinas, 1961: p. 194). This conception is profoundly transgressive of binary opposition and can, I suggest, be read as expressing a desire for difference *as* difference, similar to that touched upon in Chapter 3. The fundamental differences between this conception of alterity and that of Otherness conceived of in binary terms are that, for Levinas, the other is autonomous; the other is prior to the subject or self.

Grosz outlines four characteristics of alterity:

> First, it is a form of *exteriority*, separate from and unpredicted by the subject. The other *astonishes* and fills the subject with wonder and surprise. Second, alterity is the site of *excess*, an unabsorbable, indigestible residue the subject is unable to assimilate to itself.... Third, alterity is an *infinite* category: by this Levinas means that it exceeds all boundaries, borders, constraints and

197

limitations which the subject attempts to impose on it. Fourth, alterity is conceived by Levinas as an *activity*, in relation to which the subject is passively positioned.... In short, the other calls, beckons, summons up the subject.

(Grosz, 1989: p. 142)

Femininity, as theorized in this book, is also a form of exteriority. Femininity is also excessive and transgressive. The form of utopianism which I identify as feminine is a transgressive, infinite and active genre. It is transgressive in the senses outlined in these latter chapters: of binarity, of the Self/Other relation, of the mind/body divide, of social and scholastic conventions. It is infinite in the sense of its multiple, openended nature and approach to constructing alternative ways of living and being. It is active, first in the sense that its function is to challenge and transform perceptions of the present and of what is conceivable and possible, and secondly with regard to the nature of the texts under discussion. Reading these texts is not a passive experience; rather it is one of engagement. This move towards an active reading is provoked in some cases and forced in others by the density and complexity of their chosen style.

The understanding of alterity briefly outlined above is thoroughly fitting for transgressive feminist utopianism. Luce Irigaray explores the possibility of a new conception of the Self/Other relation in much of her recent writing. Her work on the elemental and the angel, which are transgressive of the mind/body divide, is rooted in this project and similarly should be considered within this context:

Let them have oneness, with its prerogatives, its domination, its solipsisms: like the sun. Let them have their strange division by couples, in which the other is the image of the one, but an image only. For them, being drawn to the other means a move towards one's mirage: a mirror that is (barely) alive. Glacial, mute, the mirror is all the more faithful.... We have been destined to reproduce – that sameness in which, for centuries, we have been the other.

(Irigaray, 1980: p. 11)

CONCLUSION

In my reading, the crucial tenet of the radical feminism of difference is the idea that the self-legitimation of the One rests on the exclusion of the Other, that the transcendental masculine narcissism feeds on the exclusion and fragmentation of the feminine. . . . In this framework, this infernal logic of domination by symbolic disqualification – the triumph of the One over the Other – cannot be remedied by a straight reversal of the balance of power that would counter the game of self-affirmation and the space of the projection of the One in favour of the Other. This reversal would in fact leave the dialectical opposition intact: one must tackle the very structures of the framework, not its propositional contents, in order to overcome the power relations that sustain it.

(Braidotti, 1991: pp. 213–14)

And that is what this chapter has attempted: an undermining and exposure of the structures of the framework of relations of domination with the exploration and creation of utopian theoretical alternatives. I have examined the binary, oppositional, hierarchical and competitive nature of the Self/Other relation, locating it firmly within logocentric and phallocentric symbolic orders of language. It has been argued that a logic of negativity or negation propels this relation, in that the One is dialectically opposed to the Other. The mechanics of exclusion are identified as consisting at least in part in the opposition of the universal to the particular, and the (cultural) positioning of the different, or Other, as outsider, excluded and estranged.

A utopia, it has been argued, provides a particularly useful vantage point from whence to (re)view the concept of estrangement and Otherness. The construction of Otherness is a result of an internal/external play in which one is estranged from the self through such means as that which Hélène Cixous calls the 'dark continent trick'. Thus the perception of Otherness is internalized.

Feminist attempts to provide unifying or homogenizing conceptions of the self/other relation are criticized above largely in terms of their logocentrism and affinity to sameness. Such theories, it is argued, do not challenge the structure of the framework of domination; rather, they remain enclosed within it.

Instead, this chapter has privileged a multiple or heterogeneous theorization of the self/other relation, in which the self and other are not perceived in unity. This relation has been characterized as non-possessive, non-acquisitive, open and able to let go. As such it is transgressive of the above analysis. It risks the other, encountering strangeness without fear.

A final example from feminist utopianism of a transgressive, feminine relation to the other is found in Michèle Roberts's *The Book of Mrs Noah*:

> The Ark of Women is the Other One. *The Salon des Refusées. Des Refusantes.* Cruise ship for females who are only fitted in as monsters: the gorgons, the basilisks, the sirens, the harpies, the furies, the viragos, the amazons, the medusas, the sphinxes.
>
> (Roberts, 1987: pp. 19–20)

Mrs Noah is the 'arkivist' of the Ark; she collects the stories, thoughts and creations of women. Her own story, a retelling of that of Noah, is a new story of creation and naming. Mrs Noah's daughter-in-law says: 'I want a daughter, she says: I'll love her properly. The way no one loves me. And then I'll let her leave me. I know it's got to happen' (1987: p. 81). Mrs Noah imagines a new world:

> A childish vision, impossible, I know that. I fill it with people who are as fluid as water, flowing past each other in peace and letting each other alone....
>
> For the rest of the night I wrestle with words, trying to find new ones. The names are a string with which I tie together my understanding of the God I know in this new creation, my way of connecting us all with each other and with God, humans and animals and birds and plants, none of us superior to the others however different we may look. Naming the names is a form of worship.
>
> (1987: pp. 82, 86)

Taken together, these passages express a desire for non-possessive and non-acquisitive relations to the other; relations in which difference is not feared or viewed with arrogant perception. Roberts attempts this through a new understanding of what it is to name. She names as an expression of wonder rather than one of possession. The placing of concepts in her framework is not hierarchical; rather it shows interdependence. This, I think, is an expression of greeting the other *as other* in a way similar to that theorized by Irigaray, Cixous and Young. These new ways of approaching the other are made possible by transgressive utopianism, which disrupts the opposition of self to other.

7

FEMINIST UTOPIAN TRANSGRESSION OF CODES AND GENRE

INTRODUCTION

I have suggested that feminist utopian expression is significantly deviant from the utopianism of perfection assumed by some content-based approaches. I have further suggested new ways in which we might apply theories of multiplicity to the body of contemporary feminist utopianism in order to make intelligible these moves towards an openended conception of the future and the present within the context of the complex and shifting nature of contemporary feminism itself. I have, in other words, indicated some of the ways in which my approach to utopianism might be said to be best for the 'now' of contemporary feminism.

The purpose of this chapter is to consider how and why feminist utopian texts of and since the 1970s have challenged and transgressed various aspects of social order. The structure of this chapter is determined by recurrent themes within feminist utopian literature; the theories presented are drawn from the fictional representations of women's desire for different (and better) ways of being: utopias. Discussion will be broadly divided into the following areas: transgression of stereotypes and codes of social normality such as gender, sex and the nuclear family; transgression of the concept of order itself, both sequential (linear time) and stable (truth and reality are challenged); and finally the issue of order as a form or mode of expression in consideration of genre and narrative convention. The ordering of society in feminist utopianism is found to be markedly different from that of the present. Evidence is offered to supplement that of earlier chapters that multiplicity is the mark of the contemporary text, and that this multiplicity is rooted in a rejection of dualistic and hierarchical thought.

TRANSGRESSION OF STEREOTYPES AND CODES OF SOCIAL NORMALITY

Traditionally, theories of social order tend to rest upon essentialist notions of human nature and to stereotype[1] or normalize ideals of human behaviour. The imaginative construction of the essence of humanity is commonly based on a cluster of dualisms, the function of which is to separate mankind conceptually from the animals, culture from nature. One device by which this has been attempted is that of the state of nature which imagines a (hypothetical) state in which 'man' (sic) is without government or civil society. Common themes of state-of-nature theories of human nature are an assertion of the rationality of man; the assumption of his capacity to self-improve morally or materially; and the privileging of self-interest as a primary motivating force for rational action.

In Chapter 3, I examined feminist suspicions of this approach on the grounds that it tends to establish a hierarchy of humanity, with some being considered less rational and less able to improve morally than others, by virtue of an underwritten association of the highly valued attributes with masculinity, the mind and the spirit. For my present purposes, however, it is sufficient to note the importance of this tradition in Western thought and its influence on the ideologies of liberalism and conservatism in particular.[2]

Utopian feminist responses to this tradition of essentialism vary. Most tend to focus on what could be seen to be the symptoms of an ideologically constructed society in which male and female roles are ordered according to this matrix. Some tackle the theoretical roots of patriarchal society head on: Angela Carter provides an example. Most of her work is outside of the field of utopia, but (as discussed briefly in Chapter 1) two of her books, *The Passion of New Eve* (1982) and *Heroes and Villains* (1969), can, I suggest, be firmly located within feminist utopianism. Read together, these texts provide an excellent example of satirical utopianism.

Heroes imagines two societies, those of the Barbarians and the Professors, which respectively provide an ironic perspective on the constructs of the Noble Savage and the Rational Society. The Barbarians are savage in many senses; they are, for instance, fierce and cruel, as befits the post-apocalyptic environment in which they exist. Further, they are adorned with beads and tattoos, as befits the standard imagery of a savage tribe. The stereotype of primitivism is, however, challenged by Carter, as these representatives of barbarians

202

are neither simple-minded, nor innocent in Rousseau's sense. The reader is jolted from complacency by the Barbarian Jewel's Tennysonian reference: 'It's the same everywhere you look, it's red in tooth and claw' (Carter, 1969: p. 18). The rational world of the Professors is cold and sterile, regulated strictly by time and rank. It is not an ideal any more than is its irrational counterpart.

Nan Bowman Albinski (1988) makes the interesting point that the constructs which Carter parodies and satirizes in *Heroes* are themselves of a utopian nature. *The Passion of New Eve* can, as suggested in Chapter 1, be read as an extension of this double move of satirizing. It is a satire in two senses: it establishes utopian/dystopian societies from whence to satirize the social norms of the present, and it also satirizes the concept of perfection or eutopia. As is the case elsewhere in Carter's fictions, the first person singular in *New Eve* is a man. This man is Evelyn, who is impassioned by Tristessa, a star of classic films. A primary plot of the book is concerned with desire: Evelyn's desire drives him through the book and is eventually sated when he meets Tristessa. A sub-plot is the transgression of sexuality and of the construct of gender. Evelyn becomes Eve after becoming the involuntary subject of a medical experiment by a matriarchal sect, whose members plan to impregnate him with his own semen. By the time he meets Tristessa, he is a woman. The resolution is convoluted, as Tristessa is a man, a transvestite who has parodied feminine beauty. A further and accompanying sub-plot is the satire of matriarchal society, as well as that of patriarchy. Carter challenges the concept of an ideal or perfect resolution to history. Rather, her texts privilege turbulent, unexpected and often violent transgression of those values which represent normality, constantly shaking the reader from complacency, replacing stability with a vertiginous uncertainty.

Carter tends to privilege sexual desire as the primary transgressive force and drive.[3] Sarah Lefanu has commented on this: 'Social codes fall before the imperative of desire. Sexuality, in all of Carter's work, is presented in terms of fragmentation and chaos. Her work is gloriously protean, counterposing realism with counter-realism, modernity with ancient magic' (Lefanu, 1988a: p. 79). Carter's texts are, I find, unique in their capacity to tear apart the foundations of reality with such vicious and disturbing force. Other writers, however, achieve similar ends, with different impacts and implications. Carter's style is fierce and witty and quite profoundly destructive in its upending of the symbolic order of values. Other writers offer more hopeful and, arguably, more politically useful visions of ways in which prevalent social orders might be transformed.

A common theme of feminist utopian literature (and theory) is that of the transgression of gender roles and stereotypes. Marge Piercy, for instance, in *Woman on the Edge of Time* (1979), portrays a eutopian society in which work in the public and private realms is not gender-specific; men and women, for instance, nurture, design and control technology.[4] A similar picture is sketched in Letty Cottin Pogrebin's short story: 'Born Free: A Feminist Fable' (Pogrebin, 1974). The challenging of gender stereotypes is most often attempted through the narrative device of contrasting worlds within one text. Marion Zimmer Bradley's Darkover series exemplifies this practice. In *Thendara House* (1983), for instance, the worlds of Darkover and Terran are contrasted. Terran might, at a superficial level at least, be taken as a feminist eutopia. It is a democratic society in which the dominant culture does not recognize biology as a strictly socializing force. Darkoveran culture, in contrast, is structured according to traditional gender roles, which are reinforced by a caste-type system of social ordering through feudal hierarchy. In the Dry Towns, where Jaelle (one of the central characters) was born, for instance, women are the chattels of men, kept in chains. The Thendara Guild House is a training establishment for and of Amazon renunciates. That which the Amazon sect renounce is the protection of men (the expected return for which is a submissive relation). The oath begins thus: 'From this day I renounce the right to marry save as a freemate; no man shall bind me *di catenas* and I will dwell in no man's house as a *barragana*' (Bradley, 1983: p. 65).

The story is centred partly at least on Jaelle, a Free Amazon, and Magda, a Terran. These women move into each other's cultures as envoys and observers. Magda's position is ambivalent, as her brief is to gather information for the Terran authorities. She identifies with the Amazon culture and a sub-plot is her desire (and failure) to 'fit' into either culture. Through the more or less estranged eyes of these two women, the conclusion is reached that in neither society are women autonomous or free:

'In the Terran Zone, a woman is not her freemate's property, not in law,' Jaelle said, 'but there is something in a man which seems to drive him to *possess*. I never knew this existed before.'

Magda: 'I think it is a game they like to play with us, possession. They like to think they own us; they know they do

not and it makes them insecure. Women do not – do not suffer so
much from separation as men do.'

(Bradley, 1983: p. 176)

The works of Marion Zimmer Bradley are not generally considered
to be highbrow literature and, consequently, the seriousness of
any political message that they might contain tends to be missed by
commentators.[5] However, the sentiments expressed in *Thendara House*
are similar to those discussed in chapters above. The drive to possess
can be read as belonging to a masculine economy, by which social and
cultural exchange is ordered and motivated in the apparently egalitarian society of Terra. Magda is, after all (albeit reluctantly), a spy;
Terra desires knowledge and control of Darkover and particularly of
the sect described as the Sisterhood, whose telepathic 'Laran' has
healing and cohesive properties. These are an elusive group who
represent and protect the soul of Darkover, the nature of which is not
acquisitive or interventionist: representatives perhaps of a feminine
economy?

Another utopian novel in which social orders are contrasted is Joan
Slonzcewski's *A Door Into Ocean* (1987). Again, the contrast is
heightened by the utopian tactic of estrangement in the forms of
the figures Merwen, Usha, Spinel and Bernice. Spinel and Bernice
come from the respective planets Iridis and Valedon, both of which are
under the 'protectorate' of the Patriarch.[6] Merwen the Impatient and
Usha the Inconsiderate are from Shora, a planet of water which the
Patriarch's envoy intends to colonize, and from which he hopes to gain
access to certain mystical skills in healing. Not much is told of Iridis
except that it is a centre of administration. Valedon is described as
strictly policed and, like Darkover, is ordered by a caste-type system
according to a hierarchical system of work and labour. Spinel is
effectively sold by his parents to the Shorans and goes with them, not
unwillingly, to their planet. Bernice's position is similar to that of
Magda in *Thendara House*; that of the sympathetic spy in a supposedly
primitive society.

Whereas society in the Protectorates is rigidly ordered along lines
of class and gender, that of Shora is more organic. Connections to the
environment are close; there is no concept of property; even the rafts on
which the Shorans live are constructed of living material and are of a
transitory nature dependent on climate. Shorans are described as
Sharers, and the non-possessive ethics of their culture is echoed in their
language. To wordshare, for instance, is to teach and to learn, to speak

is also to listen, and all words contain a sense of their inverse meaning. In this way, crude binarism is transgressed. Shora is an all-female world, and is alien in every sense to those of Spinel and Bernice.

Ironically, the Shoran mission is to ascertain whether or not Valedons are humans with whom they should share their knowledge. Shora privileges life, and whilst life on this planet is dangerous, it is balanced ecologically. When confronted with a mechanical labourer (servitor) and a mechanical vehicle (hovercraft), Merwen and Usha are repulsed: 'Your speech cannot express what Usha thinks of this . . . object, the hovercraft. Like the servitor, it is made of "dead", of "non-life", of material that has never known the breath of life' (Slonzcewski, 1987: p. 37).

The different conceptions of social order offered in both *Thendara House* and *Door* can be translated into two contrasting conceptions of power: power over and power to, the first of which is acquisitive and grounded in appropriation (of autonomy, for instance), while the latter is to do with internal empowerment (individually or by a society). Whilst these two conceptions of power are not necessarily mutually exclusive, they can, I suggest, be read as separate as portrayed in these two novels. Francis Bartowski finds this to be a common distinction made in feminist utopian fiction:

> The feminist utopian novel is a place where theories of power can be addressed through the construction of narratives that test and stretch the boundaries of power in its operational details. Writing from the margins and coming into speech in full knowledge of the abuses of power *over*, feminists have tended to imagine instead about power *to*; they have needed and chosen to take up the materiality of language, in order to install a self as subject, knowing that the self has also been subjected.
>
> (Bartowski, 1989: p. 5)

The establishment of an autonomous identity for women as women is accomplished by Bradley and Slonzcewski in their more or less coherent depictions of the mechanisms of alternative social orders. Both Shoran and Amazonian cultures, however, are all female. The worlds of Joanna Russ's Whileaway, Monique Wittig's Guérillères, Sally Miller Gearhart's Hill Women and Suzy McKee Charnas's Riding Women also represent single-sex cultures. Many of the major texts within contemporary feminist utopianism present cohesive and autonomous, self-defining cultures as separatist to a lesser or greater degree. All contain a material or cultural memory of oppression along gender lines. Shora is, perhaps, an exception to this norm, as the planet seems to have evolved independently of men: 'Only lesser races produce men' (Slonzcewski, 1987: p. 80). This, I suggest, can be connected to the common search for subjectivity and identity as women, and to the renunciation of historico-cultural traditions that have constructed Woman as an artifice to complement (make perfect) Man. This, however, leaves feminist theorists in a dilemma which Margaret Whitford articulates in the passage below. Whitford is speaking with reference to Luce Irigaray, but the sentiment expressed and the dilemma posed are ones that I would suggest are faced by all women who engage in feminist constructive theory:

> Irigaray faces a dilemma which could be defined as follows: on the one hand, as Moi forcefully points out, 'it still remains *politically* essential for feminists to defend women *as* women in order to counteract the patriarchal oppression that precisely defines women *as* women', so to that extent it is necessary to define female specificity; on the other hand, how does one define female specificity without getting locked once again inside the patriarchal metaphysical framework one was trying to escape from?
>
> (Whitford, 1991a: p. 9)

For Hélène Cixous, ontology (asking 'What is it?') is rooted firmly in a masculine economy in which a concept, once named, described and ascribed an essence, becomes part of the dualistic and hierarchical symbolic order of representation. Yet she calls upon women to write woman; to inscribe their sexuality. This raises the familiar problem of the tension between political efficacy and political integrity, a recurrent theme of this book. Some of the texts mentioned above take essentialist stances. Sally Miller Gearhart, for instance, attributes a higher moral status to the Hill Women than to the men of the cities and even the Gentles (sexually unthreatening males) in her *Wanderground* (1979). More common is the avoidance of constructing an artifice of 'Woman' and a focus on women's shared historical experiences as ground for the articulation and affirmation of their status as female subjects. Such approaches shift focus on to 'being as existing' rather than on 'being as essence' or constitution. In other words, sensation is privileged over rationalization. In traditional radical feminist manner, these texts draw theory from experience.

The texts challenge the assumption that the future is fixed by the present, first by challenging the 'reality' of the present and secondly by challenging the concept of unitary, linear and historical 'progress'. A useful way into these debates is through Monique Wittig's treatment of tradition in *Les Guérillères* (1971). Tradition as continuity is given interesting and apparently contradictory treatment by Wittig. *Les Guérillères* is composed of a disjointed narrative with no narrator (no 'I'), of which more later. Many of the distinct paragraphs of which the book is constructed are 'the women's' (Wittig's guerillas) perspectives on the subordination – physical, social and linguistic – of women by men. A theme of these particular sections is the ways in which symbols have served this tradition of dualistic oppression:

> The women say, unhappy one, men have expelled you from the world of symbols and yet they have given you names, they have called you slave, you unhappy slave.... They write, of their authority to accord names, that it goes back so far that the origin of language itself may be considered an act of authority emanating from those who dominate. Thus they say that they have said, this is such or such a thing, they have attached a particular word to an object or a fact and thereby consider themselves to have appropriated it.... They say, the language you speak is made up of words that are killing you.
>
> (Wittig, 1971: pp. 112, 114)

> The women say that they have been given as equivalents the earth the sea tears that which is humid that which is black that which does not burn that which is negative those who surrender without a struggle. They say this is a concept which is a product of mechanistic reasoning. It deploys a series of terms so crass that the thought of them makes the women start laughing violently.
>
> (1971: pp. 79–80)

The women laugh at this and other absurdities. Laughter is a potent weapon of feminist utopianism, used also by Hélène Cixous in her interpretation of the story of Sun Tse (discussed in Chapter 4). The laughter of Wittig's guerillas at one point literally brings the house down around their ears, and it does the same to these cultural artifices: denaturalizing tradition.

The text of *Les Guérillères* is filled with alternative symbolism that positively represents the female body. The women sleep, for instance, in O-shaped cells – the circle permeates the text. Before going to sleep at night the women say 'This order must be changed' (Wittig, 1971: p. 87). It is at this point that Wittig's treatment of tradition (provider of continuity, justificatory strategy for order) steps beyond replacing 'masculine' symbolism with 'feminine' symbolism. It is not the order of their past (our present) which is the subject of the above mantra. Rather, I suggest, it is the notion of order itself that is resisted. Despite the symbolism mentioned above the women reject the idea of privileging the vulva, labia or any other part of the female body. These symbols, they say, were necessary in the past as vehicles of opposition and strength, but serve no further purpose:

> The women say that they perceive their bodies in their entirety. They say that they do not favour any of its parts on the grounds that it was formerly a forbidden object. *They say that they do not want to become prisoners of their own ideology.*
> (Wittig, 1971: p. 57; my emphasis)[7]

For this reason the women burn the Feminaries, books which contain knowledge and history, and favour instead the Register, which is constantly being written and updated. The Register, in my reading, represents the change, flux and process of this society's development. 'They say that they foster disorder in all its forms' (1971: p. 93). Disorder, however, is not fetishized or romanticized; its negative aspects are embraced alongside its more positive elements:

> Confusion troubles violent debates disarray upsets disturbances incoherencies irregularities divergencies complications dis-agreements discords clashes polemics discursions contentions brawls disputes conflicts rants debacles cataclysms disturbances quarrels agitation turbulence conflations chaos anarchy.
> (1971: p. 93)

There is, then, in Wittig's *Les Guérillères*, no creation of a new essence of Woman. The function of the utopian society is that of the dispossession or dislodgement of power from the hands of men – not, however, to erect a new totem of femininity, but to render the concept of power *over* defunct. To paraphrase Cixous, the desire expressed is the one to destroy the space of domination: 'If I take over the world, let it be to dispossess myself of it immediately, let it be to forge new links between myself and the world' (Wittig, 1971: p. 107). Wittig's *Les Guérillères* is a transgressive utopian text. It disrupts and negates binarisms, it rejects a dualistic conceptualization of 'Woman' and/or femininity. Moreover, it celebrates *process*, representing a dynamic and ever-changing society which conceives of itself in new ways that do not rest on old universalisms.

209

TRANSGRESSION OF REALITY AND TRUTH (TIME AND SEQUENTIAL ORDER)

The following passage is from Rosi Braidotti's essay 'The Politics of Ontological Difference' (1989). Braidotti is addressing the question of becoming a woman – 'becoming' rather than 'being' because, she says, thinking about subjectivity and/or identity as a woman must take place in a tense and a sense that are profoundly different from the past/present modes of thought:

> I would like us to adopt a special mode of thinking, trying to leave behind the centuries-old habit that consists of thinking in terms of identity and oppositions, thesis and antithesis. Let us think differently about this, in a mode that I would call, following Irigaray, the conditional present.
>
> If you look back to the early feminist theory of the 1960s and 1970s you could say that it is written in the simple future tense, expressing a deep sense of determination, of certainty about the course of history and the irresistible emancipation of women. The future is the mode of expressing an open-ended game of possibilities: half prophecy and half utopia and, above all, blueprint for action. The conditional mode, however, goes beyond the logic of ideology and of teleological progress. More akin to dreamtime, it is the tense of open potentiality and consequently of desire in the sense of a web of interconnected conditions of possibility. The conditional present posits the continuity of desire as the only unifying agent between self and other, subject and history. Desire determines the ontological plane on which the subject defines her-/him-self. Therefore the conditional is the mode of inscription of desire into the present, in the here and now of our speaking stance.
>
> (Braidotti, 1989: p. 103)

I have quoted this passage in full as Braidotti's implementation of Irigaray's conditional mode is of particular relevance to the question of challenging our perceptions of the material present. It is this shift in what Braidotti calls 'enunciative nuance' (1989: p. 103) that is mobilized in much of the feminist utopian literature discussed in this book. Indeed, I would go further than Braidotti and state that it is a change not just of nuance but of enunciative position. Feminist utopianism challenges the reality and solidity of the present. The sense of disorientation evoked by texts such as those of Angela Carter's

Heroes and Villains (1969) and *The Passion of New Eve* (1982) is, I suggest, a result of the mobilization of a new tense: one that does not allow the present to be read as the logical outcome of the past and from which a similar future will emerge. It is rather a tense, as Braidotti says, of open potentiality. The present itself is not solid or impermeable to infiltration and subversion.

Dorothy Bryant's *The Kin of Ata are Waiting for You* (1971) evokes a sense of dreamtime (discussed in Chapter 6) that can, perhaps, be read through the conditional mode. Bryant's feminism is subsumed in her holistic ecologism: the emancipation of women is not a central theme of this text. The 'hero' is a thoroughly dislikeable character who, during the story, causes the deaths of two people and rapes one of his hosts (a woman). *The Kin of Ata* merges dream with reality on a number of levels. The central character wakes up in Ata after a car accident (fleeing his flat where he has just killed a woman). When, at the end of the story, he returns to his own 'reality', he is unsure whether he ever really left it. The inhabitants of Ata privilege their dream life over their waking one, which they consider to be illusory. Speech is minimal, and dance and song are the preferred modes of everyday communication. Their language is limited in vocabulary but syntactically complex: 'Their verbs lacked tenses – literally, as they spoke, there was no sense of past or future, only of now, the present moment' (Bryant, 1971: p. 50). Speech in Ata is described as fluid; a few words suffice, with meaning varying according to context. The word 'ka', for instance, refers to a dwelling or hut, and to all content and parts therein; a single pronoun refers to all humans, this pronoun being plural or singular according to context. There is no writing or other graphic representation in which this language and culture are enclosed. Their culture is not an inscribed text. Our 'hero' *attempts* to inscribe the ritualistic monologues of the community's history (for posterity) but becomes increasingly frustrated as he realizes that the story varies with the teller. There is, he comes to recognize, no permanence in 'the complex and shifting mythology of Ata'. (1971: p. 164).

Considered in such a way, the dreamtime of the conditional mode is not mere escapism. Rather it has a transformative function. The narrator of *The Kin of Ata* is motivated to change his own perceptions and hence his position in his own reality. A famous writer, almost of cult standing, he could, his lawyer insists, successfully plead not guilty to the charge of murder to which he returns. (The flight from the scene of this crime precipitated his visit to Ata.) Instead he chances death and accepts his guilt. He has, to paraphrase Margaret Whitford, undergone a paradigm shift in consciousness.

Likewise, Connie, in Marge Piercy's *Woman on the Edge of Time* (1979), is motivated by her experience of life in other 'presents' (for neither the eutopia nor the dystopia of *Woman on the Edge* is distanced temporally from her own present in any strict sense) to risk all and challenge the authorities to which she is subject in her own time. Either the eutopia of Mattapoissett or the dystopia *could* exist as the result of her own time, since the future is not fixed and nor, as mentioned above, is the present. Transgression of our acceptance of reality provokes truly openended attitudes towards both the here-and-now and the not-yet.

For Carol Pearson, the strength of some recent science fiction and utopian writing is that its political theory is based on new hypotheses of time and the nature of history. I referred to Pearson's work in Chapter 2 above, but will briefly rehearse the three central points of her thesis here. In the essay 'Of Time and Space: Theories of Social Change in Contemporary Feminist Science Fiction' (1984), she identifies three paradoxical principles drawn from this new theory:

> 1) Time is linear; *and* it is relative. To the degree that we live only in linear time, we are locked into a world governed by laws of causality, dualism, linearity, and struggle. But we also have available to us a reality based upon relativity. In this dimension, time and space are not separate, but time/space is curved. It then becomes possible to understand that we can change not only the future but the past. Such analyses focus on concepts like paradox, synchronicity, responsibility, commitment, and transformation.
>
> (Pearson, 1984: pp. 260–1)

I do not have the time or ability to pursue the branch of theoretical physics from whence these ideas come. Briefly, though, I will attempt a pedestrian explanation by way of illustration. Quantum mechanics, albeit momentarily, shook the certainties of physical science by showing that light, previously considered to be a wave, could, under certain circumstances, behave as a particle. It was thus neither a wave nor a particle, but both or either, depending on circumstance. It transgressed the binary dilemma of either/or. Pearson's reference to time/space curves is connected, in my understanding, to the following idea. If I were to speak to you, even if we were in the same room, by the time the sound of my voice reaches your ears and is transmitted to your brain, the time will be my past, albeit your present. Hence, again, as I understand it, past and present co-exist.

From this, Pearson draws her second and third principles:

2) Although past, present and future co-exist and are equally real in the present, the only point of action in which anything can be changed is in the present. Paradoxically, widespread social change occurs only as a result of the solitary decisions of individuals to step outside linear time into the 'eternal now'. Yet, at the same time, no one moves fully into the new world alone. No one is fully there, until we all are.

3) The move into a new, utopian future occurs when we simultaneously take responsibility for our own lives and relinquish all illusions that we control anything – others, the flow of history, or the effects of our own actions.

(Pearson, 1984: p. 261)

This theory of time can be applied to *Woman on the Edge of Time* and to *The Kin of Ata* – indeed, Pearson herself begins to work in this direction. It can also be couched in the less scientifically complex but perhaps more theoretically difficult terms of the conditional present. (The 'futures' visited by Connie exist in parallel with her own present. Their manifestation is conditional; dependent on her actions.) Indeed, I would suggest that a feminine economy can be seen at work here in the move away from certainty and 'truth' as such, towards a more openended and less acquisitive understanding of ourselves and our relations to others.

TRANSGRESSION OF GENRE AND NARRATIVE CONVENTION

Carol Pearson's comments are directed at the genre of science fiction, within which she identifies utopian traces. Many of the fictional utopian texts under discussion in this book are situated within this genre. The intervention of feminist writers in the genre of science fiction has, it is argued by commentators, significantly changed that genre.

Luce Armitt suggests that science fiction, whilst challenging received notions of reality, has not historically been a progressive genre: 'Unfortunately, irrespective of its superficially futuristic stance, mainstream male-orientated science fiction has traditionally been a genre obsessed with nostalgia and conservatism' (Armitt, 1991: p. 2).

This sentiment is expressed in other feminist commentaries on the genre of science fiction. Hilary Rose, for instance identifies two traditions in mainstream science fiction (Rose, 1988). One she calls the 'technicist' tradition, which is socially unreflecting. The other she finds to be preoccupied with the social implications of science and technology. This second tradition often comes in the form of u/dystopias. Even this tradition Rose finds to be conservative, offering little that is attractive to women. Her perspective is similar to that of Carol Pearson, namely that a text cannot be considered truly eutopian unless it addresses the concerns of all people. She finds that women are often oppressed in men's utopias. The difference, for Rose, that feminist science fiction represents is found in the tension between the conservatism of traditionalist science fiction and the radicalism of women's contributions. Male science fiction perpetuates existing concepts of control (power over), and to an extent the social order in which this is presently manifested; women's science fiction represents active and total revolt against the structuring of the status quo. She cites Luciente from Marge Piercy's *Woman on the Edge of Time* (1979) as most articulately expressing this tension:

> It's that race between technology in the service of those who control, and insurgence – those who want to change society in our direction (Piercy, . . . p. 228).
>
> Because a continuing preoccupation is with the construction of gender and the connections between masculinity and the science and technology of exploitation and control, regardless of political perspective, of whether the writer is realist, post-modernist, or propagandist, the [feminist] novels return again and again to Luciente's crux.
>
> (Rose, 1988: p. 122)

I addressed these issues in greater depth in the chapters above. My current interest is in how these concerns have changed or transgressed the boundaries of the genre of science fiction. For Luce Armitt, one consequence is the heightened degree of utopianism in women's science fiction:

> Women are not located at the centre of contemporary culture and society, but are almost entirely defined from the aforementioned perspective of 'otherness' or 'difference'. As such, the need to *escape from* a society with regard to which they already hold an ex-centric position is clearly an irrelevant one. More appropriate

perhaps is the need to *escape to* – that is, to depict – an alternative
reality within which centrality is possible.

(Armitt, 1991: p. 9)

This leaves utopia in an interesting position from a generic
perspective. Ruby Rohrlich and Elaine Baruch introduce their study
Women in Search of Utopia thus: 'The genres of utopian fiction and
science fiction have long been as different as men and women's
utopias.... Now that more women are writing science fiction, the
boundaries between the genres are becoming fluid' (Rohrlich and
Baruch, 1984: p. xiii). Like Rose, Rohrlich and Baruch identify two
traditions within men's writing. Men's science fiction, they say, has
been traditionally concerned with the uses and abuses of science; men's
utopian fiction has focused on the depiction of alternative social
structures. Feminist science fiction, however, has a more 'human'
edge, putting greater emphasis on characterization, and feminist
utopian fiction often makes use of technology, exploring and testing
the ways in which it might be used to satisfy human needs. As it
stands, this interpretation leans towards simplification, and I propose,
in the discussion that follows, to explore these connections a little
further by reference to the places at which science fiction and
utopianism overlap. I am going to focus, in the first instance, on
two essays written by Anne Cranny Francis, both of which are generic
studies: 'Feminist Futures: A Generic Study' (Francis, 1990b) and
Feminist Utopias (in Francis, 1990a). 'Feminist Futures' is concerned
explicitly with science fiction, in which Francis identifies two broad
trends:

> Like all fictional (sub)genres, science fiction is a composite of
> conventions negotiated by writers and readers with varying
> degrees of orthodoxy. [We can] engage with the contemporary
> articulation of generic conventions in a liberal, non-transgres-
> sive way, so constructing a text which is orthodox – generically,
> and therefore discursively.
>
> (Francis, 1990b: p. 219)

Or, she says, we can challenge the conventions:

> thereby problematising the text and its readings.... Generic
> conventions are themselves, of course, sites of ideological
> contestation; so that when writers engage with the conventions,
> they also necessarily engage in an ideological textual practice.
>
> (1990b: p. 219)

215

The transgression of generic conventions then, for Francis, is not a matter of (political) innocence or coincidence. Rather it is an ideological and hence political practice. The generic form of a text then can be read as a literal manifestation of the transgressive perspective and desire of the writer/reader.

The conventions that Francis identifies as belonging to the genre of science fiction are, first, engagement with and critique of scientific and technological discourses; secondly, the use of narrative strategies of estrangement and displacement in time or space (within recent feminist science fiction this is accomplished through complex narrative strategies); and thirdly, the presence of the alien, whose ideological distance from the found world enables what Francis calls a 're-visioning' of that world (1990b: p. 223).

Under a subtitle 'Generic history of utopian fiction' in the article 'Feminist Futures', Francis outlines the following conventions of the utopian genre: estrangement through the utopian figure; realism, that is, connection of the reader to her/his own society; and the utopian traveller as active subject. I have, in earlier chapters, undertaken closer readings of the conventions of utopianism. This example is, however, illuminating, as the conventions identified by Francis as pertaining to science fiction are not so different from those she finds appropriate to utopia. The boundaries do indeed appear fluid, and utopian thought spills into science fiction and vice versa. If, as Francis suggests, this is the result of active engagement in ideological contestations, then the facts of these transformed boundaries belong to the larger project of feminist utopianism.

Feminist utopianism is transgressive of the boundaries that separate it, as a form of literary expression, from science fiction. This is a fact of transgression in itself. The adoption of conventions of science fiction into utopian writing allows other transgressions. Linear time and reality can, for instance, be undermined by the convention of transgressive narrative technique. Monique Wittig's *Les Guérillères* (1971) is illustrative of this. Divided into discrete paragraphs, the text does not represent a unitary or 'straight'(!) narrative. Interspersed amongst the narrative text are pages of capitalized poems, lists of women's names, and symbols, all of which can, I suggest, be read as regarding the cultural history of the women. Further, the text within the paragraphs is not punctuated according to grammatical norms. The result is that words and concepts are not divided; they are not, in other words, made discrete by grammatical interruptions. Connections between concepts, overlaps and dissonances, can thus be perceived. This is a different way of writing that is transformative of the language in which it is couched, and of our reception of it.

Michèle Roberts's *The Book of Mrs Noah* (1987) is another example of a fragmented narrative, as is Joanna Russ's *The Female Man* (1986), both of which are explored in greater depth in the chapters above. The 'problematization' of the text is also a tactic of *écriture feminine*, self-conscious and overtly transgressive writing that aims, amongst other things, to disrupt the symbolic order of representation. This is not, however, change for change's sake, or an inversion of the order/disorder opposition, but rather, I suggest, representation of the conscious manifestation of the desire for a dynamic and open attitude towards apparent certainties. This desire is a characteristic of what I have called transgressive utopian thought. In earlier chapters I cited Margaret Whitford as identifying two 'types' of utopianism: static utopianism, and utopianism of process, the intention of which is to bring about (paradigm) shifts in consciousness (Whitford, 1991a: pp. 19–20). This, again, brings us back to Carol Pearson, whose second paradoxical principle is that whilst widespread change occurs as a result of individual activities that are outside of linear time, no one moves fully into the utopian future alone (Pearson, 1984: p. 261).

Feminist utopian fiction makes sorties into other genres – Frances Bartowski, in her study *Feminist Utopias*, puts it thus: 'What I am calling utopian fiction also verges on science fiction, myth, history, and theory' (Bartowski, 1989: p. 14). Myths are stories or narratives of imagined or supernatural figures that embody popular ideas on natural or social phenomena. Myths commonly form part of the cultural traditions or ideology of society. Feminist utopian literature and theory commonly mobilize reconstructed (Wittig, Daly) or deconstructed (Irigaray, Cixous) myths as forces of empowerment and/or critique. Treatment of myth is frequently metaphorical: if myth has (historically) embodied ideological values and aspirations, re/deconstructed myth perhaps can embody or at least inscribe different values. Metaphor conventionally functions to replace the name of an object with another – to apply a name to a thing to which it is not literally applicable. Paul Ricoeur and Drucilla Cornell have problematized the function of metaphor in thought and language. Cornell is concerned with the affirmation of sexual difference. Her work directly addresses the concerns of and tensions between feminism and postmodernism:

If there is a central tenet in this book, it is that the condition in which the suffering of all women can be 'seen' and 'heard', in all our difference, is that in which the tyranny of the established reality is disrupted and the possibility of further feminine resistance and the writings of a different version of the story of sexual difference is continually affirmed.

(Cornell, 1991: p. 2)

Seeking the affirmation of a different version of sexual difference in the space of what has yet to be rendered, Cornell finds a certain utopianism to be indispensable to feminist theory. She cites Cixous and Irigaray as thinkers of change who operate from within/without this space of 'not yet' or 'as if'. She finds the utopianism that she seeks in postmodernism:

We have to dance differently with the old distinctions [for example, of either/or], distinctions that have indeed been displaced by 'postmodern' philosophers.

(1991: p. 18)

This [postmodern] writing is explicitly utopian in that it evokes an elsewhere to our current system, in which sex is lived within the established 'heterosexual' matrix as a rigid gender identity which creates our separation and identifies us as girls and boys.

(1991: p. 19)

The importance of metaphor in Cornell's project is located in the surplus of meaning that it creates: 'Thus, in Irigaray and Cixous, the practice of re-metaphorisation – but without a replacement of the phallus as the primary metaphor of desire – is to mark the unrepresentable sexual difference that is erased by the current gender hierarchy' (1991: p. 168). Cornell offers close readings of Cixous and Irigaray, and suggests that Cleopatra, in Cixous's 'Sorties', is the mythical figure for a consciously mimetic women who is playing out the role of the ideal woman but also affirming her presence:

She is not the distant object, the signifier of absence, she is 'there', enacting in herself the art that makes love possible.... At the end of her quest Cleopatra 'finds' a lover who does not demand that she be less, or so the story goes as Cixous tells it.

(1991: p. 176)

For Ricoeur (1986), the paradox of metaphor is the tension between 'is' and 'is not': the metaphor is evocative, its function is to evoke an absent, or metaphysical 'truth' or 'us', which paradoxically 'is not'.

This can be disentangled by way of analogy with the term 'etcetera'. In her essay 'The Linguistic Transformation of Womanhood', H. Lee Gershuny states the following:

> In general semantics, *etc.* acknowledges the non-allness of language. For a feminist, however, *etc.* doesn't go far enough since the omitted secondary details of 'and others', and 'and so forth', have often referred to the unheard and invisible female experience.
>
> (Gershuny, 1984: pp. 191–2)

The metaphor, as I read Ricoeur and Cornell, can give shape to the contents of *etc.*. Like *etc.*, the metaphor invokes 'something' else: a surplus. We must, says Ricoeur, recognize a 'truth' in the metaphor for it to 'work'. By suggesting alternative truths, realities and values through metaphor and myth, feminist utopian theory and fiction, I suggest, both challenge and create, by stimulating questions and perhaps discordance in the mind of the reader. In this way, remetaphorization functions similarly to a disjointed narrative technique, jolting and intercepting the normal (traditional) chain of associative thought. Tradition, for instance, is denaturalized, symbolic order upturned, and new spaces for/of exploration opened:

> The 'as if' of the imagination is implicated in the very act of 'seeing' the real.
>
> (Cornell, 1991: p. 168)

> The necessary utopian moment in feminism lies precisely in our opening up the possible through metaphoric transformation.... Here, I am using utopia in a ... traditional way, but not in the sense of the establishment of a blueprint of an ideal society. Utopian thinking demonstrates the continual exploration and re-exploration of the possible and yet also the unrepresentable. Without utopian thinking, however, feminism is inevitably ensnared in the system of gender identity that devalues the feminine.
>
> (1991: pp. 168, 169)

In the article mentioned above, Gershuny provides a simple but, I suggest, useful schematic representation of how feminist women have attempted the linguistic transformation of womanhood.

Consideration of this can pull together many of the themes introduced in this chapter. The following extract is the opening paragraph of the article, in which Gershuny locates the linguistic transformation of womanhood at the centre of feminist utopian attempts to create paradigm shifts in consciousness:

> In criticizing patriarchal institutions, feminist writers have generated a *parole feministe* both to transform and transcend patriarchal paradigms. To perceive herself as a subject in present or future worlds first requires what Mary Daly calls an 'exorcism' of masculinist language and, secondly, a means of expression that reveals and unravels feminist consciousness. Starting from different perspectives, feminist writers are developing that language in forms as varied as philosophical treatises and utopian literature. The result is that feminist metaphors, models, myths, and methods not only reflect a unified sensibility, but an integration of three phases of feminist consciousness: analysis and criticism, transformation, and transcendence.
>
> (Gershuny, 1984: p. 189)

In this statement Gershuny is addressing the question 'why?' – why do feminist writers share the perceived need to attempt to transform linguistically the construct of womanhood? She also gestures towards the question 'how?' The three phases identified above are not spatially or temporally discrete – all three can be located at work in many of the texts in this chapter. Analysis and criticism identify what Gershuny calls 'patterns of linguistic sexism' (1984: p. 189), such as gendered hierarchies and the privileging of masculinity: 'Dualism, opposition, difference, and domination characterise patriarchal myths and metaphors that echo throughout the Judeo-Christian cosmology and moral order' (1984: p. 191). Transformation occurs, for instance, in the depiction of alternatively grounded societies, real or imagined; though such artifices as Marge Piercy's 'per' and Bryant's use of the word 'kin' to replace the 'pseudogeneric he' (1984: p. 191). Gershuny's conception of transcendence is not incompatible with my use of the word transgression: 'In discarding masculinist maps that polarize female and male into hierarchies, feminist writers have attempted to blend reason and feeling into a unified sensibility' (1984: p. 192). I have argued that it is the construct of oppositional conceptualization as a vehicle of oppression, domination and hierarchy that is the primary target of some feminists. This I prefer to express in terms of transgression rather than those of transcendence as, for reasons outlined in Chapter 5, the latter has implications of detachment from the body that do not appear altogether appropriate.

The following remark by Jenny Woolmark (1985) was intended to apply to the short stories in the anthology *Despatches from the Frontiers of the Female Mind* (Green and Lefanu, 1985). It is, however, particularly apposite to this discussion of the strategies (of form and content) employed by women attempting to perceive or construct themselves as subjects in present or future worlds: 'they are neither wholly pessimistic nor wholly optimistic. They are entirely open-ended and this is where their radicalism lies' (Woolmark, 1985: p. 99). Deconstructive textual practices, tactics of remetaphorization, and transgression of social codes and of the notions of truth and reality allow feminist utopianism to create openended textual and conceptual attitudes towards the present and the future. This, I suggest, is where *its* radicalism lies.

In the following reading of Hélène Cixous's *Portrait of Dora* (1983), which I discussed briefly in Chapter 4, I propose to draw together the themes introduced in this chapter. The field of utopianism is transgressive of generic boundaries, and utopian expression of desire is manifested in many forms. *Portrait of Dora* provides an excellent example of utopian boundary transgression. It is a play written originally for the radio and adapted for theatre. Its inspiration, as outlined earlier, is Freud's Dora Case. Thus already we have psychoanalysis, normally a private practice, transferred to the public stage through the medium of radio and theatre. These are the most obvious of a complex set of layers of multiplicity that comprise the play.

In the original case, Dora is diagnosed by Freud to be suffering from hysteria. Hysteria floods the play, and Martha Noel Evans describes it as being written in the hysterical mode. (Evans, 1987: p. 165). This mode, for Evans, is particularly appropriate to the theatre: ' "Protean", "seductive", "histrionic", "theatrical", "given to multiple identifications" – all of these terms have been used to describe hysterics over the years' (1987: pp. 166–7). The play, like much of Cixous's writing, can be described in all of these terms. It is a staging of the arts of pretence and seduction; it is variable and versatile, like the Greek sea god Proteus (who appears in many forms). Proteus serves as a useful metaphor for utopianism. Proteus is the changing or inconstant person or thing; the word 'protean' can also refer to amoeba, kinds of bacteria and amphibians. Utopianism too can be read as a body that lives in more than one environment (fiction and reality, literature and theory) and takes many shapes, as do the amphibian and the amoeba.

Hysteria is closely associated with the body, and particularly with the female body. It was, as mentioned in Chapter 4, originally thought to derive from a disturbance of the womb. In its characteristics of multiplicity and proximity to the body, hysteria is a fitting mode for 'feminine' expression. Dora is taken to Freud in a state of aphonia (total loss of voice), a typical symptom of hysteria. Caught in silence, she has no access to language. I have not seen the play performed, but the script as published in *Diacritics* (Cixous, 1983) indicates that film and voice-overs as well as on-stage acting enhance the sense of dislocation between the body and the voice of the hysteric.

The uncertainty of Dora's position is further mirrored in the multiple and conflicting narratives of the players. I commented earlier on the ambiguity of Dora's position as an adolescent. The phrases 'Dora is a child' and 'Dora is no longer a child' are frequently uttered by the adults, but it is never clear to whom these statements are addressed. The narratives of the adults conflict and conflate, as do their actions: 'As the adults in the play behave in a duplicitous fashion, cynically protecting themselves by taking multiple points of view, their duplicity is shadowed by another doubleness of their actions' (Evans, 1987: p. 172). Earlier in this chapter I discussed the ways in which utopianism, particularly when manifested in the common form of science fiction, is transgressive of the boundaries of time and space. *Portrait of Dora* has no chronology at all, in that time and space are jumbled. It is, moreover, hysterically excessive and overwhelming, even to read. As a piece of *écriture feminine* it contributes to a new utopian approach of seeking new ways of expression and communication.

Cixous's voice is present in the play but not in an authoritative position. In the original case, Freud fills in Dora's aphonic gaps and silences with his own scientific discourse. Cixous, however, does not take the stance of the diagnostic, or assume the authority to speak for anyone. Rather her voice seems to melt into those of the characters in a way that implies a loss (or gift) of her own sense of self. Evans describes the tone of the work in the following terms: 'Her voice is no longer hers, or no longer just hers: it is at the same time the voice of Dora or of Freud or of the K's' (Evans, 1987: p. 162). As an expression of the ultimate impotence of the diagnosed hysteric, the play is dystopian/ realist. There is no 'moral' or message to *Portrait of Dora*. But it does transgress the boundaries of science and fiction, reality and illusion, dream and consciousness, eutopia and dystopia, masculine and feminine economies: it does create a new space in which conceptualization can take place. It is an enactment of Cixous's utopian desire to make fiction exist. In an Oxford Amnesty lecture (14 February 1992), Cixous described her work as poetic. This word has special force for her, as she attributes to it a subversive function. Its density and transgressive nature contribute to this force. For Cixous, then, a transgressive prose that is self-consciously poetic has subversive potency in itself.

Utopian transgression of the barriers between fiction and reality is similarly potent. The preoccupation amongst women writers with this field is connected to the conviction that legend, myth and fairy tale all function to structure and legitimate reality. These 'fictions' construct 'reality'. Their purpose is to expose this link, and such exposure forms a familiar utopian technique. It denaturalizes as well as denies the desirability of the reality (partly) constructed on/by myth and legend. The socializing role of the fairy tale, for example, forms a common theme of explicit (Cixous) and implicit (Carter) critique. Within Carter's utopian text, *Heroes and Villains* (1969), for instance, there is an implicit mirroring of the tales of Sleeping Beauty, who awakens and is thus transformed from passivity to activity (albeit limited) with her first sexual encounter, and Beauty and the Beast, reflected in the characters of Marianne and Jewel. Sarah Lefanu points out that whereas Sleeping Beauty's story ends with the kiss, 'Marianne's story, in *Heroes and Villains*, in a sense *begins* with her marriage; although it is precisely then that her coherence as an individual begins to fragment' (Lefanu, 1988a: p. 79). *Heroes and Villains* serves as an illustration of the connection of fairy tale (fiction) to ideas about the way in which the self is constructed; in other words, of the transgression of the boundaries between fiction and theory.

Science fiction, the form taken by many utopian novels, is cited by Lefanu as a site of transgression itself (Lefanu, 1988a: p. 87). It allows, she says, simultaneous occupation of the positions of authoritarianism and anti-authoritarianism. As an anti-authoritarian genre, she says:

> It is able to break through the parameters of realism: in literary terms to enjoy the freedom of the fantastic mode, or to employ modernist techniques to challenge the hegemony of the main-stream novel, or again, importantly, to centralize the short story as a literary form that is both viable and popular. In social or

political terms, it is able to extrapolate from, to comment on, to satirise the real.

(Lefanu, 1988a: p. 87)

Conversely, she argues, science fiction has always reflected the authority of men over women. It is thus at once a repressive and an emancipatory genre. Similar points have been made by other feminist commentators. Hilary Rose, whose work was mentioned earlier, notes the common association of women with nature in what she calls 'mainstream masculinist SF', of which rape is a central metaphor (Rose, 1988: p. 124). Various responses are made by feminist writers to this scenario, including the assumption of the mantle of authority in a simple reversal of roles by some; others, such as Ursula Le Guin, stay within the mainstream tradition of science fiction whilst shifting the emphasis towards people and politics, emphasizing the 'soft' sciences of ecology and psychology. Lefanu's preferred approach (which I have also privileged in Chapters 5 and 6) is the disintegrationist one in which authority and sentiment (as c/overtly masculine and feminine (social) positioning) are rejected, and in which 'not just an apparent reality but its very construction' are questioned (Lefanu, 1988a: p. 87).

I mentioned the work of Anne Cranny Francis earlier in this chapter, and the reworking of generic conventions is the theme of her essay 'Feminist Futures: A Generic Study' (1990b). According to Francis, some women (feminist) writers have challenged the conventions of science fiction and produced unorthodox texts, 'thereby problematizing the text and its readings' (1990b: p. 219). Such texts are, she says, shifting and produce 'wholly *new meanings*, new knowledge' (1990b: pp. 219–20). The utopian feminist writer can thus exploit the freedoms already existing within science fiction and can then subvert an already subversive genre.

CONCLUSION

The move discussed in earlier chapters away from static approaches to utopianism is, of course, a transgression of the form and function of blueprint utopianism. Margaret Whitford has argued that the effects of feminist intervention in the genre of utopia are similar to those which have been provoked in that of philosophy: that programming the future has become undesirable:

A genuinely different future cannot be entirely foreseen,

224

certainly not predicted in any detail; it can only be the product of freeing our genuine creative abilities. However, at the same time, this view itself is subject to uncertainty, in its belief in the possibility of a radically different future.... Feminist utopian visions, then, are mostly of the dynamic, rather than the programmatic kind; they do not seek to offer blueprints of the ideal future, still less of the steps towards attaining it.

(Whitford, 1991a: p. 20)

I have cited this passage before, but include it again as it identifies an important denial – of a determinist, teleological link between past, present and future. Hélène Cixous, in 'The Laugh of the Medusa' (1981a), states that:

The future must no longer be determined by the past. I do not deny that the effects of the past are still with us. But I refuse to strengthen them by repeating them, to confer upon them an irremovability the equivalent of destiny, to confuse the biological and the cultural. Anticipation is imperative.

(Cixous, 1981a: p. 245)

The future cannot be programmed in terms of the present, as constructed by the past. It must be dreamt and imagined according to desire. This utopian break is perhaps the most transgressive and is illustrative of the scope of such a feminist project. Not only does the present need to be critiqued but its status, and that of women within it, need to be questioned. Transgression of social codes, of the concept of order, and of generic conventions all comprise elements of a practice, which I have called radical and transgressive utopianism, that seeks to subvert and exploit the ways in which our perceptions of reality (and the concepts that enable us to make sense of reality) are constructed. By dislocating the present, we can, I suggest, create new conceptual space which allows challenges to the present to be made, and permits the desire for change to become manifest and 'meaningful'.

CONCLUSION

The word 'conclusion' is etymologically linked to the concept of closure: it shuts or fastens the doors on the debate in hand. A conclusion terminates a discussion and presents the final result or decision, judgement of which has been reached (ideally) by reasoning. A utopia, as represented by the standard view, also represents closure; it marks a desired end to history, terminates progress, and presents the final result of politics. I have argued that this view is flawed, and a subtext of this book has argued for the need to resist unnecessary and unacknowledged closure on the grounds of political and intellectual integrity. With this irony in mind, then, I shall attempt to pull together the various strands of thought and argument pursued in this book and bring this particular contribution to debate to a close.

I have argued in the course of this book that utopianism needs to be reapproached, because this view of utopian thought as closed and enclosing is inappropriate to what has been identified as the new (and radical) transgressive utopianism emerging from feminism and other contemporary discourses, as well as being inappropriate to many historical utopias. My argument has linked approach and conceptualization, and through a *different* approach to utopian thought I have created and practised what I call a new utopianism – the concept is (in)formed by the process of openended conceptualization. My approach is embedded in contemporary feminisms and is informed by the transgressive discourses of Derridean and Cixousian poststructuralism. My conclusion, if you like, is that the new utopianism represents the manifestation of a conscious and necessary desire to resist the closure that is evoked by approaches to utopia as perfect, and that this has far-reaching implications.

Transgressive utopianism is, for instance, of a political nature, but is fundamentally transgressive of not only the political present but also the ways in which it is normally studied. Feminist political theory, for instance, has broadened the meaning of the concept of politics – feminist content-based analyses illustrate this point quite adequately, and near-unanimity exists amongst commentators as to the political concerns of women. Annette Keinhorst (1987), for example, identifies common concerns with group relations, non-hierarchic social structures, the recollection of an alternative consciousness which celebrates the 'female principle', non-abusive use of technology, consensual decision-making, and the primacy of social bonding over biological ties as characteristic of the feminist utopia. I have discussed the value and dangers of such analyses at some length and will not go over this ground again. Keinhorst's 'list' is introduced merely as an example of the extension of politics from its original and restricted public and organizational senses.

More interesting, and perhaps more radical, is the transgressive effect of the new (approach to) utopianism on the field of political theory itself. Study of utopian thought has always involved the traversing of generic and disciplinary boundaries – this is both the beauty and the beast of the field. The study of utopianism is an inexhaustible and fascinating process but requires a broad-ranging background and can lead to the 'Jack of all trades' syndrome. This tension is exploited by the new utopianism, the radicalness of which I have suggested is its self-conscious and resourceful transgression of boundaries. In this way, *process* becomes the focus of political theoretical research, rather than result or consequence. Put another way, conceptualization is privileged over concept. Study of contemporary feminist utopianism forces political theory beyond its normal parameters into, for example the field of the fantastic. Patrick Murphy, in his essay 'Feminism Faces the Fantastic', states that 'Still too often, feminist writers in treating an author like Marge Piercy or Margaret Atwood ignore or downplay the fantastic element of the fiction in the course of emphasizing feminist thematics' (Murphy, 1987a: p. 83). The point here, for political theory, is that attention to form in the narrow sense, traditionally the realm of literary theory, becomes an integral part of research. The poststructuralist work of Derrida leads in the same direction: the internal construction of the literary text and its components are shown to be shaped by political factors.

Furthermore, the transgression or subversion of generic conventions can be seen stylistically to enact transgressive political desires. Form in the shape of the openended text or utopia has also been focused upon in this book as a fundamental point of divergence from tradition. In this sense, the critical function of utopia is inverted on to the genre itself as the concept of universalism is challenged. I have traced concerns regarding the nature and function of the concept of difference in feminist (and poststructuralist) theory, and a further subtext of this book has been an examination of the dilemma which desires to preserve difference whilst establishing and articulating coherence. This tension also addresses the field of political theory. The suggested, albeit problematic, solution to this dilemma consists in holding concepts and categories open and resisting the desire for closure. This I have suggested is most convincingly achieved by moving away from standard mechanisms of conceptualization and analysis, and specifically by resisting dualistic thought, in such a way as to open new conceptual spaces (utopias) in which different ways of being and thinking can be envisaged and practised. Again, there are implications in this assertion for the genre of political theory – theory has traditionally sought to offer full and complete explanation and, like philosophy, to name the truth. I have suggested that we let go of these goals and resist conclusion in favour of openended and creative theorization.

It should, perhaps, be mentioned again at this juncture that resistance to closure is informed by certain convictions regarding the repressive function of the dominant mode of conceptualization. Oppositional thought requires negation in order to operate: the fear of negation is encapsulated in the passage below, wherein Hélène Cixous expresses the desire for a new place that is no place – utopia:

> There will be some elsewhere where the other will no longer be condemned to death. But has there ever been any elsewhere, is there any? While it is not yet 'here', it is there by now – in this place that disrupts social order, where desire makes fiction exist. Not any old fiction, for, of course, there is classical fiction caught in the oppositions of the system, and literary history has been homogeneous with the phallocentric tradition, to the point of being phallocentrism-looking-at-itself, taking pleasure in repeating itself.
>
> (Cixous and Clement, 1986: p. 97)

In the creation of new conceptual space, utopianism performs a creative function that displaces that of creating a blueprint for the perfect society. In the first instance, as stated above, new understandings of and approaches to politics are provoked. This can be related to the Derridean conviction that there is nothing outside the text: that we can speak of a cultural text that is inscribed in and by language, at the heart of which is a system of thought which operates by binary opposition and which is profoundly and essentially hierarchical. Much of the bulk of this book has been devoted to an exploration of how and why feminist utopian thinkers have worked to undermine these mechanics. I have identified a new utopian function as being variously manifested but as having the effect of provoking a paradigm shift in consciousness (Whitford, 1991a: p. 20). This phrase of Margaret Whitford's resonates throughout the book. Whitford never expands the phrase, but for me it encapsulates what makes so many feminist utopian texts and theories – and indeed my new reading of utopianism *per se* – so radically different and potent. Peter Alexander was cited in the first chapter as describing philosophy as the art of the possible because it is concerned with questions of conceivability. Philosophy, utopia and the fairy tale, he says, play on fears and longings to shift values and give insight of political and moral matters (Alexander, 1984: p. 41). I have suggested that in provoking paradigm shifts in consciousness, utopianism can enable us to repattern and restructure our thought; to dance differently to the same tune, which is language; and to foresee the previously unforeseeable (Cixous, 1981a: p. 245). This is utopian thought, and it can be observed in operation by paying attention to the subversion of narrative conventions and the upending of social myths.

Feminist utopianism operates with a subtle lightness of touch. Once its effects are noted, however, they can be seen to have profound implications. The following passage comes from Hélène Cixous, whose work has strongly influenced this book. Her description of 'feminine light' can, I suggest, be read as a metaphor for transgressive utopianism:

> Feminine light doesn't come from above, doesn't fall, doesn't strike, doesn't go through. It radiates, it is a slow, sweet, difficult, absolutely unstoppable, painful rising that reaches and impregnates lands, that filters, that wells up, and finally tears open, wets and spreads apart what is dull and thick, the stolid, the volumes. Fighting off opacity from deep within. This light doesn't plant, it spawns.
>
> (Cixous and Clement, 1986: p. 88)

This is a poignant passage, filled with physical and sexual imagery. In this sense, it illustrates the practice, discussed in Chapter 5, of embodying the text and of making consideration of the body a theoretical act. If, as stated above, there is nothing outside the text, and if, as implied in Chapter 5, women's bodies represent the embodiment of their cultural experience, then drawing the (female) body into the previously masculine-dominated fields of philosophy and political theory is a revolutionary move. It is so because it transgresses and renders meaningless the division between mind and body, and creates a new kind of political theory that does not ignore or devalue the physical, the emotional or the 'feminine'. The touch of this light upon our skin would not burn, but rather would deeply infuse heat and energy.

The passage further serves to illustrate the complexity and subtlety of feminist utopian thought. It spawns; it is multidirectional and prolific, elusive and difficult to contain. It is embedded in the text which it critiques; it does not come from above, or outside. Questions of subjectivity and objectivity can be introduced at this point. A text which critiques from *inside*, but which introduces a perspective that is *outside*, external or O/other, cannot be objective. Nor, however, can it be said to be purely subjective. Rather, I suggest, this kind of complicity with the (cultural) text is subversive of the boundary between these two approaches. No external 'truth' is imposed on the text, no normative conclusions are drawn, but rather the text is opened to enquiry. Truths and norms are challenged, and flux and ambiguity displace certainty.

What I have called the new (approach to) utopianism does not desire perfection but dynamism and unending process. For some, utopia is interpreted as desiring the death of politics and the end of change, in return for which it offers perfection. I have suggested that this can be read in terms of masculine economics of social exchange, and that the perfect gift of death which is the blueprint utopia be rejected in favour of the more difficult and slippery, openended vision which contemporary feminist utopianism represents.

> Malachite: 'The Patriarch is the perfect judge of humankind. His perfect judgement has been demonstrated for a thousand years of human survival.'
> Merwen: 'Then he must be dead.'
> ... 'Listen,' Merwen went on, annoyed at having to lecture, 'What is the name of perfect good? Is it freedom? Perfect freedom is death. Is it peace? Perfect peace is death. Is it love? Perfect love is to choose to love death, that others may live.'
> (Slonzcewski, 1987: p. 151)

NOTES

INTRODUCTION

1 Bloch wrote *The Principle of Hope* between 1938 and 1947. I am using the 1986 English translation of his 1957 revised edition.

2 Levitas finds the essentialism of this approach to be problematic. Sargent is less concerned. I myself tend to find the assumption that (most) people at some time dream of or desire a better life to be unproblematic. I do not, however, consider this activity to be a defining human characteristic, and believe that as long as the nature of that desire is left undefined, then problems of essentialism do not arise.

3 The varied usage of the term 'utopia' is due in part to the tendency amongst commentators to use this word in unspecific ways. It is, for instance, common to use the term as Levitas does, but other writers are not always as clear as to their intent.

4 The definition comes from the *Oxford English Dictionary*, which I cite in order to illustrate dominant colloquial views of the meaning of the concept.

5 'Contemporary' and 'recent', in the context of this book, refer to the period 1970–90.

6 One source for the new utopianism that is advanced in this thesis is Derridean deconstructive theory, which can only operate from within a (literary or cultural) text. This approach denies the possibility of objectivity and insists that rigorous critique must recognize itself as rooted inside the discourses on which it works.

7 Marge Piercy's work provides the clearest example of this approach: her utopian novel *Woman on the Edge of Time* (1979) is clearly an exploration of Shulamith Firestone's theory as advanced in *The Dialectic of Sex* (1971), and her recent novel *Body of Glass* explores ideas raised in Donna Harraway's 'Manifesto for Cyborgs' (1990).

1

FORM-BASED AND CONTENT-BASED APPROACHES TO UTOPIANISM

1 Chapters 1 and 2 will be concerned largely with the first two of these claims, and Chapters 3 and 4 will refer more to the latter.

2 I shall, wherever possible, confine my discussions of the existing approaches to utopianism to these headings. In places, however, there will be some seepage from one approach to another, as commentators often combine focus on form, content and function.

3 My pluralization of the term 'feminism' is indicative of my belief that 'feminism' is a multiple and diverse body of thought best considered in the broadest and most plural sense. These points are pursued at some length in Chapter 3.

4 Barbara Goodwin does not: 'The road to utopia is devious. I set out with political philosophy and a liking for literary utopias, and arrived with the conviction that utopianism is a distinctive form of social science' (Goodwin, 1978: p. vii). This approach still privileges form, albeit a different one from the literary genre.

5 Colloquial understandings of terms, dictionary definitions and everyday usages are important to this book because I am interested to ask whence they originate. The dominant colloquial meaning is, I shall be arguing, in many cases the product of a certain academic approach or methodology. I shall be concerned to unravel and challenge the mechanics by which these products are constructed.

6 See n. 4 regarding Barbara Goodwin's approach, which could be read in this way.

7 Likewise, the assumption of any 'formulaic' definition of utopianism results in a narrow approach – even Goodwin's (1978) 'utopianism as social science' is too restrictive. We may study utopianism as part of an exercise in social science, we may approach utopianism as social scientists, but we cannot claim the phenomenon itself. To attempt to do so would surely prevent and deny the richness of a multidisciplinary tradition. More's *Utopia*, for instance, has to be read for its fictional form *and* its potentially socially scientific content. I shall address these concerns again later in the chapter.

8 The topic of genre is further explored in Chapter 7.

9 I use Morton's spelling of the poem in order to attempt to distinguish between the poem and the tradition.

10 Morton lists other variants of this form of expression as including the French Coquaigne, Pomona and Hy in Brasil, Venusberg and the Country of the Young, Lubberland, Sclaraffenland, Poor Man's Heaven and Rock Candy Mountains (Morton, 1952: p. 10).

11 In making this point I do not wish to strip Cokaygne of its fun and humour. The playfulness of utopias is something to which I return later in the chapter and again in Chapter 7.

12 I shall expand on this point later. Briefly, though, instances of utopias that contain multiple worlds are Piercy, *Woman on the Edge of Time*

(1979); Russ, *The Female Man* (1986); Lessing, *The Marriages between Zones Three, Four and Five* (1980); Carter, *The Passion of New Eve* (1982), and *Heroes and Villains* (1969); Slonczewski, *A Door into Ocean* (1987); and Roberts, *The Book of Mrs Noah* (1987).

13 I shall be saying more on the topic of the function of utopian thought in the next chapter, and on Carter in Chapter 7.

14 Of course, this phenomenon is not 'new' at all. More's *Utopia* (1975) also transgresses definitions which rely on perfection and the blueprint as characterizing features. Morris's *News from Nowhere* (1891) does likewise. What is new is the approach which allows utopianism to be considered as a transgressive phenomenon. I shall be introducing other facets of this transgression later.

15 I do not mean to suggest that More's *Utopia* (1975) is an uncontroversial or straightforward text, but rather that it is commonly accepted without dispute to *be* a utopia (that is, of the literary genre) and to *contain* a Utopia (a vision of a better way of being).

16 Morris's *News from Nowhere* (1891) is similarly imperfect. Indeed, Morris, in the above-mentioned review of *Looking Backward*, implies that utopias *must* be read as flawed (Morris, 1889: p. 248).

17 This argument forms the focus of Chapter 3, which establishes an openended conception of feminism as the grounding for utopian feminist thought that does not insist on closure.

18 In Chapter 2 I begin to establish a definition of the utopian function as provoking a shift in consciousness. If this is understood as the primary function of utopia, then the two approaches identified by Rudnik-Smalbraack can be more constructively considered as complementary rather than oppositional.

19 This is noted by Ruth Levitas (1990), Krishan Kumar (1991) and Tom Moylan (1986).

20 See Chapter 3 for a fuller exploration of the nature of contemporary feminism.

21 This argument is pursued further in Chapter 3.

22 The libidinal economies of masculinity and femininity are explained in Chapter 4 and explored in Chapters 5, 6 and 7.

23 Black feminists have made the point that it does not matter whether or not these moves of exclusion are intentional; the result is the same.

24 These are Mary Bradley Lane's *Mizora: A Prophesy* (Boston: Gregg Press; 1st edn 1890; 1975 edn); Charlotte Perkins Gilman's *Herland* (New York: Pantheon; 1st edn 1915; 1975 edn); Dorothy Bryant's *The Kin of Ata are Waiting for You* (1971); and Mary Staton's *From the Legend of Beil* (New York: Ace Books; 1976).

25 Assuming of course that the function of a definition is to provide universally applicable criteria. See Chapters 3 and 4 for further commentary on this feature of the concept of definition.

26 In that this approach is so common and in that it informs the dominant colloquial understanding of utopian expression as being normally manifested in a fictional form, we can say that it contributes to the standard view of what constitutes (a) utopia.

27 An example, perhaps, of a porous definition.

2
FUNCTION-BASED APPROACHES TO UTOPIANISM

1 This statement applies with particular force to those approaches which focus on narrative content; formulaic content is discussed further in the next section.

2 This is particularly likely to have been the case in historical periods such as that of sixteenth-century England, when a despotic crown made political critique especially dangerous.

3 Krishan Kumar notes that many writers of historical utopias were imprisoned and/or tortured as political subversives (Kumar, 1991).

4 The notion of utopia as an estranged text is considered in further depth in Chapter 4.

5 The idea that utopia can be read as a 'feminine' genre is explored in Chapter 4.

6 I should like to note here that I am not buying into this 'fiction = trivial, philosophy = serious' dichotomy, but use it ironically as an explanatory device.

7 The subject of the function and effect of diversity on contemporary feminist thought is explored in greater depth below. See especially Chapters 3 and 4.

8 The transgressive function of utopian thought is a theme that is pursued throughout the remaining chapters of this book.

9 It is interesting to note that Mannheim, like Bloch, refers to utopia initially as a state of mind, and subsequently as a concrete action. (Bloch also sees socialism as the concrete utopia.) Utopian desire, when tied to a social movement (that of socialism in this case), is transformed into political activity. The passivity associated with the utopian dreamer is thus similarly transformed. In this way socialist critiques attempt to address questions of agency.

10 I am using the 1977 edition of Thompson because I wish to refer to the postscript added to the volume in that year. The statement above comes from the earlier, 1955 edition.

11 I cite Miguel Abensour here, but see too John Goode (1977), who also objects to the term 'scientific utopianism'. For Goode, what makes Morris's work so powerful is his approach to art and politics – the utopianism of his work should not therefore be devalued.

12 Fuller discussion of the ways in which feminist utopianism relates to feminist theory and to the contemporary feminist movements is undertaken in the next chapter.

13 Jean-Jacques Rousseau's *The Social Contract* is an example of a piece of political theory which is both utopian and informed by this view of 'humanity'. The noble savage, in Rousseau's state of nature, is a slave to his passions; full humanity comes only when reason conquers these 'animalistic' desires and acts as a precursor to the attainment of morality.

14 In the next two chapters I suggest that utopia needs to be reapproached *and* reconceptualized, and that the latter cannot be achieved without engaging in the former. I also propose that this new approach should be engaged with and in the utopianism which it builds. These arguments are informed by poststructuralist theories of deconstructive reading techniques.

15 The texts with which Moylan is concerned are Marge Piercy's *Woman on the Edge of Time* (1979), Ursula Le Guin's *The Dispossessed* (1975), Joanna Russ's *The Female Man* (1986) and Samuel Delany's *Triton*.

16 Fredric Jameson advances this view in *The Political Unconscious* (1981).

17 I shall return to discussion of this trend in feminist thought in Chapter 3.

18 'Letting go' (of power and claims to it) is a theme of Chapter 4, which explores Hélène Cixous's theory of libidinal femininity.

3
FEMINISM

1 I have called this the standard view because the content-based approach, which privileges the perceived conventions of perfection, and the function-based approach, which identifies a blueprinting function to utopianism, have constructed the dominant (hence standard), colloquial understanding of the term 'utopia'.

2 This oppositional function is further explored and exploited in the chapters that follow.

3 I shall be examining the relation of self to other in Chapter 6.

4 See below for a rough categorization of some of the ways in which difference is conceptualized.

5 See, for example, Keith Joseph and Joseph Sumption's *Equality* (1979).

6 See, for instance, Cherrìe Morga and Anzaldua (1981), Patricia Hill Collins (1990) and bell hooks (1984).

7 For an example of divisions and heterogeneity amongst such groups, see Alice Walker's discussion of the friction between light- and dark-skinned Afro-Caribbean women (Walker, 1984).

8 Here I employ Bhikhu Parekh's term in preference to those of 'culture' and 'race' so as to avoid the generalization of the former and the reductionism of the latter. See Parekh (1991).

9 These points are not new to feminist thought, or to this century. Aristotle's principle of proportional equality, in which it is thought to be just to treat equals equally (the same) and unequals unequally (differently), in proportion to their respective inequalities, raises the same issues and questions. Mary Wollstonecraft's *Vindication of the Rights of Woman* (1792) was concerned to expose how Rousseau's (1974) depiction of Emile as naturally different to Sophie legitimized (unfair) unequal treatment.

10 See Chapter 6 for a discussion of femininity defined as other to masculinity.

11 I shall be arguing below that wanting to establish identity as 'identical-ness' is indicative of a certain desire to appropriate the possibility of 'pure' difference.

12 I shall be looking at the transgressive effects of these conceptual–structural denials in my discussions of the relation of self to other and mind to body (Chapters 5 and 6).

13 Not really 'opposed to', of course, merely 'prior to'.

14 I am conscious of the dangers of false homogenization involved when referring to feminism and postmodernism as discrete and total move-ments, but do so here for the sake of clarity.

15 The discussion that follows continues to explore this point.

16 Following Bertens's scheme for conceptualizing postmodernism, I should, perhaps, point out that what I call 'Derridean poststructural-ism' he calls 'deconstructionist postmodernism' (Bertens, 1995: p. 7).

17 Such a move also supports racism: see, for instance, Parekh (1991) and Collins (1990).

18 For an early account, see Mary Wollstonecraft's *Vindication of the Rights of Women* (1792).

19 In the sections that follow, however, I caution against naivety (political and intellectual) when introducing postmodernism to feminism.

20 The readings below of the works of Jacques Derrida and Hélène Cixous are just that: readings, interpretations in which the reader (myself) is self-consciously present.

21 These two elements are not discrete from one another and do not operate in succession. Rather they work simultaneously in a double-edged manner.

22 Derrida's neologism *'différance'* is discussed more fully in the next chapter.

23 *'Proper*: 1. own. 2. (astron.) ~motion, that part of the apparent motion of fixed star supposed to be due to its actual movement in space. 3. Belonging, relating, exclusively or distinctively (to). 4. (gram) ~noun or name, name used to designate an individual person, animal, town, ship, etc. 5. Accurate, correct. 6. strictly so called, real, genuine. 7. Thorough, complete. 8. Handsome. 9. Fit, suitable, right. 10. In conformity with demands of society, decent, respectable.
Property: 1. owning, being owned; thing owned, possessions(s). 2. (theatr.) Article of costume, furniture. 3. Attribute, quality; (Logic) quality common to a class but not necessary to distinguish it from others.
Appropriate: 1. Belonging, peculiar (to); suitable, proper. 2. Take possession of; take to oneself; devote to special purposes' (*Oxford English Dictionary*).

24 Elizabeth Spelman's (1990) work illustrates the dangers encountered when such a project is naively undertaken: white women have named (described and defined) feminism to the exclusion of others – they have thus constructed Others and denied them voice, effectively delegiti-mizing their existence and experiences. Once this is accomplished, the desires and utopias of the excluded group become similarly invisible and redundant.

25 A dualistic conception of choice limits the range of possibilities to one of two alternatives.
26 I made a similar point in the last chapter regarding approaches to utopianism that privilege narrative content.
27 Literally, for if binary opposition has henceforth created meaning, to surpass the position of either/or is to pass beyond opposition towards a new multiplicity.
28 Not, at least, if the question (the approach) is framed in such a way as to elicit a single and universally applicable response.
29 Problematic because of the essentializing implications of this term.

4
UTOPIA AS NO PLACE

1 Conceptions of precisely what constitutes the political have of course been transformed by feminist thought.
2 Silence was identified in the chapter above as one possible outcome of treading a deconstructive path.
3 An illustration of this can be found in the discussions of the relation of sameness and difference in Chapter 3.
4 Derrida does not, to my knowledge, incorporate the second meaning of the word 'defer': were he to do so, the hierarchical nature of oppositional thought might perhaps become more apparent.
5 This passage was also cited in Chapter 3.
6 I chose to include the extracts above chiefly because they allude to flight. Hélène Cixous has encouraged women to be the bird that flies and steals (Cixous and Clement, 1986). Rather than working in opposition to deconstructive contextualizing tactics, though, I suggest that she can be read as echoing the lack, in Derrida's writing, of any ideologically political stance. Cixous's is an eclectic stance, one that I have suggested in Chapter 3 is appropriate to contemporary feminism. She has also described her work, in *The Newly Born Woman* (Cixous and Clement, 1986), as that of a talpa or mole, burrowing into the text. In this sense her work is deconstructive. Cixous's work will be explored more fully later.
7 Amen: 'so be it' – etymologically Greek and Hebrew *amen*, 'certainly'.
8 These ideas are pursued further in Chapter 6, which focuses on relations between self and other.
9 See Chapter 6 for further exploration of how the relation between self and other is constructed.
10 This essential conservatism of historical (male) utopias is a theme of Chapter 7, which examines ways in which feminist utopian thought attempts to undermine and subvert the concept of order and social codification.
11 The choice of the terms 'masculine' and 'feminine' to describe these economies is somewhat problematic because of their essentialist implications. Cixous has commented on this in interview (in Sellers, 1986). Masculinity and femininity, and their associated attributes, do

frequently coincide with men and women respectively, but Cixous undermines the assumption that this is inevitable. Throughout the remainder of this book the terms are used with these problematics in mind.

12 The case is commonly referred to as 'the Dora Case'.

13 This new relation to the other is explored further in Chapter 6.

14 This area is approached by looking at the varied responses to the problematics of developing a female subjectivity. A tension is identified between those writers whose approach results in separatist (women-only) utopian visions and those who prefer to envisage societies of more than one gender.

5
FEMINIST UTOPIAN TRANSGRESSION OF THE SPIRIT/MATTER RELATION

1 See Chapter 3 for an introduction to the preoccupations of contemporary feminist theory.

2 In the discussions that follow, 'Woman' as cultural or mythical construct is capitalized to distinguish this concept from 'women' (real, historical beings) and 'a woman' (one real, historical being).

3 See Chapter 6 for the construction of femininity as a complement to the masculine.

4 Here Griffin can be seen to address a central theme of this book, which identifies utopian thought as transgressing dominant modes of conceptualization and thus destroying, transforming and reviving the concepts in question.

5 Relations between the body and the cultural text are examined in the section below, which analyses some utopian feminist theories of language.

6 These ideas are expanded further in the section below on envisaged social organizations and societies.

7 Cixous's propositions cannot be read through a dualistic matrix of 'either/or'; hence the simultaneous 'both/and'.

8 Whilst her theoretical work is grounded on different premises to that of Wittig, Cixous takes a similar stance regarding these 'labels' or signifiers.

9 See Chapter 6 for more on the Gaffer.

10 My awareness of these concerns was heightened recently by attendance at the Morrel Conference on Political Theory and Literature (University of York, September 1993) and especially by Maureen Whitebrook's unpublished paper, 'Taking the Narrative Turn'.

11 A similar tactic is used by Joanna Russ in *The Female Man* (1986) in an exploration of female subjectivity. Russ portrays four characters, all of whom are the various potentialities of one woman. (See Chapter 6.)

12 See Chapter 4 for an introduction to the concept of a masculine economy of exchange which is driven by fear of, and the desire to appropriate, difference.

13 Cixous's reading of the story of Sun Tse is discussed in Chapter 4.

6
FEMINIST UTOPIAN TRANSGRESSION OF THE SELF/OTHER RELATION

1 The 'O' of the terms 'Other' and 'Otherness' is capitalized in this chapter when the *concept* of Otherness as constructed through a binary opposition to sameness is indicated. The mechanics of this construction are explored in the discussions below.
2 This text was introduced in Chapter 5.
3 This text was also introduced in Chapter 5. 'Fems' are women and 'Dirties' are non-white men.
4 The other two models identified by Ferguson are Difference Theory and Aspect Theory, discussed later in this chapter.
5 I should perhaps provide a reminder at this juncture that 'Utopia' (capital 'U') is used in this book to refer to a vision of a better place, and 'utopia' (lower case 'u') to refer to a literary genre.
6 I say this with caution as I am anxious to avoid the trap of essentialism and universalism into which Shulamith Firestone (1971) falls when she uses these terms.
7 Monique Wittig's construction of an autonomous subjectivity is the result of careful political theoretical analysis (see above, this chapter). Gearhart's is not.
8 Carol Gilligan has made similar observations, finding an 'ethic of care' to be present in women's speech (Gilligan, 1983, 1993: pp. ix–xxvii).
9 See, for instance, the oft-quoted section from 'Sorties', 'Where is she?', cited earlier in this chapter.
10 'Human' in the sense of human-constructed, such as culture/nature.
11 See Luce Irigaray's *Speculum of the Other Woman* (1985b); also Chapter 3.
12 The city idealized by Young is fairly small: 10,000–20,000 inhabitants.

7
FEMINIST UTOPIAN TRANSGRESSION OF CODES AND GENRE

1 I use the word 'stereotype' in this section in strict adherence to its literal meaning, which is not restricted to its more common derogatory sense. In the printing industry a stereotype is a plate which is cast and used to make a fixed and lasting impression. To stereotype, then, is to make a thing unchangeable (Greek *stereos*, 'solid'; Greek *tupus*, 'impression, figure, type').
2 Socialism can also be argued to have been influenced by this tradition, for, whilst taking a flexible approach to human nature, the contribution of thinkers such as Rousseau cannot be ignored: that is, the primacy of

reason, and the higher moral freedom that self-improving man can achieve by accepting the general will of society.

3 See also *The Infernal Desire Machines of Doctor Hoffman*, *The Bloody Chamber* (1981) and *Nights at the Circus*.

4 See Chapters 5 and 6 for further consideration of *Woman on the Edge of Time*.

5 An attitude that is perhaps promoted by the sleeves of her books, which generally represent muscular women partially dressed in leather and thongs. The appearance is that of a text of soft pornography.

6 Like Bradley, Slonzcewski uses the word 'protect' as a satirical euphemism for 'control'.

7 This passage was also quoted in Chapter 6.

BIBLIOGRAPHY

Adler, Margot (1989) 'The Juice and the Mystery' in Plant (1989).

Albinski, Nan Bowman (1988) *Women's Utopias in British and American Fiction* (London: Routledge).

Alexander, Peter (1984) 'Grimms' Utopias: Motives and Justifications' in Alexander and Gill (1984).

Alexander, Peter and Gill, Roger (eds) (1984) *Utopias* (London: Duckworth).

Allen, Jeffner (1989) 'Women who Beget Women must Thwart Major Sophisms' in Garry and Pearsall (1989).

Andrews, Geoff (ed.) (1991) *Citizenship* (London: Lawrence & Wishart).

Armitt, Luce (1991) *Where No Man has Gone Before: Women and Science Fiction* (London: Routledge).

Atwood, Margaret (1986) *The Handmaid's Tale* (London: Cape).

Augustine, St (1961) *The Confessions* trans. R.S. Pinecoffin (Harmondsworth: Penguin).

Bacon, Francis (1629) *New Atlantis* in Morley's Universal Library (1889).

Baker-Smith, Dominic and Barfoot, C.C. (eds) (1987) *Between Dream and Nature: Essays on Utopia and Dystopia* DQR Studies in Literature 2 (Amsterdam: Editions Rodopi).

Bammer, Angelika (1991) *Partial Visions: Feminism and Utopianism in the 1970s* (London: Routledge).

Barr, Marleen S. (1981) *Future Females: A Critical Anthology* (Cincinnati: Bowling Green State University Press).

—— (1987) 'Feminist Fabulation; Or, Playing with Patriarchy vs. the Masculinization of Metafiction' in Murphy (1987a).

Barrett, Michèle and Phillips, Anne (1992) *Destabilizing Theory* (Cambridge: Polity Press).

Bartowski, Francis (1989) *Feminist Utopias* (Lincoln, Nebr., and London: University of Nebraska Press).

Baruch, Elaine and Lucienne, Serrana (1983) 'Interview with Luce Irigaray' in Todd (1983).

Bellamy, Edward (1951) *Looking Backward 2000–1887* (New York: Random House), 1st edn 1887 .

Bertens, Hans (1995) *The Idea of the Postmodern: A History* (London: Routledge).

Best, Steven and Kellner, Douglas (1991) *Postmodern Theory: Critical Interrogations* (London: Macmillan).

Bloch, Ernst (1986) *The Principle of Hope* vols 1, 2, 3, trans. Neville Plaice, Stephen Plaice, Paul Knight (Oxford: Blackwell), revised 1957, 1959.

Bordo, Susan (1990) 'Feminism, Postmodernism, and Gender-Scepticism' in Nicholson (1990).

Bowie, Malcolm (1991) *Lacan* (London: Fontana).

Boyne, Roy (1990) *Foucault and Derrida: The Other Side of Reason* (London: Unwin Hyman).

Bradley, Marion Zimmer (1980) *The Ruins of Isis* (London: Arrow Books).

—— (1983) *Thendara House* (London: Arrow Books).

Braidotti, Rosi (1989) 'The Politics of Ontological Difference' in Brennan (1989).

—— (1991) *Patterns of Dissonance* (Cambridge: Polity Press).

Brennan, Teresa (ed.) (1989) *Between Feminism and Psychoanalysis* (London: Routledge).

Bryant, Dorothy (1971) *The Kin of Ata are Waiting for You* (New York: Random House).

Bryson, Valerie (1992) *Feminist Political Theory* (Basingstoke: Macmillan).

Bunch, Charlotte (1988) 'Making Common Cause: Diversity and Coalitions' in McEwan and O'Sullivan (1988).

Campanella, (*c.* 1600) *The City of the Sun* in Morley's Universal Library (1889).

Carter, Angela (1969) *Heroes and Villains* (Harmondsworth: Penguin).

—— (1981) *The Bloody Chamber and Other Stories* (Harmondsworth: Penguin).

—— (1982) *The Passion of New Eve* (London: Virago).

Charnas, Suzy McKee (1979) *Walk to the End of the World* (London: Victor Gollancz).

—— (1980) *Motherlines* (London: Victor Gollancz).

Churchman, C. West (1984) 'Utopias' in Alexander and Gill (1984).

Cixous, Hélène (1981a) 'The Laugh of the Medusa' in Marks and Courtivron (1981).

—— (1981b) 'Castration or Decapitation?' trans. Annette Kuhn, *Signs* vol. 7, no. 11.

—— (1983) *Portrait of Dora*, *Diacritics: A Review of Contemporary Criticism*, Spring.

—— (1990) *Reading with Clarice Lispector* ed. and trans. Verena Andermatt Conley (London: Harvester Wheatsheaf).

Cixous, Hélène and Clement, Catherine (1986) *The Newly Born Woman* trans. Betsy Wing (Manchester: Manchester University Press).

Claeys, Gregory (1994) *Utopias of the British Enlightenment* (Cambridge: Cambridge University Press).

Collins, Patricia Hill (1990) *Black Feminist Thought* (Boston, Mass.: Unwin Hyman).

Cooper, J.C. (1983) *Fairy Tales: Allegories of the Inner Life* (Wellingborough: Aquarian Press).

Conley, Verena Andermatt (1984a) 'Appendix: Exchange with Hélène Cixous' in Conley (1984b).

Conley, Verena Andermatt (1984b) *Hélène Cixous* (Lincoln, Nebr.: University of Nebraska Press).

Cornell, Drucilla (1991) *Beyond Accommodation: Ethical Feminism, Deconstruction and the Law* (London: Routledge).

Daly, Mary (1985) *The Church and the Second Sex* (Boston, Mass.: Beacon Press), 1st edn 1968.

—— (1987) *Gyn/Ecology: The Metaethics of Radical Feminism* (London: Women's Press), 1st edn 1979.

—— (1991) *Beyond God the Father: Toward a Philosophy of Women's Liberation* (London: Women's Press), 1st edn 1986.

Davis, J.C. (1981) *Utopia and the Ideal Society: A Study of English Utopian Writing 1516–1700* (Cambridge: Cambridge University Press).

—— (1984) 'The History of Utopia: The Chronology of Nowhere' in Alexander and Gill (1984).

—— (1987) 'Utopia, Science and Social Science' in Kamenka (1987).

D'Eaubonne, Françoise 1981 'Feminism or Death' in Marks and Courtivron (1981).

Deferrari, Roy J. (1957) *Treatise on Marriage and Other Subjects* (New York: Fathers of the Church).

Derrida, Jacques (1972a) ' "Difference" from *Margins of Philosophy* in Kamuf (1991).

—— (1972b) ' "Tympan" from *Margins of Philosophy*' in Kamuf (1991).

—— (1974) 'From *Glas*' in Kamuf (1991).

—— (1978a) 'From *Spurs: Nietzsche's Styles*' in Kamuf (1991).

—— (1978b) 'Structure, Sign and Play in the Discourses of the Human Sciences'.

—— (1982) 'Choreographies' in Kamuf (1991).

—— (1985) 'Des Tours de Babel' in Kamuf (1991).

—— (1987) ' "At this Very Moment in this Work Here I Am" from *Psyche*' in Kamuf (1991).

Dinnerstein, Dorothy (1989) 'Survival on Earth: The Meaning of Ecofeminism' in Plant (1989).

Docherty, Thomas (1993) *Postmodernisms: A Reader* (Hemel Hempstead: Harvester Wheatsheaf).

Dowling, William C. (1984) *Jameson, Althusser, Marx: An Introduction to the Political Unconscious* (London: Methuen).

During, Simon (1993) 'Postmodernism or Post Colonialism Today' in Docherty (1993).

Elgin, Suzette Hadin (1987) 'Women's Language and Near Future Science Fiction: A Reply' in Murphy (1987a).

Esfandiary, F.M. (1974) 'Transhumans – 2000' in Tripp (1974).

Eugene, Toinett M. (1989) 'While Love is Unfashionable: Ethical Implications of Black Spirituality' in Garry and Pearsall (1989).

Evans, Martha Noel (1987) *Masks of Tradition: Women and the Politics of Writing in Twentieth Century France* (Ithaca, N.Y.: Cornell University Press).

Fairburns, Zoe (1979) *Benefits* (London: Virago).

Farley, Tucker (1984) 'Realities and Fictions: Lesbian Visions of Utopia' in Rohrlich and Baruch (1984)

Ferguson, Ann (1989) 'A Feminist Aspect Theory of the Self' in Garry and Pearsall (1989).

Finley, M.I. (1975) *The Uses and Abuses of History* (London: Chatto & Windus).

Firestone, Shulamith (1971) *The Dialectic of Sex: A Case for Feminist Revolution* (St Albans: Paladin).

Francis, Anne Cranny (1990a) *Feminist Fiction* (Cambridge: Polity Press).

—— (1990b) 'Feminist Futures: A Generic Study' in Kuhn (1990).

Fraser, Nancy, Nicholson Linda J. (1990) 'Social Criticism without Philosophy: An Encounter between Feminism and Postmodernism' in Nicholson (1990).

Freud, Sigmund (1905) 'Three Essays on the Theory of Sexuality' in Freud (1977).

—— (1925) 'Some Physical Consequences of the Anatomical Distinction Between the Sexes' in Freud (1977).

—— (1931) 'Female Sexuality' in Freud (1977).

—— (1977) *On Sexuality* trans. J. Strachey, Pelican Freud Library vol. 7 (Harmondsworth: Penguin).

Frosch, Stephen (1987) *The Politics of Psychoanalysis: An Introduction to Freudian and Post-Freudian Theory* (London: Macmillan).

Frye, Northrop (1973) 'Varieties of Literary Utopias' in Manuel (1973)

Gallop, Jane (1986) *Feminism and Psychoanalysis: The Daughter's Seduction* (London: Macmillan), 1st edn 1982.

Garry, Ann and Pearsall, Marilyn (eds) (1989) *Women, Knowledge, and Reality: Explorations in Feminist Philosophy* (London: Unwin Hyman).

Gatens, Moira (1991) *Feminism and Philosophy: Perspectives on Difference and Equality* (Cambridge: Polity Press).

Gearhart, Sally Miller (1979) *The Wanderground: Stories of the Hill Women* (Watertown, Mass.: Persephone Press).

—— (1984) 'Future Visions: Today's Politics: Feminist Utopias in Review' in Rohrlich and Baruch (1984).

Geoghegen, Vincent (1987) *Utopianism and Marxism* (London: Methuen).

Gershuny, H. Lee (1984) 'The Linguistic Transformation of Womanhood' in Rohrlich and Baruch (1984).

Gilligan, Carol (1993) *In a Different Voice: Psychological Theory and Women's Development* (London: Harvard University Press), 1st edn 1982.

Goode, John (1977) 'William Morris and the Dream of Revolution' in Lucas (1977).

Goodwin, Barbara (1978) *Social Science and Utopia: Nineteenth Century Models of Social Harmony* (Brighton: Harvester).

—— (1984) 'Economic and Social Innovation in Utopia' in Alexander and Gill (1984).

—— (1987) *Using Political Ideas* (Chichester: John Wiley), 1st edn 1982.

Green, Jen, Lefanu Sarah (eds) (1985) *Despatches from the Frontiers of the Female Mind* (London: Women's Press).

Griffin, Susan (1989) 'Split Culture' in Plant (1989).

Grosz, Elizabeth (1989) *Sexual Subversions: Three French Feminists* (London: Allen & Unwin).

—— (1990a) 'A Note on Essentialism and Difference' in Gunew (1990).

—— (1990b) *Jacques Lacan: A Feminist Introduction* (London: Routledge).

Gunew, Sneja (ed.) (1990) *Feminist Knowledge: Critique – and Construct* (London: Routledge).

Haber, Honi Fern (1994) *Beyond Postmodern Politics: Lyotard, Rorty, Foucault* (London: Routledge).

Hall, Joseph (1776) 'Mundus Alter et Idem', a fragment, trans. William King, in Morley's Universal Library (1889).

Halpern, Richard (1991) *The Poetics of Primitive Accumulation: English Renaissance Culture and the Genealogy of Capital* (London: Cornell University Press).

Harding, Sandra (1990) 'Feminism, Science, and the Anti-Enlightenment Critiques' in Nicholson (1990).

Harraway, Donna (1990) 'A Manifesto for Cyborgs: Science, Technology and Socialist Feminism in the 1980s' in Nicholson (1990).

Hein, Hilde (1989) 'Liberating Philosophy: An End to the Dichotomy of Spirit and Matter' in Garry and Pearsall (1989).

hooks, bell (1984) *Feminist Theory: From Margin to Centre* (Boston, Mass.: South End Press).

Humm, Maggie (ed.) (1992) *Feminisms: A Reader* (London: Harvester Wheatsheaf).

Irigaray, Luce (1977a) 'Women's Exile', interview, *Ideology and Consciousness*, no. 1.

—— (1977b) 'The Poverty of Psychoanalysis' in Whitford (1991b).

—— (1980) 'When Our Lips Speak Together' trans. Caroline Burke, *Signs*, vol. 6, no. 1.

—— (1981a) 'And the One Doesn't Stir Without the Other' trans. Hélène Viviene Wenzel, *Signs*, vol. 7, no. 1.

—— (1981b) 'This Sex Which is not One' in Marks and Courtivron (1981).

—— (1982a) 'The Limits of Transference' in Whitford (1991b).

—— (1982b) 'Sexual Difference' in Whitford (1991a).

—— (1985a) 'Women-Amongst-Themselves: Creating a Woman-to-Woman Sociality' in Whitford (1991b).

—— (1985b) *Speculum of the Other Woman* trans. G.C. Gill (New York: Cornell University Press).

—— (1985c) *This Sex Which is Not One* trans. C. Burke and C. Porter (New York: Cornell University Press).

—— (1986) 'Equal or Different' in Whitford (1991b).

—— (1987a) 'The Bodily Encounter with the Mother' in Whitford (1991b).

—— (1987b) 'The Neglect of Female Genealogies' in Irigaray (1993a).

—— (1987c) 'Religious and Civil Myths' in Irigaray (1993a).

—— (1990) 'Questions to Emmanuel Levinas' in Whitford (1991b).

—— (1993a) *Je, Tu, Nous: Towards a Culture of Difference* trans. Alison Martin (London: Routledge).

—— (1993b) *An Ethics of Sexual Difference* trans. Caroline Burke and Gillian C. Gill (London: Athlone Press).

Jackson, Rosemary (1981) *Fantasy: The Literature of Subversion* (London: Methuen).

Jagger, Alison (1983) *Feminist Politics and Human Nature* (Brighton: Harvester Press).
—— (1989) 'Love and Knowledge: Emotion in Feminist Epistemology' in Garry and Pearsall (1989).
Jameson, Fredric (1981) *The Political Unconscious: Narrative as a Socially Symbolic Act* (London: Methuen).
Jordan, June (1984) 'A Song of Sojourner Truth' in Rohrlich and Baruch (1984).
Joseph, Keith and Sumption, Jonathan (1979) *Equality* (London: Murray).
Kamenka, Eugene (1987) *Utopias* (Oxford: Oxford University Press).
Kamuf, Peggy (1991) *A Derrida Reader: Between the Blinds* (Hemel Hempstead: Harvester Wheatsheaf).
Keinhorst, Annette (1987) 'Emancipatory Projection: An Introduction to Women's Critical Utopias' in Murphy (1987a).
Kourany, Janet A., Sterba James T., Tong Rosemarie (1993) *Feminist Philosophies* (London: Harvester Wheatsheaf).
Kramarae, Cheris (1987) 'Present Problems with the Language of the Future' in Murphy (1987a).
Kramer, Leonie (1987) 'Utopia as Metaphor' in Kamenka (1987).
Kuhn, Annette (1990) *Alien Zone: Cultural Theory and Contemporary Science Fiction Cinema* (London: Verso).
Kumar, Krishan (1991) *Utopianism* (Buckingham: Open University Press).
Lacan, Jacques (1987) 'God and the *Jouissance* of the Woman' in Mitchell and Rose (1987).
LeBow, Diane (1984) 'Rethinking Matriliny Amongst the Hopi' in Rohrlich and Baruch (1984).
Lechte, John (1994) *Fifty Contemporary Thinkers* (London: Routledge).
Lees, Susan H. (1984) 'Motherhood in Feminist Utopias' in Rohrlich and Baruch (1984).
Lefanu, Sarah (1988a) *In the Chinks of the World Machine: Feminism and Science Fiction* (London: Women's Press).
—— (1988b) 'Robots and Romance: The Science Fiction and Fantasy of Tanith Lee' in Radstone (1988).
Le, Guin Ursula (1975) *The Dispossessed* (London: Grafton).
—— (1989) 'Lost Arrow and the Feather People' in Plant (1989).
Lessing, Doris (1979) *Shikasta*, Canopus in Argos: Archives I (London: Cape).
—— (1980) *The Marriages Between Zones Three, Four, and Five, as Marked by the Chroniclers of Zone Three*, Canopus in Argos: Archives II (London: Cape).
Levinas, Emmanuel (1961) *Totality and Infinity* (Pittsburgh: Duquesne University Press).
Levitas, Ruth (1990) *The Concept of Utopia* (Hemel Hempstead: Philip Allan).
Lloyd, Genevieve (1989) 'The Man of Reason' in Garry and Pearsall (1989).
Lorde, Audre (1984a) 'Open Letter to Mary Daly' in Lorde (1984b).
—— (1984b) *Sister Outsider* (New York: Crossing Press).
Lucas, John (1977) *Literature and Politics in the Nineteenth Century* (London: Methuen).
Lugones, Maria (1989) 'Playfulness – "World"-Traveling and Loving Perception' in Garry and Pearsall (1989).

Lyotard, Jean-François (1993) *Political Writings* trans. and foreword Bill Readings (London: UCL Press).

Makward, Christine (1976) 'Interview with Hélène Cixous', *Sub-Stance*, no. 13.

Mannheim, Karl (1936) *Ideology and Utopia* (London: Kegan Paul).

Manuel, Frank (ed.) (1973) *Utopias and Utopian Thought* (London: Souvenir Press).

Manuel, Frank and Manuel, Fritzie (1979) *Utopian Thought in the Western World* (Cambridge, Mass.: Belknap Press).

Marin, Louis (1990) *Utopics: The Semiological Play of Textual Spaces* trans. Robert A. Vollrath (Philadelphia: Humanities Press), 1st edn 1984.

Marks, Elaine, Courtivron Isabelle de (1981) *New French Feminisms* (Brighton: Harvester).

McDowell, Linda, Pringle Rosemary (1992) *Defining Women: Social Institutions and Gender Division* (Cambridge: Polity Press).

McEwan, Christian, O'Sullivan Sue (1988) *Out the Other Side: Contemporary Lesbian Writing* (London: Virago).

Metzger, Deena (1989) 'Invoking the Grove' in Plant (1989).

Moi, Toril (1985) *Sexual/Textual Politics: Feminist Literary Theory* (London: Methuen).

Montefiore, Jan (1987) *Feminism and Poetry: Language, Identity, Experience in Women's Writing* (London: Pandora Press).

More, Thomas (1975) *Utopia* trans. G.M. Logan, intro. Robert M. Adams (Cambridge: Cambridge University Press), 1st edn 1516.

Morley's, Universal Library (1889) *Ideal Commonwealths* (London: Routledge).

Morga, Cherrie and Anzaldùa (eds) (1981) *This Bridge Called My Back: Writings by Radical Women of Color* (Watertown, Mass.: Persephone Press).

Morris, William (1889) 'On *Looking Backward*', review, in Morton (1984).

—— (1891) *News from Nowhere* in Morris (1986).

—— (1986) *Three Works by William Morris*, intro. A.L. Morton (London: Lawrence & Wishart).

Morton, A.L. (1952) *The English Utopia* (London: Lawrence & Wishart).

—— (ed.) (1984) *The Political Writings of William Morris* (London: Lawrence & Wishart).

Moulton, Janice (1989) 'A Paradigm Reality: Feminist Ontology' in Garry and Pearsall (1989).

Moylan, Tom (1986) *Demand the Impossible: Science Fiction and the Utopian Imagination* (London and New York: Methuen).

Mitchell, Juliet, Rose Jacqueline (eds) (1987) *Feminine Sexuality, Jacques Lacan and the Ecole Freudienne* trans. J. Rose (London: Macmillan).

Murphy, Patrick (1987a) 'Feminism Faces the Fantastic', *Women's Studies: An Interdisciplinary Journal*, special issue, vol. 14, no. 2.

—— (1987b) 'Feminism Faces the Fantastic' in Murphy (1987a).

Nead, Lynda (1992) 'Framing and Freeing: Utopias of the Female Body', *Radical Philosophy* no. 60.

Neustatter, Angela (1990) *Hyenas in Petticoats: A Look at Twenty Years of Feminism* (Harmondsworth: Penguin).

247

Nicholson, Linda J. (ed.) (1990) *Feminism/Postmodernism* (London: Routledge).

Nielsen, Joyce McCarl (1984) 'Women in Dystopia/Utopia', *Women's Studies: An Interdisciplinary Journal*, vol. 7, no. 2.

Norris, Christopher (1982) *Deconstruction: Theory and Practice* (London: Methuen).

Nye, Andrea (1989) *Feminist Theory and the Philosophies of Man* (London: Routledge).

Parekh, Bhikhu (1991) 'British Citizenship and Cultural Difference' in Andrews (1991).

Parturier, Françoise (1981) 'An Open Letter to Men' in Marks and Courtivron (1981).

Pearson, Carol (1981) 'Coming Home: Four Feminist Utopias and Patriarchal Experience' in Barr (1981).

—— (1984) 'Of Time and Space: Theories of Social Change in Contemporary Feminist Science Fiction' in Rohrlich and Baruch (1984).

Piercy, Marge (1979) *Woman on the Edge of Time* (London: Women's Press).

—— (1992) *Body of Glass* (Harmondsworth: Penguin). (*He, She and It* in US publications.)

Plant, Judith (ed.) (1989) *Healing the Wounds: The Promise of Ecofeminism* (London: Merlin Press).

Pogrebin, Letty Cottin (1974) 'Born Free: A Feminist Fable' in Tripp (1974).

Radstone, Susannah (ed.) (1988) *Sweet Dreams: Sexuality, Gender, and Popular Fiction* (London: Lawrence & Wishart).

Reuther, Rosemary Radford (1989) 'Towards an Ecofeminist Theology of Nature' in Plant (1989).

Ricoeur, Paul (1986) *The Rule of Metaphor: Multi-Disciplinary Studies and the Creation of Meaning in Language* trans. Robert Czerny, Kathleen McLaughlin, John Costello (London: Routledge), 1st edn 1978.

Roberts, Michèle (1987) *The Book of Mrs Noah* (London: Methuen).

Rohrlich, Ruby, Baruch Elaine Hoffman (eds) (1984) *Women in Search of Utopia: Mavericks and Mythmakers* (New York: Schocken Books).

Rose, Hilary (1988) 'Dreaming the Future', *Hypatia*, vol. 3, no. 1.

Rousseau, Jean-Jacques (1974) *Emile* trans. B. Foxley (New York: Dutton).

Rowbotham, Sheila (1973) *Hidden From History* (London: Pluto Press).

Rudnik-Smalbraack, Marijke (1987) 'Woman and Utopia: Some Reflections and Explorations' in Baker-Smith and Barfoot (1987).

Russ, Joanna (1978) 'When it Changed' in Sargent (1978).

—— (1981) 'Recent Feminist Utopias' in Barr (1981).

—— (1986) *The Female Man* (Boston, Mass.: Beacon Press), 1st edn 1975.

Sargent, Lyman Tower (1975) 'Utopia – The Problems of Definition', *Extrapolation*, vol. 16, no. 2.

Sargent, Lyman Tower (1988) *British and American Utopian Literature, 1516–1985: An Annotated, Chronological Bibliography* (London: Garland Publishing).

—— (1994) 'The Three Faces of Utopianism Revisited', *Utopian Studies*, vol. 15, no. 1.

Sargent, Pamela (ed.) (1978) *The New Women of Wonder* (New York: Random House).

248

Sarup, Madan (1988) *An Introductory Guide to Post-Structuralism and Postmodernism* (London: Harvester Wheatsheaf).

Saxton, Josephine (1986a) *The Travails of Jane Saint and Other Stories* (London: Women's Press), 1st edn 1971.

—— (1986b) 'The Travails of Jane Saint' in Saxton (1986a).

—— (1986c) 'Woe, Blight and in Heaven, Laughs' in Saxton (1986a).

—— (1986d) 'Gordon's Women' in Saxton (1986a).

Schklar, Judith (1973) 'The Political Theory of Utopia: From Melancholy to Nostalgia' in Manuel (1973).

Scott, Joan (1992) 'Deconstructing Equality-versus-Difference: Or, the Uses of Post-Structuralist Thought for Feminism' in McDowell and Pringle (1992).

Sellers, Susan (1986) 'Hélène Cixous', interview, *Women's Review*, no. 7.

—— (1991) *Language and Sexual Difference* (London: Macmillan).

Shanley, Mary Lyndon, Pateman Carole (1991) *Feminist Interpretations and Political Theory* (Cambridge: Polity Press).

Shiach, Morag (1989) 'Their "Symbolic" Exists, it Holds Power – We, the Sowers of Disorder, Know it Only Too Well' in Brennan (1989).

—— (1990) 'Hélène Cixous: Staging History', unpublished paper delivered at Keele University.

—— (1991) *Hélène Cixous: The Politics of Writing* (London: Routledge).

Slonzcewski, Joan (1987) *A Door into Ocean* (London: Women's Press), published 1986 in the USA.

Spelman, Elizabeth (1990) *Inessential Woman: Problems of Exclusion in Feminist Thought* (London: Women's Press).

Spretnak, Charlene (1989) 'Towards an Ecological-Feminist Theory of Nature' in Plant (1989).

Stefano, Christine de (1990) 'Dilemmas of Difference: Feminism, Modernity and Postmodernism' in Nicholson (1990).

Stenstad, Gail (1989) 'Anarchic Thinking: Breaking the Hold of Mono-theistic Ideology on Feminist Philosophy' in Garry and Pearsall (1989).

Stephens, Anthony (1987) 'The Sun State and its Shadow: On the Condition of Utopian Writing' in Kamenka (1987).

Suvin, Darko (1973) 'Defining the Literary Genre of Utopia', *Studies in the Literary Imagination*, vol. 6, no. 2.

Thompson, E.P. (1977) *William Morris: Romantic to Revolutionary* (London: Merlin Press), 1st edn 1955.

Thorne, Barrie, Kramarae Cheris, Henley Nancy (1984) 'Imagining a Different World of Talk' in Rohrlich and Baruch (1984).

Tiptree, James Jnr (1978) 'The Women Men Don't See' in Sargent (1978).

Todd, Janet (ed.) (1983) *Women Writers Talking* (London: Holmes & Meier).

Tripp, Maggie (ed.) (1974) *Woman in the Year 2000* (New York: Arbor House).

Walker, Alice (1984) *In Search of Our Mothers' Gardens* (London: Women's Press).

Weitzman, Leonore J. (1981) *The Marriage Contract, Spouses, Lovers, and the Law* (New York: Macmillan).

Wells, H.G. (1905) *A Modern Utopia* (London: Collins).

Whitbeck, Caroline (1989) 'A Different Reality: Feminist Ontology' in Garry and Pearsall (1989).

Whitford, Margaret (1991a) *Luce Irigaray: Philosophy in the Feminine* (London: Routledge).

—— (1991b) *The Irigaray Reader* (Oxford: Blackwell).

Wiemer, Annegret J. (1987) 'Foreign L(anguish), Mother Tongue: Concepts of Language in Contemporary Feminist Science Fiction' in Murphy (1987a).

Wilcox, Helen, McWatters Keith, Thompson Ann, Williams Linda (eds) (1990) *The Body and the Text: Hélène Cixous, Reading and Teaching* (London: Harvester Wheatsheaf).

Wittig, Monique (1971) *Les Guérillères* trans. David Le Vay (London: David Owen).

—— (1973) *The Lesbian Body* trans. R. Owen (Boston: Beacon Press).

—— (1976/1982) 'The Category of Sex' in Wittig, (1992).

—— (1980a) 'The Straight Mind' in Wittig (1992).

—— (1980b) 'The Point of View: Universal or Particular?' in Wittig (1992).

—— (1981) 'One is Not Born a Woman' in Wittig (1992).

—— (1990) 'Homo Sum' in Wittig (1992).

—— (1992) *The Straight Mind and Other Essays* (Hemel Hempstead: Harvester).

Wood, David (ed.) (1992) *Derrida: A Critical Reader* (Oxford: Blackwell).

Woolmark, Jenny (1985) '*Despatches from the Frontiers of the Female Mind*', review, *Foundations*, no. 35.

Yeatman, Anna (1994) *Postmodern Revisionings of the Political* (London: Routledge).

Young, Iris Marion (1986) 'Impartiality and the Civic Public: Some Implications of Feminist Critics of Modern Political Theory', *Praxis International*, vol. 5, no. 4.

Young, Iris Marion (1990) 'The Ideal of Community and the Politics of Difference' in Nicholson (1990).

Zaki, Hoda M. (1990) 'Utopia and Ideology in *Daughters of a Coral Dawn* and Contemporary Feminist Utopias' in Murphy (1987a).

Zoline, Pamela (1978) 'The Heat Death of the Universe' in Sargent (1978).

INDEX

Printed in the United Kingdom
by Lightning Source UK Ltd.
125427UK00001B/19/A